Trials of Arab Modern

LITERARY AFFECTS AND THE NEW POLITICAL

Tarek El-Ariss

FORDHAM UNIVERSITY PRESS *New York* 2013

the
modern language
initiative

THIS BOOK IS MADE POSSIBLE BY A COLLABORATIVE GRANT
FROM THE ANDREW W. MELLON FOUNDATION.

Library of Congress Cataloging-in-Publication Data

El-Ariss, Tarek.
   Trials of Arab modernity : literary affects and the
new political / Tarek El-Ariss. — First edition.
      pages cm
   Includes bibliographical references and index.
   ISBN 978-0-8232-5171-1 (cloth : alk. paper)
   ISBN 978-0-8232-5172-8 (pbk. : alk. paper)
      1. Arabic literature—20th century—History and
criticism. 2. Arabic literature—21st century—History
and criticism. 3. Literature, Experimental—Arab
countries—History and criticism. 4. Modernism
(Literature)—Arab countries. I. Title.
PJ7538.E43   2013
892.7'09006—dc23
                                    2012050166

Printed in the United States of America

15 14   5 4 3 2

First edition

Trials of Arab Modernity

CONTENTS

ACKNOWLEDGMENTS

This book is the outcome of hard work, perseverance, random encounters, encouragements, displacement, luck, love, and the kind of support that a junior faculty can only dream of. But my special thanks goes first to my editor, Helen Tartar, and to the editorial team at Fordham University Press; I'm grateful for the great work they've done.

At the University of Texas at Austin, I would like to thank the Humanities Institute and its director, Pauline Strong, for providing the course release (Spring 2010) and the forum to work on the book. The Graduate School's Summer Research Assignment (2010) and the College of Liberal Arts' Research Assignment (Fall 2011) gave me the time to complete the manuscript. I thank Dean Randy Diehl and Associate Deans Richard Flores and Esther Raizen for their ongoing support. I'm also grateful to the generous subventions from the College, and from President Bill Powers, which made this publication possible.

I thank my colleagues for their incredible support and generous feedback. I'm grateful to my chair and mentor Kristen Brustad, for giving me the space to write and for making the ground on which I walk firmer, every step of the way. I thank Mahmoud al-Batal for his generosity and motivation, and for taking the Mercedes out of the alley. I thank Kamran Aghaie for the wisdom and time, and for showing me the ropes. I'm indebted to Barbara Harlow for her generous mentorship; Yoav Di-Capua for the stimulating conversations and thorough feedback on the book proposal and various chapters; Samer Ali for his feedback and encouragement; and Benjamin Brower for commenting on my work. I thank as well Hannah Wojciehowski, Geraldine Heng, and Wendy Moore for their feedback on my proposal and continued support. I also thank John Hartigan for inviting me to give a talk based on chapter 3, and Middle East librarian Roberta Dougherty for opening the gates of learning to us all. I'm also grateful to Elizabeth Richmond-Garza, Kamran Ali, Sofian Merabet, Karen Grumberg, Na'ama Pat-El, Faegheh Shirazi, Michael Johnson, Igor Siddiqui, Carl Mathews, and all those at the university who helped this project come to fruition.

Special thanks go to my students—my current and future colleagues. I thank Zeina G. Halabi for her invaluable feedback on the chapters and for helping me keep it real at every level. I thank Angela Giordani for editing the manuscript and pushing me to make the argument pop at the end—the conclusion is dedicated to her. I also thank Benjamin Koerber, Drew Paul, Rachel Levine, Johanna Sellman, Michal Raizen, Katie Logan, and Anna Ziajka, including those who were in my travel narrative seminar in Spring 2009. Our discussions helped me shape the book's argument and provided me with the excitement and the passion to go on writing.

I owe a great deal to my teachers and colleagues at Cornell and to the intellectual environment of the Society for the Humanities. I'm deeply grateful to Natalie Melas, Jonathan Culler, Anne Berger, Emily Apter, Shawkat Toorawa, Dominick LaCapra, Geoffrey Waite, Milad Doueihi, and all those who have taught and inspired me in Ithaca. I also thank my teachers at the University of Rochester and American University of Beirut: Sharon Willis, Eva Geulen, Tom DiPierro, Tim Walters, John Michael, Seta Dadoyan, Mona Amyuni, Saleh Agha, Suzanne Kassab, Waddah Nasr, and Nadeem Naimy. What they taught me made its way into the book in various shapes and forms. I also would like to thank Hoda Barakat and Rashid al-Daif for inspiring me through their friendship and brilliance to see the world in new ways.

I thank my interlocutor and dear friend Moneera al-Ghadeer, whose generosity and support are the not-so-secret ingredients of this book. Chapter 6 particularly benefited from feedback from David Damrosch and Sabry Hafez at a conference she organized at Qatar University in Spring 2010. I'm deeply grateful to John Borneman for the intellectual stimulation and infinite support, Mona Zaki for her warmth and insight, and William Granara for his feedback on the project and continued encouragement. I thank Muhsin al-Musawi for his guidance and vision, and for his generous invitations to the Arabic Seminar and other conferences at Columbia, which are creating the platform for new Arabic studies. I thank Michael Allan for his feedback and generosity. I'm also grateful to Anny Bakalian from the City University of New York–Graduate Center and Nadia Maria el-Cheikh from the American University of Beirut for "bringing me home" by inviting me to give talks based on chapter 3 at their respective institutions. I thank Samuel Shimon and Margaret Obank for publishing in *Banipal* my review of Ahmed Alaidy's *Being Abbas el Abd*, the subject of chapter 6. I thank as well Waïl Hassan and Amal Amireh for editing and including an earlier version of chapter 6, "Hacking the Modern," in their special issue of *Comparative Literature Studies*, Vol. 47, No. 4, 2010. Copyright © 2010 by the Pennsylvania State University Press. Reprinted by permission of the Pennsylvania State University Press. I also thank Sara Pursley for her editing of chapter 5, "Majnun Strikes Back," which appeared with slight modifications in the *International Journal of Middle Eastern Studies*, Vol. 45, No. 2, 2013. Copyright © 2013 by Cambridge University Press. Reprinted by permission of Cambridge University Press. I'm also grateful to Christine Tohme, Walid Raad, and Emily Jacir for inviting me for a talk at *Ashkal Alwan* based on chapter 6, and to Akram Zaatari and the *Arab Image Foundation* for the cover image.

I owe it all to my friends: Maamoun Jabali, who took me in and set me free; my beautiful Ramzi (Zakharia), who passed away yet lives in me; and Christophe and Léa Sloan as well as my goddaughter Mia and her sister Lucy, je vous aime! I thank my friends and colleagues Richard Calichman, Camille Robcis, Judith Surkis, Dore Bowen, Aissa Deebi, Bassam Abed, Kathleen Hulley, Laura Metzler, and Clif Hubby for the love and intellectual stimulation. I thank Tania Haddad, Hatim El Hibri, Huda Saigh, Mazen Khaled, Nada Haddad, Walid Ghandour, Paul Ribnicker, Amira Solh, Nizar Alauf, Lucienne Vidah, Nancy Wolf, Nishan Kazazian, and Jack Drescher for the nourishment, the breath, the insight, and the pleasure of being. My sincere gratitude goes to my friends in Texas, Aziz and Arwa Shaibani, for their warmth, generosity, and freedom.

I would like to thank my family, my mother Elham, my brother Raed, my sister Anita, and my brother Maher who saw it all coming so clearly. I thank my beautiful nephews and nieces; I'm as proud of them as I hope they are of me.

I dedicate this book to my father, Dr. Adnan Ariss (1930–1987), and to the memory of those like him who wandered west. May we finally recognize their trials!

NOTE ON TRANSLATION AND TRANSLITERATION

I followed style and transliteration guidelines of the *Chicago Manual of Style* (15th ed.) and the *International Journal of Middle Eastern Studies* (*IJMES*). For Arab authors' names, I followed the most commonly used transliteration in English. Whereas my transliteration of poetry included all the accents on word endings (e.g., *kitābi, yuḥāwilu*), my transliteration of prose text generally included none (e.g., *kitāb, yuḥāwil*). I used transliteration and referred to the Arabic text only to call attention to language variation and important metaphors. I used published translations of Arabic texts when available. I indicated either in the body of the text or in the endnotes when the translation is my own.

Trials of Arab Modernity

CHAPTER ONE

Introduction

Debating Modernity

I wonder whether we may not envisage modernity rather as an *attitude* [bodily posture] than as a period of history. And by "attitude," I mean a mode of relating to contemporary reality; a voluntary choice made by certain people; in the end, a way of thinking and feeling; a way, too, of acting and behaving that at one and the same time marks a relation of belonging and presents itself as a task.

—MICHEL FOUCAULT, "What Is Enlightenment?"

The events of Rashid al-Daif's (b. 1945) novel *Tablit al-Bahr* (Paving over the sea) (2011) begin in 1860, following the sectarian massacres that claimed the lives of thousands in Lebanon and Syria and led to a French military intervention. Al-Daif's main character, Faris, whose family survives the killing in Mount Lebanon, is meant to represent the subject of Arab Enlightenment in the nineteenth century who goes on to study medicine at the Syrian Protestant College, later known as the American University of Beirut. Faris's childhood friend and future classmate is none other than Jurji Zaidan (1861–1914), precursor of Arabic literary modernity. In one episode, the narrator explains how Faris and Jurji, in need of a corpse for their autopsy class, conspire to smuggle Faris's deceased aunt on a mule through Ottoman checkpoints from the village to their college in Beirut. Dissecting corpses in autopsy class and exploring the body in sexual encounters interspersed throughout the narrative anchor the discourse on Arab modernity in the relation to the body.

Al-Daif's treatment of modernity does not directly engage 1860 as the historical turning point that set in motion various social

and political movements that led, eventually, to the creation of
Lebanon. Nor does he present Zaidan as the modern Arab author
and master of the historical novel. Nor does he situate the study
of medicine and debates about Darwinism as the cornerstone of
an Arab scientific modernity. Instead, al-Daif's modernity is constituted through various accidents and encounters centered on the
body that take place in between Beirut and the countryside, Lebanon and the Americas, and medicine and literature. Modernity
is performed in acts of smuggling corpses at night, autopsy ses-
sions, sexual experimentation between two teenage friends, and
missing home cooking while abroad. It also takes shape in the
effects of the French military intervention in Beirut on prostitution and, in turn, on the sexual mores of the local population. Al-
Daif's work stages modernity through symptoms and affects that
require diagnosis and interpretation, thereby questioning modernity's association with the political and cultural project of Arab
Enlightenment starting in the nineteenth century.

Focusing on the body as a site of rupture and signification,
Trials of Arab Modernity shifts the paradigm for the study of
modernity in the Arab context from questions of representation and cultural exchange to an engagement with a genealogy of symptoms and affects. It traces a series of experiences
and encounters arising from leaving home, aversion to food,
disorientation, anxiety attacks, and physical collapse embodied in travelogues, novels, poetic fragments, and anecdotes
from the nineteenth century to the present. Bridging the gap
between *Nahda* or the so-called Arab project of Enlightenment,
or Renaissance, and postcolonial and postmodern fiction, this
study challenges the prevalent conceptualizations of modernity,
both those that treat it as a Western ideological project imposed
by colonialism, and others that understand it as a universal narrative of progress and innovation.

In literature, the Arab poet and critic Adonis (b. 1930) interprets modernity (*ḥadātha*) as innovation (*iḥdāth*) vis-à-vis tradition, thereby tracing it to the Abbasid poet Abu Nuwas (756–814),
among others. Questioning its treatment as a time period and a

project originating in Europe, Adonis argues that modernity is a process of renewal that systematically supplants traditional forms of literary production.[1] Engaging Adonis's understanding of modernity as a process of innovation (*iḥdāth*) in relation to tradition, I read modernity in the event (*ḥadath*) or events (*aḥdāth*)[2] in order to simultaneously engage nineteenth-century travel narratives and Arabic writing in the virtual age. An event (*ḥadath*), according to Gilles Deleuze and Félix Guattari, "is not another moment within time, but something that allows time to take off on a new path."[3] In the Arab context, *ḥadath* is intertwined with *ḥādith* (accident) and *ḥāditha* (episode). The plural, *aḥdāth* and *ḥawādith*,[4] have been used to denote conflict. Such conflicts as the war and genocide of 1860 as well as the Lebanese civil war (1975–90), for instance, are referred to as *al-aḥdāth*—sites of catastrophic unfolding that could not be named and thus reveal themselves only through a process of interpretation and analysis. *Aḥdāth* also mean scattered news and anecdotes that circulate within and across texts and registers.

This study reframes Arab modernity (*ḥadātha*) as a somatic condition, which takes shape through accidents and events (*aḥdāth*) emerging in and between Europe and the Arab world, the literary text and political discourse. Focusing on travelers and literary characters as they wander, run, take shelter, crouch, faint, panic, and go mad, I identify the simultaneous performances and contestations—or trials—of modernity in experiences and encounters in Cairo and London, in the interstices of the novel and the travelogue, writing and blogging. This book reveals the unfolding of these trials as a violent and ongoing confrontation with and within modernity, decentering yet also redefining and producing it. Through modes of revealing (*kashf*) and hacking (*ikhtirāq, tanṣīf*)—notions I carefully explore in various chapters—these trials take shape in intervals and instantaneous flashes. Modernity emerges from these trials and events—asymmetrical and fleeting *aḥdāth*. I engage texts at the level of uncertainty, ambiguity, and incoherence. Rather than presenting an exhaustive account of Arab literary modernity, this book offers close readings of specific encounters and texts in which modernity is performed.

DEBATING MODERNITY

The question of modernity has dominated Arab intellectual thought from Qasim Amin's (1863–1908) call for the "liberation" of women[5] to Taha Hussein's (1889–1973) situating Egypt's civilizational trajectory within that of the West.[6] Other thinkers address the relation between cultural development and the production of Arab subjectivity and social and political institutions.[7] Georges Tarabishi (b. 1939), for instance, undertakes a psychoanalytic reading of Arab modernity, situating it in structures of trauma and lack. According to Tarabishi, Arab intellectual debates about progress, authenticity, and tradition are conditioned by lack. This lack permeates Arab discursive production and shapes the relation to the Arab past on the one hand and to the West on the other.[8] For his part, Sadiq Jalal al-Azm (b. 1934) undertakes a Marxist critique of Arab society's blind embrace of *Nahda* liberation discourse without adequately scrutinizing traditional forms of authority and beliefs. According to al-Azm, the 1967 Arab defeat against Israel, or *Naksa*, exposed the absence of this radical critique and exacerbated the discrepancy between the discourse on modernity and Arab social and political structures.[9]

Debates about Arab modernity from the nineteenth century onward have recently had to contend with new social and political practices that generate different concerns and require new interpretive models. Talal Asad has shown that the association of modernity with secularism in the context of the postcolonial nation-state has shifted dramatically.[10] From Islamist institutions and alternative communities to the social movements that brought about the events of the Arab Spring starting in 2010, modernity is refigured and reimagined across the Arab world. The avatars of an Arab "modernity in trial" organize and mobilize through social media, imagine communities through online fatwa banks and dating sites, and produce literary works wherein English and Arabic, tweets and verse, seamlessly coexist. These trials systematically question modernity's association with humanism and secularism and its opposition to tradition.[11] They also create the possibility for rethinking modernity in the nineteenth century by identifying its production in writing practices and community activism, which involve texts and events that are traditionally excluded from modernity's master narrative.

Trials of Arab Modernity draws on both classical and modern Arabic literature and thought, and contemporary theory and philosophy. Reading affects as a counterpart to the question of representation, which has governed literary studies for so long, is key for identifying new crossings between the literary and the political, experience and writing. These links are inscribed in the body, a site of literary and cultural narratives and histories. In *Body Consciousness: A Philosophy of Mindfulness and Somaesthetics* (2008), Richard Shusterman reads the body as the "organizing core of experience."[12] He introduces the notion of "somaesthetics," employing the word "soma" to denote "the living, feeling, sentient, purposive body rather than a mere physical corpus of flesh and bones."[13] "The body," according to Shusterman, "expresses the ambiguity of human being, as both subjective sensibility that experiences the world and as an object perceived in that world."[14] The body has agency and thus could not be reduced to a medium, prison, or object of representation in critical discourse. In *Neuropolitics: Thinking, Culture, Speed* (2002), William Connolly creates a dialogue between neuroscience and cultural theory, critiquing the body's dismissal as a scientifically predetermined object of study.[15] He claims that "culture involves practices in which the porosity of argument is inhabited by more noise, unstated habit, and differential intensities of affect."[16] Understanding culture thus requires acts of listening, experiencing, and closely examining the sensorial and the somatic as they take shape in texts and practices, moments of collapse and projection.[17]

In *The Ethical Soundscape: Cassette Sermons and Islamic Counterpublics* (2009), Charles Hirschkind examines the function of Muslim sermon tapes by exploring the human sensorium as site of production and proliferation of social, ethical, and political practices. Elaborating on William Connolly's analysis of "visceral modes of appraisal" that cannot be assessed at conscious and intellectual levels, Hirschkind argues that the "new Islamic political" cannot be reduced to revivalist ideology and texts but rather must be explored in listening acts. It is to be found in Cairo's "acoustic architecture," which impinges on the human sensorium and thus orients believers "within the modern city *as a space of moral action*."[18] In line with Talal Asad's argument about secular practices that take shape through forms of bricolage that defy secular/religious binary, Hirschkind argues that "the senses are not a stable foundation upon which a singular and unassailable truth can be erected, as an empiricist epistemology would claim, but rather a space of inderteminacy, heterogeneity, and possibility."[19] Elaborating on Leigh Eric Schmidt's reading of the rise of modern subjectivity through the proliferation of auditory technology and practices starting in the eighteenth century,[20] Hirschkind argues that the question of visuality and the mistrust of hearing are constitutive of the Enlightenment project with which Arab modernity is associated as well. The emphasis on seeing, mapping, and reading the text and recognizing its letters thus marginalizes other sensory forms and experiences wherein new meaning is produced and, as I argue, the trials of Arab modernity take shape. Thus, the attention to listening in Hirschkind's study allows him to explore a wider sensorium that is visceral yet not irrational. Suffice it to say that this critical model displaces both the Enlightenment's oculocentricity and the primacy of the "Western gaze" when examining Arab modernity.[21] This is not to claim that listening or tasting has replaced seeing, but that the trials of Arab modernity are activated at a variety of sensorial levels embodied in the texts I examine.

The critique of modernity as an intellectual project that could be engaged only through a specific set of binaries involving the rational and the irrational, the representational and the material, is echoed in theoretical departures from questions of duality and the figurative in contemporary theory. In *Parables for the Virtual Moment* (2002), Brian Massumi argues that a return to the body without the fear of the metaphysics of presence is key to moving beyond stultified forms of criticism.[22] Reading bodily affects through Spinoza, Bergson, and Deleuze, among others, Massumi argues that affect and resistance, intensity and rupture should be reinscribed in a dynamic space of transformation. Distinguishing it from emotion, Massumi argues that affect is "resistant to critique"[23] and to signification. Affect is force and duration, which bind space-time through an "impingement" on the body. This emphasis on affect breaks with dialectical engagement with texts and ideas, and, as Massumi argues, with the figurative framework of literary criticism and its emphasis on representation.

In a similar vein, Melissa Gregg and Gregory J. Seigworth argue that affect theory introduces new sites of embodiment and performativity.

> Affect arises in the midst of *in-between-ness*: in the capacities to act and be acted upon. Affect is an impingement or extrusion . . . of forces or intensities . . . that pass body to body . . . in those resonances that circulate about, between, and sometimes stick to bodies and worlds. . . . [Affects are] visceral forces beneath, alongside, or generally *other than* conscious knowing, vital forces insisting beyond emotion— that can serve to drive us toward movement, toward thought and extension. . . . Indeed, affect is persistent proof of a body's never less than ongoing immersion in and among the world's obstinacies and rhythms, its refusals as much as its invitations.[24]

Given this formulation, the bodily, the physical, and movement itself are sites of transformation and new meaning. This attempted definition, which simulates the affective, moves the debate beyond representation. While Rei Terada's *Feeling in Theory: Emotions after the "Death of the Subject"* (2003) engages works by Paul de Man and Jacques Derrida in order to read affects as nonsubject-centered intensities,[25] in *Flesh of My Flesh* (2009), Kaja Silverman interrogates the binary framing of subjectivity through modes of difference, otherness, and emphasis on "individuality." Reexamining the relation to the *other* in terms of analogy, mortality, and finitude, Silverman reads Freud through

Lou Andrea Salomé in order to recuperate such Freudian notions as "the oceanic feeling," often dismissed for its perceived incoherence and irreducibility to the binary of self/other, crucial in psychoanalysis.[26] For Silverman, analogies do not simply replace the binaries of difference in the works of Freud and Lacan but offer instead a new terrain of investigation.

My reading of affects is in dialogue with Terada and Silverman, and Eve Sedgwick as well, who deploys affect to question poststructuralist emphasis on representation. Specifically, the question of performativity, which has been crucial to Judith Butler's deconstruction of sex and gender, has been treated "as if its theoretical salience all came directly from work on speech acts following Austin."[27] In *Touching Feeling: Affect, Pedagogy, Performativity* (2003), Sedgwick argues that this framework also extends to nonverbal acts, suggesting that "the line between words and things or between linguistic and nonlinguistic phenomena is endlessly changing, permeable, and entirely unsusceptible to any definitive articulation."[28] Specifically, such notions as performance, theater, and stage are fundamental to the framing of the performative in the works of Butler and others.[29] Affect, in this context, could not be reduced to a discursive moment subsumed in a model of representation but rather engaged as something that is constantly going in and out of representation, text, and modes of embodiment. It is precisely this permeability of texts and the dynamic character of affect wherein the narrative I read takes shape.

THE COMPARATIVE PROJECT

In dialogue with affect theory, deconstruction, psychoanalysis, Michel Foucault, and Walter Benjamin, this book interrogates the reading of modern Arabic literature through teleological narratives of progress or anticolonial struggle. In this light, *Trials of Arab Modernity* diverges from the linear genealogy of Arab modernity starting with Napoleon's invasion of Egypt (1798) and Haykal's *Zaynab* (1913), which is considered to be the first

Arabic novel.[30] It also interrogates traditional East/West comparative models that disseminate modern Arabic literature in the American academic context. In *Death of a Discipline* (2003), Gayatri Spivak challenges "Eurocentric" categories of nation and class in order to offer an alternative reading of the question of collectivity in "Third World literature." Drawing on the Derridean notion of *telepoesis* (reading from a distance), Spivak claims that "literature contains the element of surprising the political."[31] According to Spivak, the literary text is a site of tension, a scene of writing and reading, encoding and decoding, thereby staging a dynamic back and forth with which the critic engages with no guarantees or certainties. Natalie Melas reads Spivak's project as a movement away from a traditional comparative mastery of *other* texts— representative of *other* cultures—offering instead a new comparative "ethic of reading" that "foregrounds the unverifiable quality of literary textuality as a crucial, if unpredictable and unsystematic, access to collectivities."[32] In this context, Melas argues that "close reading offers an important approach to cross-cultural engagement, because it points toward an open model of interlocution rather than mastery."[33] Identifying modernity in sites of trial is an attempt to gauge new meaning and recognize textual forms that do not fit neatly into Arabic literary canons in the Arab world and beyond.

Naguib Mahfouz's (1911–2006) earning of the Nobel Prize in 1988 has driven the interest in modern Arabic literature among literary scholars and the public in the United States especially. However, observes Roger Allen, this interest has been restricted to Mahfouz's trilogy from the 1950s.[34] The teaching and translation of modern Arabic literature have traditionally ignored current literary production and bypassed texts from the *Nahda*. In this context, modernity has been confined to and associated with a specific time period, reflecting specific political and social struggles. Studies of Arabic literature and culture within this framework predominantly focus on the political dynamics of the Arab-Israeli conflict and the colonial legacy. These studies approach texts through the binaries of tradition and modernity, Islam and the West, and trace works to the intentions of their authors by situating them within uncomplicated historical and cultural contexts. This perspective has reduced texts to sociological accounts and elided their literary complexity. Treated as an objective representation of Arab culture and Islam or as the "true word" of the native informant, "Arabic literature is not allowed to have aesthetics," claims Marilyn Booth.[35]

Since the publication of *Orientalism* (1979), postcolonial theory has become the prevalent framework for engaging modern Arabic literature in American academia, especially in English and comparative literature departments. Though Edward Said himself rails against the deaestheticization of Arabic texts,[36] postcolonial studies often reduce them to the practical politics of colonialism and the neocolonial dynamics of global capital. These discussions treat texts as sites of resistance to or deployment of Western cultural models, thereby engaging modernity as a narrative of complicity with a hegemonic West, which suppresses, one way or another, Arab-Islamic tradition and practices. Relegating novels, films, and short stories to debates about nationalism, secularism, and religion without adequately challenging the binaries of modernity/tradition and East/West sidelines the creative transformations of Arabic texts. In this context, Muhsin al-Musawi argues that critical focus on questions of "identity, migration, change of location, tradition and modernity" in contemporary Arabic literature has become inadequate.[37] This calls for the investigation of complex narrative thresholds and a multitude of sociopolitical models and forms of consciousness that collectively chart a new critical direction, "debate ambivalence," and interrogate binaries. In this context, al-Musawi remarks that the erosion of the East/West dichotomy was particularly emphasized in Abd al-Hakim Qasim's *The Seven Days of Man* (1969). Al-Musawi argues that the Arab subject's crisis in the novel unfolds in a confrontation with state power and authority and thus bypasses city/countryside and East/West binaries.[38] However, the critique of duality, as Eve Sedgwick reminds us, is never final or conclusive. The interrogation of binary oppositions ought to emphasize adjacent spaces—*beside*—that yield alternative meaning and direction.[39]

A dynamic exploration of modernity *in between* and *beside* East and West requires close yet lateral readings that are philological and comparative at the same time. Such readings are addressed and practiced in Edward Said's reevaluation of humanism in a series of posthumously published lectures. In *Humanism and Democratic Criticism* (2004), Said observes that "attacking the abuses of something [humanism] is not the same thing as dismissing or entirely destroying that thing."[40] In light of Said's formulation, rather than reduce modernity to the European colonial project deployed through an identifiable set of social, political, and discursive practices, it's necessary to perform instead a careful exploration of spaces of critique within its literary manifestations and instances of unraveling in Arabic texts. Said undertakes "an extended meditation on the useable scope of humanism as an ongoing practice and not as a possession,"[41] thereby "treating this subject not in order to produce a history of humanism, nor an exploration of all its possible meanings."[42] Without collapsing it with humanism, my treatment of modernity, rather than seeking to consolidate a literary genre by tracing all its possible occurrences, investigates instead practices and mechanisms through which questions of genre are addressed. In this context, *Trials of Arab Modernity* examines philological play in a series of key notions such as *ḥadātha* (modernity), *kashf* (revealing), and *ikhtifā'* (disappearing) as a way of "getting inside the process of language already going on in words and making it disclose what may be hidden or incomplete or masked or distorted. . . . Words are not passive markers or signifiers standing in unassumingly for a higher reality; they are, instead, an integral formative part of the reality itself."[43] The deconstruction of concepts and words throughout this book serves to activate their dynamic potential, which allows us to recognize different kinds of texts and registers.

My exploration of modernity in Arabic literature calls attention to traces in language, intertextuality, omitted connections, and suppressed narratives and experiences.[44] The literary thus

designates a space of slippage, irreducible to representation and
to materiality yet arising in between them and from their interaction. Reading the literary is a way to occupy this space and fol-
low traces, stage ruptures, and reintroduce in the process questions of agency, performance, and movement (traveling, running,
fainting). The literary ushers in scenes characterized by the proliferation of writing practices, genre crossing, intertextuality, and
physical and virtual encounters. The texts I examine, which are
set strategically in between cultural contexts ranging from nineteenth-century travel narratives to contemporary fiction, perform the modern in instances of play and deconstruction. A close
reading of affect in these works allows us to identify the literary
embodiment of Arab modernity's trials.

Challenging descriptive and historical discussions of Arabic
travel narratives,[45] my study examines the encounter with Europe
in instances of rupture and collapse in order to displace Europe
as the origin of Arab cultural, political, and literary modernity.
In this context, the book engages the intellectual project of "provincializing Europe," which calls for displacing the West from
its central position in the cultural and literary comparative axis
(Europe/Middle East, Europe/Africa, etc.).[46] By introducing a
variety of frameworks that operate across historical and cultural
contexts both within the Arab world and in relation to Europe as
well, I deconstruct the way European centrality has been established through the predominance of questions of borrowing,
resistance, tradition, and representation. Engaging this encounter
in all its complexity rids the Arabic text of the "anxiety of influ-
ence" vis-à-vis European literature to which traditional comparative studies have subjected it for so long.[47]

Albert Hourani argues that the *Nahda*, which is associated
with Arab modernity, arises from the violent shock embodied in
the French invasion of Egypt in 1798.[48] However, the violence
incurred in this encounter is often described and studied in colonial and military terms, pitting a Western aggressor against a
helpless native. It is important to investigate literary staging of
personal struggle, collapse, disorientation, and crisis as sites of

questioning and unraveling of the historical narratives and intellectual debates dealing with this encounter. The experience of Arab writers and travelers in European cities and towns, forced to endure different weather and food, and learn new languages and customs, are key for identifying multiple sites of the modern. In this light, my exploration of modernity's affects in Arabic literature draws on Walter Benjamin's discussion of the shock experience, Michel Foucault's discursive production of sexual norms, and Judith Butler's performativity, among others. These theoretical frameworks have shaped, for better or worse, our understanding of modernity both in the Euro-American context and beyond. Specifically, the rise of industrialization and urban development in nineteenth-century Europe is a crucible for the Arab experience of modernity in the works of such travelers and residents of European cities as Ahmad Faris al-Shidyaq (1804–1886), Rifaʿa Rafiʿ al-Tahtawi (1801–1873), and Fransis Fath-Allah al-Marrash (1836–1873). My comparative study challenges the Eurocentric framework that treats Arab modernity as borrowing from the West, or as a process that started in the Arab-Islamic world independently of Europe.

CHAPTERS

Trials of Arab Modernity starts by examining the production of a modern Arabic textuality in the encounter with Europe in the nineteenth century. Focusing on travel narratives as sites of staging and deconstruction of concepts of culture and civilization, I examine works by Rifaʿa Rafiʿ al-Tahtawi and Ahmad Faris al-Shidyaq. While al-Tahtawi was an Azharite imam who became a state bureaucrat and reformer of Egypt's educational system, al-Shidyaq was an exiled intellectual from Mount Lebanon who rebelled against church authority and lived in Europe and across the Ottoman world. In chapter 2, "Fantasy of the Imam," I analyze al-Tahtawi's encounters in France from 1826 to 1831 by focusing on poetic associations in *Takhlis al-Ibriz fi Talkhis Bariz aw al-Diwan al-Nafis bi-Iwan Baris* (*An Imam in Paris:*

Al-Tahtawi's Visit to France [1826–1831]) (1834). A close reading of al-Tahtawi's anxiety, which he expresses in literary fragments and anecdotes throughout his otherwise descriptive travel
narrative, reveals a hitherto unexplored articulation of the relation between power, sexuality, and knowledge. My reading of
al-Tahtawi's work anchors the relation between Europe and the
Ottoman world in the fantasmatic, the associative, and the affective. Questions of tradition, education, and political authority—
key *Nahda* topics— are examined in the staging of the young
scholar's (*'ālim*) anxiety in nineteenth-century Europe.

The investigation of fantasy and imagination emphasizes the
importance of literature as the *scene* of conflict and fascination.
This *scene* casts Arab modernity in a state of trial, which literature performs and exposes simultaneously. Specifically, I argue
that al-Tahtawi's appropriation and transformation of such Arabic genres as *madḥ* (praise ode) and *riḥla* (travel narrative) ties in
political fantasy with the text's aesthetic transformation. I interpret al-Tahtawi's literary staging of his experience in France as
a form of embodiment that disrupts the all-too-common linear
and descriptive narrative of the Arab encounter with Europe in
the nineteenth century. In this vein, chapter 2 also aims at situating al-Tahtawi's text as part of a European urban experience
that gave rise to the theories of modernity deployed in Benjamin's work. This particular framing challenges the resistance to
theory in reading Arabic literature. This analysis dismantles the
treatment of the *Nahda* as a site of borrowing and incorporating
European ideas and genres.

In chapter 3, "Aversion to Civilization," I examine al-Shidyaq's
parody of the association between modernity and progress on the
one hand and civilization on the other in *Kashf al-Mukhabba' 'an
Funun Urubba* (Revealing the hidden in European arts) (1863). Al-
Shidyaq's parody arises from his systematic attempts to diagnose
and explain the way the British define and practice civilization.
He treats civilization as a proliferation of symptoms manifested
on the body, in city streets, and in food consumption and preparation. Focusing on episodes (*aḥdāth*) of ingestion and expulsion,

I argue that al-Shidyaq's aversion to British food, embodied in his physical collapse and intellectual crises, inverts the civilizational model by casting the British as uncivilized in comparison to the sophisticated and cosmopolitan Ottoman subject. Ultimately, this inversion allows al-Shidyaq to satirically deconstruct the notion of civilization as an exclusionary structure and expose its inherent contradictions and epistemic violence.

Through a dialogue with theoretical articulations by Louis Marin and Deleuze and Guattari, I argue that the narrative and affects of the Arab traveler's body enact in the text a form of deterritorialization that depicts in this context processes of *kashf* (revealing, unveiling) and *ta'riya* (stripping naked) of language and cultural discourse. Specifically, through its systematic interrogation of orientalism and colonialism, al-Shidyaq's *Kashf* dismantles, once and for all, the perceived passivity of the *Nahda* text, alleged receptacle of European ideas and cultural models. Arab modernity takes shape in al-Shidyaq's work in sites of confrontation and unveiling that highlight Arab modernity's specificity, potential, and trials. I argue that confusion and frustration, embodied in al-Shidyaq's interactive text, which calls on the reader to witness and experience what the author is subjected to in England especially, are productive and critical sites that give rise to different trajectories of the *Nahda*.

The modes of negotiation and trial I identify in *Nahda* texts are framed through narratives of disorientation and fragmentation in postcolonial and diasporic writing as well. Chapters 4 and 5 investigate modernity in instances of sexual anxiety and madness in works by Tayeb Salih (1929–2009), Hanan al-Shaykh (b. 1945), and Hamdi Abu Golayyel (b. 1967). In chapter 4, "Staging the Colonial Encounter," I examine questions of experience and trauma in Tayeb Salih's *Mawsim al-Hijra ila al-Shamal* (*Season of Migration to the North*) (1966). Fictionalizing the Arab-African encounter with European colonialism and technology, Salih aligns England and the Sudan, colonial wars and World War I, in order to highlight the colonized man's attempts to witness, return to, and capture the colonial encounter. Confronting ghosts and memories, recognizing voices and tracing smells oozing from decomposing bodies, Salih's narrative deploys a postcolonial sensorium that leads the reader to expose the fantasmatic production of the East/West relation.

Engaging the Sudan in this study of Arab modernity *in trials* calls attention to its exclusion from modern Arab political and cultural models. Salih's text reintroduces the Sudan into the narrative of Arab modernity by destabilizing the Europe-*Mashriq* (Middle East, Levant) and Europe-*Maghrib* (Northwest Africa) axes through which Arabic literature, thought, and history are investigated in a comparative context. The Sudan is reintroduced alongside Arab modernity's accidents, trials, and events that were also excluded, made absent (*mughayyabīn*), or forced to disappear (*makhfiyyīn*) in order for a specific master narrative of Arab modernity to maintain its coherence and linearity.

From the Sudanese cultural and racial *other* within the narrative of Arab modernity, chapter 5 sheds light on queer subjectivity. While Salih's engagement with European civilization unleashes a plethora of violent sexual impulses that lead to murder and destruction, expressions of queer desire and identity in al-Shaykh's and Abu Golayyel's works operate as spaces of subversion of social and political normativity in between Europe and the Arab world. Chapter 5, "Majnun Strikes Back," reads modernity's trials in fits of madness, disguise, and collapse. The chapter focuses on the association of homosexuality with madness in Hanan al-Shaykh's *Innaha London ya 'Azizi* (*Only in London*) (2000) and Hamdi Abu Golayyel's *Lusus Mutaqa'idun* (*Thieves in Retirement*) (2002). Discussing the aesthetic transformations of the Arabic novel from the 1960s onward, I argue that Majnun, the quintessential figure of the obsessive lover who is consumed by his desire in the Arabic tradition, reappears as a queer subject in contemporary fiction. In his modern role, he does drag, acts out, protests, and resists incarceration. I argue that the affects and trials of the queer Majnun unsettle the debate about homosexuality in the Arab world along the neatly defined binaries of local and global, decentering modernity as a Western onslaught on endangered Arab tradition and practice. My reading explores the way both modernity and tradition are in fact produced through modes of violence, incarceration, and erasure.

Probing these models by engaging Michel Foucault's critique of modern regimes of power, my reading of affects and performativity in al-Shaykh and Abu Golayyel serves to align these novels with *Nahda* texts. This allows for the transition from critical approaches that privilege exchange, representation, and cultural difference to new theoretical possibilities able to investigate Arabic literature in the twenty-first century from a different standpoint. The emphasis on locating and denouncing modes of complicity with all that is associated with the West, from queer nomenclature and GLBT rights to social media, thus points to these approaches' scholarly blind spots and inability to engage the sensorium of Arab subjectivity manifested in dress and actions and interactive writing that are essential components of contemporary cultural production and social and political change.

In chapter 6, "Hacking the Modern," I analyze processes of hacking (*ikhtirāq, tansīf*) in Arabic fiction's multiple sites of production across media and cultural contexts. Focusing on Ahmed Alaidy's (b. 1974) iconoclastic manifesto of new writing, *An Takun 'Abbas al-'Abd* (*Being Abbas el Abd*) (2003), I argue that the main preoccupation of this hacker-like author, who also writes scripts for television and cinema, and political poems and comic strips for newspapers, is with the immediacy of authoritarian Arab regimes. Challenging their political and cultural legitimacy, Alaidy's text stages a new scene of violence, meticulously deployed against Arab modernity's signifiers in social, educational, and literary contexts. Examining acts of desecrating books and state institutions, I argue that Alaidy's new-generation antihero supplants the disoriented Arab traveler in Paris and London that one finds in al-Shidyaq, al-Tahtawi, and al-Shaykh. Displacing experiences of disorientation and fragmentation onto the text itself, this new writing manifesto ushers in a reconceptualization of the relation between the literary and the political in the Arab world. I elaborate on this in the concluding chapter 7, "Writing the New Political," and argue that a comparative analysis of contemporary fiction, *Nahda*, and diasporic and postcolonial texts serves to frame the social and political transformations associated with the Arab Spring.

CHAPTER TWO

Fantasy of the Imam

Tomorrow we leave for Marseilles; we do not mean to stay there
long, for Rica's plan, and mine, is to travel on without delay to Paris,
which is the seat of government of the empire of Europe. Travelers
always seek out the great cities, which provide a kind of homeland
common to all foreigners. Farewell, be assured of my faithful love.

—MONTESQUIEU, *Persian Letters* (1721)

Adonis traces Arab literary modernity to Abu Nuwas (756–814),
al-Mutanabbi (915–965), and other Abbasid poets who refigure *jāhilī*, or pre-Islamic poetry, by displacing it from the register of personal loss and sentiments and inscribing it in a universal human condition. This modernity is anchored in new urban
contexts brought about by Muslim expansions in the seventh
and eighth centuries. For instance, in his reading of ʿAli ibn al-
Jahm's (804–863) *madḥ* (praise ode) *Rusafiyya*, Samer Ali argues
that the city of Baghdad itself conditions the poem's modernity.
Dedicated to the Abbasid Caliph al-Mutawakkil (reigned 847–
861), the ode stages the literary effects of Ibn al-Jahm's civilizing encounter with the Abbasid metropolis. The immersion of
this allegedly Bedouin poet in Baghdad's urban sophistication
serves to refine the poet's style by melding it "with cosmopolitan
aesthetic."[1] The poem, which derives its name from Rusafa, "a
vibrant neighborhood . . . and emblem of the Abbasid metropolis,"[2] moves teleologically from the description of separation with
the tribe, the tribulations of the poet, to reunion and redemp-
tion at the end. Working "toward the patron and [marking] the

poet's tribute to him as the culmination of maturity and knowledge,"[3] the poem, like a *voyage vers soi* (voyage toward oneself), presents a personal and literary transformation that intervenes in and redirects al-Mutawakkil's desire from dismissal and mockery toward Ibn al-Jahm to appreciation and praise. This model of literary modernity thus aligns a system of patronage with the urban encounter in the Abbasid metropolis, thereby determining the poem's meaning and significance.

This encounter, in which aesthetic transformation is meant to coincide with a modern urban experience, frames comparatively many nineteenth-century Arabic travel narratives as well. Specifically, travel as a quest for knowledge in the "Arab rediscovery of Europe"[4] genre involves poetic and allegorical elements that capture the encounter with modernity in the European metropolis, ushering in new articulations of literary and political relations. Experiencing new locales and undergoing the vagaries of travel, authors incorporate into their travelogues poetry, satire, and allegory. These literary elements serve to critique, placate, and seek the patronage of various rulers. From Ahmad Faris al-Shidyaq's famous *madḥ* for Queen Victoria to Rifaʿa Rafiʿ al-Tahtawi's systematic evocation of his patron, Muhammad ʿAli (reigned 1805–1849), poetry and literary fantasy occupy a central role in *Nahda* texts. The investigation of these literary landscapes is thus an inquiry into morphing of genres and sociopolitical shifts hitherto ignored by the scholarship in the field.

Al-Tahtawi's *Takhlis al-Ibriz fi Talkhis Bariz aw al-Diwan al-Nafis bi-Iwan Baris (An Imam in Paris: Al-Tahtawi's Visit to France [1826–1831])* (1834, henceforth: *Takhlis*)[5] occupies a liminal position at the intersection of historical contexts and genres, from the medieval Arab *riḥla* to eighteenth-century European travelogues and works on history and culture. Published following al-Tahtawi's return from the student mission in France, *Takhlis* contains descriptions of Paris and discussions of French people's beliefs, customs, technological development, popular culture, and judicial system. Al-Tahtawi lauds the Parisians' freedom of religious practice, rule of law, superior arts and sciences, and patriotism (*ḥub al-waṭan*). Having studied French politics, literature, and language, he translates a variety of books and essays by Georges Depping (1784–1853), Montesquieu (1689–1755), and Jean-Jacques Rousseau (1712–1778), and engages with such scholars as Silvestre de Sacy (1758–1838), Armand-Pierre Caussin de Perceval (1759–1835), Joseph Reinaud (1795–1867), and Edmé-François Jomard (1777–1862), editor of *Description de l'Egypte* (1810–1828) and the mission's supervisor. Al-Tahtawi was the first to translate such key terms as "democracy" (*shūra*) and "Enlightenment" (*tanwīr*).[6] Having witnessed the political events of 1830, he translates the new French constitution, commenting on its various clauses while emphasizing that the origin of laws in France is political rather than divine.

Al-Tahtawi's social and political writings such as *Manahij al-Albab al-Misriyya fi Mabahij al-Adab al-ʿAsriyya* (The paths of Egyptian hearts in the joys of contemporary letters) (1869) and *Kitab al-Murshid al-Amin li-l-Banat wa-l-Banin* (Honest guide on the education of boys and girls) (1872), as well as writings by other Arab thinkers about Europe in the second half of the nineteenth century, receive much critical attention by *Nahda* historians.[7] It is important, however, to shed light on al-Tahtawi's earlier work, full of poetic associations and allegories. At the intersection of political and literary transformations, *Takhlis* requires a close analysis of its incongruities and ruptures, ambiguities and intertextual references. I read al-Tahtawi's physical collapse, disorientation, and hallucination as an embodiment of the encounter with modernity in nineteenth-century Paris.

As noted by Muhsin al-Musawi, in *Takhlis* al-Tahtawi introduces a new metropolitan scape through a specific consciousness and experience.[8] Walter Benjamin argues that the condition of modernity in the European city is one of alienation but also of shock, which the modern poet cushions and attenuates. According to Benjamin, poetry captures if not endures this new experience. This is not to suggest that Charles Baudelaire's (1821–1867) poetry—the object of Benjamin's analysis—and the poetic fragments interspersed in *Takhlis* could be compared in a clear and unproblematic fashion. Rather, I suggest that al-Tahtawi's encounter with European modernity, often expressed in poetic association, needs to be examined through a comparative lens informed by modernity's various theoretical frameworks, including Benjamin's.

I investigate al-Tahtawi's experience in France in *Takhlis*'s spaces of fantasy and dissonance. My reading challenges the scholarship that ignores literary and poetic elements in al-Tahtawi's text, or dismisses them as customary ornamentation in his otherwise descriptive narrative.[9] I argue that it is precisely in these literary spaces—the ornament or superfluous text—that a new understanding of al-Tahtawi's embodiment of a modern experience emerges. This analysis exposes both the personal struggle of the imam in Paris and his literary negotiations between such Arabic genres as *rihla* (travelogue) and *qasida* (ode) on the one hand, and literary and philosophical articulations of modernity in nineteenth-century texts on the other. Examining al-Tahtawi's encounter serves to explain the logic of juxtaposition and comparison in *Takhlis*, thereby providing a new interpretation of this body of writing, thought, and culture at that historical juncture.

Though it is Hasan al-'Attar (1766–1835), al-Azhar's rector and al-Tahtawi's teacher, who asks his student to keep an account of his trip to France, al-Tahtawi dedicates *Takhlis* to Muhammad 'Ali, thereby seeking his acknowledgment, approval, and further patronage.[10] Thus, "much is implicit" in *Takhlis*, which makes it difficult to identify a clear position on politics and government.[11] This implicitness leads us to examine the text's *unconscious* or literary spaces, which stage the *Nahda* problematic through modes of trials and embodiment. I read these spaces in a series of ruptures that fantasmatically refigure the relation between al-Tahtawi, the mission's imam and seeker of European knowledge, and Muhammad 'Ali, Egypt's ruler, the mission's patron, and desirer of technological development. Al-Tahtawi casts Egypt's pasha in the roles of the virile conqueror and sacker of cities, disciplining father, insatiable lover, and modern ruler. Respectively, he casts himself in the roles of the inadequate son, blind imam, impotent man, and heroic lover. I argue that in these literary spaces, the new ʿālim (religious scholar) (al-Tahtawi) deconstructs the advent of Arab modernity as a site of exchange with and borrowing from Europe. Shedding new light on the significance of the process of modernization that swept through the Ottoman Empire in the nineteenth century, this chapter demonstrates that *Takhlis*'s narrative of collapse, dissonance, and fragmentation systematically unsettles and interrupts modernity's epistemological closure in this early *Nahda* text. My comparative approach connects this body of works to various genres and historical contexts from the pre-Islamic period to the present, thereby interrogating the binary opposition of tradition and modernity that long dominated *Nahda* scholarship and Arabic literary criticism.[12]

THE PASHA AND THE IMAM

The "appointment" of Muhammad ʿAli as Egypt's governor in 1805 led to a gradual centralization of political and economic power, which resulted in the expropriation of the traditional ruling class, including that of the ʿulamāʾ (religious scholars).[13] A Mamluk of Albanian descent, Muhammad ʿAli consolidated his rule by eliminating rival Mamluk factions and building a modern army.[14] He formed a class of "westernizers"[15] by hiring European engineers and scientists and sending students to France in order to acquire European "practical sciences."[16] These modernization policies led to the creation of various military academies and a school of languages (Madrasat al-Alsun), established in 1836. The founder of this school, Rifaʿa Rafiʿ al-Tahtawi, was an Azharite (Azhar scholar) turned state bureaucrat, who eventually held key posts in Egypt's new institutions of learning, and left his mark on educational and intellectual development throughout the Arab-Ottoman world.

Al-Tahtawi was born in 1801, in Upper Egypt (Tahta), to an Arab family of *ashrāf* (descendants of the Prophet), ultimately impoverished by Muhammad ʿAli's land and taxation reforms. At the age of sixteen, he enrolled at al-Azhar in order to study under a family friend, Hasan al-ʿAttar. Al-ʿAttar introduced his student to Arabic love poetry, history, and the secular knowledge that was no longer taught at this center of Islamic learning at the time.[17] Soon after al-Tahtawi's graduation in 1824, al-ʿAttar placed him as a preacher (waʿiẓ) in the growing state army. In 1826, al-ʿAttar proposed the name of his protégé to Muhammad ʿAli, suggesting he serve as the spiritual guide for the first student mission to Paris that same year.[18] Al-ʿAttar, who was interested in European modernity and had visited L'Institut d'Egypte and collaborated with its scholars during the French occupation, encouraged his student to record and analyze his encounters in Paris and to produce a travel guide that would serve Egyptian students on future missions.[19] Thus, Takhlis emerged from a structure of patronage that involves al-Tahtawi's family connections, his Azhar training under al-ʿAttar, and Muhammad ʿAli's sponsorship of the mission to France.

TAKHLIS'S PUBLICATION AND LITERARY CONTEXT

One of the first Arabic books to be published at Bulaq[20] in 1834, Takhlis was widely read throughout the Ottoman world.[21] Specifically, it "had found much favor with the ruler," Muhammad ʿAli, who ordered its translation to Turkish in 1839, and then had it circulated among his officials.[22] The book is composed of six essays (maqāla), each divided into various sections (fuṣūl). Though rooted in the Islamic medieval travel narrative (riḥla), Takhlis is written in a simple language, devoid of rhymed verse (sajaʿ).[23] In his preface (khuṭba), al-Tahtawi states that he travels to Paris to witness and report on the perfection (kamāl)[24] of European arts and sciences. Furthermore, he suggests that his work is groundbreaking in its reporting on some fundamental European practices, beliefs, and knowledge.[25] He boasts that his account of a modern European nation is unparalleled in the Arabic tradition. Melding riḥla and Arabic poetry with the ethnographic style of eighteenth-century European travel narratives, Takhlis should be positioned in relation to other riḥla texts in the nineteenth century, namely Niqula ibn Yusuf al-Turk's (1763–1828) work *Histoire de l'expédition des Français en Egypte* (1839),[26] and Muhammad al-Saffar's *rihla*.[27] This "Arab rediscovery of Europe," which will subsequently include fictionalized narratives such as Ahmad Faris al-Shidyaq's *Al-Saq 'ala al-Saq* (Leg over leg) (1855) and *'Alam al-Din* (1888) by 'Ali Mubarak (1823–1893), involves stylistic innovations and various articulations of European culture and discussions of its relevance to Ottoman social and political contexts.

Takhlis offers a key comparative framework for thinking through Arab and European cultures and languages in the first half of the nineteenth century. Mohammed Sawaie engages al-Tahtawi's translation strategies in rendering such terms as "theater" (*tiyatru*), "opera" (*ubira*), and "spectacle" (*sbaktakil*).[28] Sawaie notes that al-Tahtawi resorts to arabicization at times, and produces neologisms by drawing on "the model-of-translation program during the Abbasid era."[29] Considering the book as an early kind of "Occidentalism,"[30] Myriam Salama-Carr focuses on al-Tahtawi's "mediating agency" as a translator negotiating various cultural and political pitfalls in his account of Europe and discussion of the rise of science and secularism in a new age.[31] She reads his translation of such terms as "freedom" (*hurriyya*) and "citizen" (*muwatin*) as sites of negotiation that enable al-Tahtawi to express his opinion yet avoid censorship and reprimand. This mediation lies in a strategy of familiarization of the foreign by constantly discussing the similarities between Egypt and France, Arab-Islamic and European cultures. She argues that his work "does not convey a sense of rupture between the Islamic tradition and European culture, but . . . needs to be read in the context of the Reformist movement to which he belongs and the relationship that the movement was striving to establish between Islam and Modernity."[32]

Emphasizing the comparative aspect of al-Tahtawi's text, Shaden Tageldin reads *Takhlis*'s linguistic and cultural negotiations as an expression of an Arabic comparative practice in the nineteenth century. She analyzes al-Tahtawi's systematic attempts to both juxtapose Arabic and French languages and identify the danger in this juxtaposition. For instance, Tageldin argues that al-Tahtawi's understanding of French language structure and history makes him question the superiority of Arabic language and confront issues of universality, translatability, and linguistic and cultural kinship in new ways.[33] Drawing on Walter Benjamin's 1923 essay "The Task of the Translator," Tageldin situates *Takhlis*'s comparative practices in instances of danger, translation, and comparison. These instances operate both in relation to language and to the encounter with European modernity and urban settings in the nineteenth century.

In *Takhlis*, al-Tahtawi presents the encounter with French culture and learning within the framework of Muhammad 'Ali's desire for European technological modernity.[34] His encounter with Europe thus coincides with the encounter with the ruler's desire, both involving forms of danger. Therefore, understanding al-Tahtawi's encounter in France and his translation of concepts across languages and cultural contexts requires an investigation of the grueling experiences endured by al-Tahtawi and his colleagues.[35] The emergence of a modern Arab experience and textuality in *Takhlis* thus lends itself to Benjamin's analysis of the immediacy of experience in the nineteenth century.

ON SOME MOTIFS IN AL-TAHTAWI

In his essay "On Some Motifs in Baudelaire" (1939), Walter Benjamin posits shock experience as the necessary condition of modern poetry. He distinguishes individual experience (*Erlebnis*) from a collective or historical one (*Erfahrung*), i.e., the wisdom passed on across generations. In *Erlebnis*, consciousness plays the essential role of cushioning external stimuli: "Perhaps the special achievement of shock defense may be seen in its function of assigning to an incident a precise point in time in consciousness at the cost of the integrity of its contents."[36] *Erlebnis* has the potential of attenuating the shock incurred in a specific encounter by containing its effect "retroactively." In the context of literary production, the author recaptures through his/her experience what the urban setting of the nineteenth-century European metropolis has successfully managed to disintegrate, namely the possibility of experience itself.

According to Benjamin, the poet "completes in time" and concretizes the experience of the modern.[37] This concretization operates as a temporal closure to which any sequel can only be fortuitous. In Benjamin's reading of Baudelaire, the poet—a heroic figure likened to a fencer—expresses the experience in his violent confrontation with modernity. Baudelaire states that "by modernity I mean the ephemeral, the fugitive, the contingent, the half of art whose other half is the eternal and the immutable."[38] The ephemeral and immediate constitute the condition of modernity captured by the poet experiencing the crowded European metropolis. Discussing Benjamin's reading, Michael Jennings argues that *Erlebnis* is "in fact parried by consciousness and leaves a trace in the unconscious. Of particular interest to Benjamin is the case in which this defensive mechanism fails—that is, the case in which the shock is *not* parried by consciousness, but instead penetrates and deforms it."[39] The failure of the mechanism of consciousness to contain the shock is precisely what constitutes the modern for Benjamin. This violent and dangerous encounter gives rise to Baudelaire's poetic modernity. This experience, associated with the "evocation of a life of plenitude—of 'luxe, calme, et volupté'—is instead for Benjamin in large part a *repoussoir*, a perspective device that allows Baudelaire to 'fathom the full meaning of the breakdown which he, as a modern man, was witnessing.'"[40]

Baudelaire's poetic embodiment of modernity operates in a similar fashion in al-Tahtawi's text. Throughout *Takhlis*, al-Tahtawi systematically attempts to contain the shock experience that Benjamin identifies. *Takhlis*'s poetic associations, which often invoke Muhammad 'Ali, presents al-Tahtawi as the heroic fencer who physically confronts modernity by allowing his body to be assailed and scared by it. Thus, in order to understand the trials of Arab modernity at the intersection of the literary and the political, in between the Azharite ʿālim and Egypt's ruler, and between Europe and the Arab-Ottoman world in the nineteenth century, it is important to focus on *Takhlis*'s poetic associations. Focusing on these *other* texts within *Takhlis* allows us to explore the way individual experience both stages the breakdown that Benjamin theorizes and constitutes an intervention in and a manipulation of the ruler's desire for technological modernity. Modernity's embodiment in *Takhlis*'s literary spaces casts in a new light the meaning and implications of the processes of Westernization and modernization sweeping through the Ottoman Empire in the nineteenth century. This alters as well our understanding of the *Nahda*, with which these processes are generally associated.

MODERNITY ON A BOAT

Tahtawi's initial encounter with European modernity occurs on board the French battleship *La Truite*, which transports the students from Alexandria to Marseille.[41]

> We sailed on this sea (the Mediterranean) in the afternoon of Wednesday, the fifth day of Ramadan. We boarded [*imtaṭaynā*] a French man-of-war which does not strike fear in the heart of men [*lā tughādir fī fuʾād al-insān ruʿb*]. The seriousness [*razāna*] of its craftsmanship so captivates the heart of the traveler that he becomes a child [*ṣibā*] when he is on board of this vessel [*fī wisṭihā*]. It contained every piece of equipment required for all manner of crafts and professions. It also included weaponry as well as soldiers, and was fitted with 18 guns. The ship raised anchor on Thursday, the sixth day of the blessed month of Ramadan. At the time, there was a gentle breeze so that we were sailing without being aware of it and without suffering the slightest inconvenience from it. Prior to embarking, I had drunk large handfuls of salty seawater in compliance with what I had been told by one of my fellow ʿulamāʾ who had travelled to Istanbul. He said that it would ward off seasickness [*yadfaʿ alamah*]. As it happens, I did not get sick. However, at the time that I boarded the vessel I was gripped with fever, from which

I was freed only as a result of the voyage and the movement of the ship. Sometimes, the body heals through illness! We continued to sail without any violent movement or buffering for about four days, after which a storm rose and the sea began to surge and swell, playing with the bodies and souls of those on board. Most of us held on fast to the ground, and we all besought help from Him who mediates on the Day of Judgment. The words of a certain wit [ba'ḍ al-ẓu rafā'] also came to us: "*Danger befalls him who sails the sea; but more dangerous is he who sits in the company of kings without knowledge and wisdom*" [bi-ghayr 'ilm wa-ma'rifa]. It confirmed to us that which our erudite friend al-Safti inserted in a humorous poem [hazl] written by Abu Nuwas:

I saw all fears surrounded
by coitus as you—my servant girl of the sea—were pregnant
I swore on my life that I would no longer board a ship
only on the backs of animals would I travel for evermore.

Yet he who puts his trust in the Most Generous need not fear any great mishap. And how true are the following words of the poet:

Why did we sail the sea
when we all but perished from fear
On the Most Generous we relied
He will surely not leave us.[42]

Through a pre-Islamic gesture, al-Tahtawi starts with the personification of the ship (feminine), describing it as *maṭiyya* (as in *imtaṭaynā*, we rode), camel-like. However, in making the warship animate and familiar by associating it with the Arab-Islamic trajectory of travel, he employs an ambiguous idiomatic structure that further complicates this process of familiarization. In reference to the ship's construction and warring capabilities, he states that the ship *lā tughādir fī fu'ād al-insān ru'b*, which literally means, "it doesn't leave behind terror in the heart of man." He uses the verb *yughādir/ghādar* (depart, leave) in order to denote the act of travel but also to negate the emotion of fear and terror in the heart. Al-Tahtawi deploys this negation as a way of exposing the problematic of departure while simultaneously suppressing the experience of terror aboard the ship.[43] Moreover, *fu'ād* means the "tormented" and "anguished heart," which further emphasizes the form of negation with regard to terror. This calls attention to al-Tahtawi's ambivalent relation to the act of departure and to the ship's modernity. His ambivalence is further accentuated in the seduction metaphors used to render familiar that which *doesn't* terrorize him.

Locating it in the heart as well, al-Tahtawi experiences the ship's industrial perfection and power as forms of seduction and captivation. In drawing him to and engulfing him by its perfection, the ship rejuvenates al-Tahtawi and turns him into an inexperienced youth (*ṣibā*). Thus, the assumed anxiety in relation to modernity and its alleged terror is transformed and mitigated yet at the same time acknowledged and staged. Describing his terror and seduction, both threatening and rejuvenating, al-Tahtawi presents the movement of the ship, initially sailing through a gentle breeze, as curing him from his fever. The ship becomes the healing mother, cradling and lulling the inexperienced and sick youth (al-Tahtawi), but also the terrifying mother whose power he acknowledges and negates simultaneously. Incorporating and engulfing him, the *mother* ship, "fitted with 18 canons," unsettles al-Tahtawi and causes him pleasure and elation, confusion and anxiety.

The reference to the storm, which terrorizes al-Tahtawi and his colleagues, forcing them to take cover and collapse on the floor in a scene likened to one of bombardment, is juxtaposed to the lulling effect of the ship's motion. The stormy weather exacerbates the ship's terror, thereby transforming it into a stage of war. Fitted with guns and manned by soldiers, the ship gradually evolves in al-Tahtawi's description from the camel-like vessel—the cradling yet castrating mother—to a theater of war. This alignment of the stormy weather with military violence characterizes 'Abd al-Rahman al-Jabarti's (1753–1825/6) description of the French's entry into Cairo in 1798. In *'Aja'ib al-Athar* (*History of Egypt*), Egypt's last great chronicler depicts the rising waves of the Nile, the earth shaking, and people trembling with terror to the deafening sounds of French canons. As the invasion unfolds, al-Jabarti invokes God in the moment of disaster.[44] By conjuring up apocalyptic imagery, al-Jabarti suggests that the arrival of the French coincides, as it were, with that of Judgment Day. In a similar fashion, the storm al-Tahtawi experiences aboard the warship could not be separated from the colonial memory of the Egyptians who experienced the French soldiers' desecration of their city and, later on, al-Azhar itself.[45] Al-Tahtawi's experience of modernity on the ship is thus staged as an attack and a seduction, which involve turbulence and a near-death encounter. This complex site of the modern, full of ambivalence, is simultaneously a war zone, a place of youth, a city with professions and crafts, and a cause and object of desire. While it triggers al-Tahtawi's terror and anxiety, the modern is suffused with the memory and the possibility of conflict. By no means a smooth sea voyage, lulled by gentle breeze, the travel aboard *La Truite* becomes the site of a war experience. In this light, the encounter with modernity generates anguish and gives rise to multiple sites of memory, from the pre-Islamic "poet's quest" to European colonialism.

Al-Tahtawi's claim that the encounter with the ship had cured him from his fever needs to be scrutinized further. Throughout this passage, he situates this *non*-terrorizing experience within an Islamic cultural context. Having early on established the religious legitimacy of travel[46] for the pursuit of knowledge beyond Muslim lands (*al-diyār al-Islāmiyya*) by invoking the Prophet's trips to Jerusalem and Damascus, al-Tahtawi refers to the travel experience of al-ʿAttar and his fellow *ʿulamāʾ*. He thus positions his encounter within an Islamic epistemological framework and the *riḥla* genre specifically.[47] This operates as a process of familiarization that enables him to contain the experience of the modern. However, bearing in mind that Muslims are exempt from fasting in cases of sickness, impurity, or for purposes of travel, embarking on the fifth day of Ramadan interrupts al-Tahtawi's religious duties. In this light, drinking salt water prior to departure, as al-ʿAttar had advised him, forces him to break his fast. This locates the familiarization strategy within the Arab-Islamic

context yet points to its failure in enabling al-Tahtawi to obliterate his unsettling experience aboard the ship.

Al-Tahtawi's encounter generates anxieties that could not be
contained either by the ʿulamāʾ's logic of prevention or by the
Prophet's wisdom regarding travel for the pursuit of knowledge.
In this way, the riḥla genre and its underlying religious and epistemological frameworks are unsettled in al-Tahtawi's narrative.
Moving beyond *Erfahrung* as the collective experience of the
Prophet and the ʿulamāʾ, which is passed on to al-Tahtawi, his
encounter with technological modernity takes him off guard. The
encounter with the French battleship frames al-Tahtawi's individual experience (*Erlebnis*), which is dangerous and terrorizing.
Like the heroic yet childlike poet in Baudelaire who surrenders to
the experience of the modern in the hope of producing something
new, al-Tahtawi endures this encounter and bears its violence,
which forces him to collapse to the floor and prepare for Judgment Day. The stormy weather associated with the trip to Europe
causes al-Tahtawi's personal trials and reflects his psychological state. The sea's turbulence, aligned with those of the Nile at
the time of the French invasion, shatters al-Tahtawi's attempts
to familiarize and attenuate the experience aboard the ship. In
this way, al-Tahtawi's modern encounter constitutes a site of new
knowledge the acquisition of which involves trials, tribulations,
and a near-death experience.

Describing the relation to the ship through the registers of
seduction, fascination, and terror complicates al-Tahtawi's
ambivalent relation to Muhammad ʿAli's desire for technological
modernity that the ship represents. At the end of his description,
al-Tahtawi quotes a statement by a wit claiming that what is far
more dangerous than traveling by sea is sitting with kings while
lacking knowledge or having failed in acquiring it. This situates
al-Tahtawi's experience within the framework of his mission
more generally, and within Muhammad ʿAli's desire for modernity, more specifically. The danger in al-Tahtawi's encounter with
modernity thus pales in comparison to the danger involved in
his ignorance or inability to learn what is required of him. The

modern encounter is thus a necessary stage for sitting with rulers and serving as their advisor. In this way, al-Tahtawi emphasizes the question of patronage by linking Muhammad ʿAli's desire for European modernity to experiences of anxiety and seduction. Al-Tahtawi embodies Muhammad ʿAli's desire by collapsing on the ship's floor in fear of death. Desiring the ship and working toward its acquisition thus involves an encounter that terrorizes, seduces, and engulfs the young *ṭālib* (student, seeker of knowledge) on his way to France.

While al-Tahtawi's description in the text's main narrative betrays his attempts and inability to contain his emotions of anguish and terror, he introduces at the end a reflection by one of the *ẓurafāʾ* (men of wit) as well as poetic fragments from the Arabic classical tradition. Al-Tahtawi quotes both a *hazl* (humorous poem) by Abu Nuwas, the quintessential modern poet according to Adonis, who vows never to ride a ship again, and a verse from an anonymous poet invoking God's protection when traveling by sea. These poetic associations serve to further contain al-Tahtawi's experience. The reference to *hazl* anchors his attempt to both express yet undermine the powerful experience aboard the ship. As the trip evolves, he describes his anxiety and terror, almost unconsciously, in a series of poetic associations that interrupt his descriptions and analyses in the text's main narrative. These associations create spaces of literary fantasy that allow al-Tahtawi to both express and contain his powerful emotions. Thus, the experience of modernity will no longer be stifled or resisted by invoking tradition but rather engaged through an open confrontation that unfolds in poetic association. Investigating his encounters in France and examining their respective literary associations serve to frame *Takhlis* through a series of incidents and ruptures, with wide-ranging epistemological and political implications.

MIRRORS OF MARSEILLE

Arriving in Marseille after a long and perilous journey, al-
Tahtawi and his colleagues are initially quarantined for eigh-
teen days. Then, they spend two months intensively learning
French and sporadically exploring the city.[48] He describes in great
detail Marseille's wide streets, traffic, and public spaces. In one
instance, he discusses the overwhelming effect of the number of
mirrors on the wall in a café. People's reflections in the mirrors
give al-Tahtawi the impression of entering a "kasbah" (qaṣaba,
neighborhood) rather than an enclosed space. Disoriented and
confused, he experiences the mirrors' multiplication of his image
as one of visual fragmentation. Al-Tahtawi composes a poem that
describes how his reflection disappears yet reappears again as a
fleeting image, multiplied on the mirror-covered walls.

> Yaghību ʿannī fa-lā yabqā lahu atharu
> siwā bi-qalbī wa-lam yusmaʿ lahu khabaru
> Fa-ḥinā yulqī ʿalā l-mirʾāti ṣuratahu
> yalūḥu fīhā bi-dūrin kulluhā ṣuwaru.[49]

> [He disappeared from me, and not a trace of him has remained
> except in my heart, and no news is heard from him
> And when he appears, the mirror shows his appearance
> in which houses full of images become visible.][50]

While his reflection disappears without a trace, except in the
heart, it simultaneously reappears as a multiplied image. Through
the externalization of the "I" as the locus of identity, al-Tahtawi
addresses his reflection in the third-person singular (huwa, he) to
describe the discrepancy not only between him and his reflection
but also between his image and its fragmentation through visual
multiplication. The mirrors detach the signifier (the image) from
the signified (al-Tahtawi's identity or self), thereby generating an
experience of fragmentation. In this context, only the trace or the
memory of the self survives in the heart (qalb). The heart, which
functions as the locus of identity and loss in this poetic fragment, could also be compared to his heart as the site of the terror

experienced in the encounter with the battleship. This experience, which also accentuates the problematic of departure and abandonment ("he disappeared . . . and no news is heard from him"), is countered and attenuated through a fantasmatic return that takes shape poetically as well.

As al-Tahtawi experiences the loss of his "self," he retrieves it by conjuring up an Egyptian mirror through another poetic association in order to counter the experience of fragmentation in the café. Aligning his modern experience with the anguish of his own departure through travel, al-Tahtawi enacts a metaphorical return both to Egypt and to his "self," fantasized as whole, one with itself, and unfragmented.

> Ubarqi'u manẓara l-mir'āti 'anhu
> makhāfata an tuthnīhi li-'aynī
> Uqāṣī mā uqāṣī wa-huwa fadhdhu
> fa-kayfa idhā tajallā farqadayni.[51]

> [I veil the view of the mirror from him
> for fear it should double before my eyes
> I suffer what is my unique suffering
> but what if two stars should reveal themselves.][52]

Whereas the mirrors (plural) in the café multiply al-Tahtawi's image, the Egyptian mirror reaffirms it (*tuthnī*) as it consolidates its immediate relation to the body. Given the fact that the verb *tuthnī* shares the root of the word "two" (*ithnayn*), the poem highlights the meaning of *tuthnī* as praising and reassuring through a process of visual doubling and reflection. However, al-Tahtawi claims that he is able to interrupt this doubling by veiling the mirror, thereby protecting and consolidating his singularity or self. Thus, in conjuring up the Egyptian mirror in the second poem, al-Tahtawi seeks to govern the process of representation and to overcome the fragmentation incurred in the encounter with the mirrors in Marseille. The visual affects in this scene thus mark the collapse of representation as the privileged mode of the production of subjectivity in the cross-cultural encounter.

Anouar Louca performs a psychoanalytic reading of al-
Tahtawi's encounter with the mirrors. Analyzing this scene as
a Lacanian "mirror stage," Louca suggests that al-Tahtawi
acquires a new cultural identity, both Egyptian and French, that
of the imam and student, seeker of European knowledge.[53] In
Lacan's "mirror stage," when the child looks at her/himself in the
mirror, his or her bodily reflection becomes the physical locus of
identity.[54] The "mirror stage" coincides with the advent of subjectivity, i.e., the child's access to the Symbolic or language. The
identification of the child with his or her image stands, in effect,
as an inaugural moment of a particular mode of self-representa-
tion. The imago (one's reflection), according to Lacan, becomes
that with which the child identifies. In this context, the formation of subjectivity coincides with the inauguration of the self as
a fantasized whole that counters the alienation produced in the
encounter with the mirror. Fantasy characterizes the discrepancy
between one and oneself, between the child's body and his/her
reflection.

Louca argues that al-Tahtawi's encounter with mirrors exposes
the ambivalence of his task both as the mission's imam and ṭālib
(student). However, this reading dismisses the important role
of fantasy and the unconscious, fundamental to the advent of
subjectivity in Lacan. Louca suggests that al-Tahtawi realizes or
becomes "consciously" aware of his new identity and the duality of his task in Europe.[55] However, al-Tahtawi's encounter with
mirrors in Marseille disrupts and displaces the process of mis-
recognition necessary for the advent of subjectivity in Lacan. In
fact, al-Tahtawi's imago disappears and gets multiplied only to
resurface again through a process of doubling and consolidation
in the Egyptian mirror.

In the absence of a fixed or direct reflection of himself in the
café mirrors, al-Tahtawi's identity (reflection) is subsumed in his
imago, which relegates the "I" or the "self" to a forgotten trace
in the heart. This experience of absence and fragmentation arises
from the encounter with the mirrors, but also from the act of
travel or departure, which leaves the "self" unable to send news,

write, or speak. Given Lacan's model, this state of absence positions the lost and departed self out of sight and outside of language. The encounter in Marseille thus marks a form of breakdown or collapse that conditions al-Tahtawi's fantasmatic return
to the Egyptian mirror as the locus of a reaffirmed and recov-
ered "I." His experience of fragmentation in the café triggers the
return to his reflection (imago) in the Egyptian mirror as a way of
resisting and overcoming the encounter with modernity and the
trials of departure (both voyage [*riḥla*] and its pre-Islamic poetic
articulation [*raḥīl*]). Conjuring up the Egyptian mirror frames
al-Tahtawi's fantasizing his "self" as whole and misrecognized
yet affirmed and consolidated. Always in the Lacanian context,
this fantasmatic consolidation of the self in the Egyptian mirror
allows al-Tahtawi to "veil" his fragmentation in Marseille.[56]

The return to the mirror in Egypt is not only a recuperation
of a comforting structure that allows the subject of experience
to counter the unsettling effects of the mirrors in Marseille but
an activation of poetry as a site and register of this fantasmatic
return as well.[57] Al-Tahtawi's experience of fragmentation or castration in Lacanian terms leads the critic to examine both the
site of return (Egypt) and its medium (the poem). This double
return exposes the way poetry embodies al-Tahtawi's experience
in France. The relation between the experiential and the literary, between *Takhlis*'s main and descriptive narrative on the one
hand, and its poetic associations dismissed by scholars on the
other, is a critical site for investigating the historical and aesthetic
implications of desiring and encountering modernity—trials of
Arab modernity—in the nineteenth century.

Furthermore, while the poem about Egypt seeks to attenuate
al-Tahtawi's experience, the poem about the multiplied imago
or lost "self" marks the breakdown in the mechanism of consciousness. Michael Jennings argues that according to Benjamin, "heroism consists in [the poet's] constant willingness to
have the character of his age mark and scar his body. 'The
resistance that modernity offers to the natural productive élan
of an individual is out of all proportion to his strength. It is

understandable if a person becomes exhausted and takes ref-
uge in death.' Heroism thus assumes the form of a mourning
that has not yet occurred but always threatens."[58] Whereas al-
Tahtawi's return to the Egyptian mirror is an attempt to contain
the shock experience, his experience of fragmentation in Marseille brings about the collapse of the mechanism of consciousness and of its ability to parry shocks. Just like the interplay
between expressing the experience of terror aboard the ship
and trying to suppress or contain it, two complementary experiences of modernity are juxtaposed in this scene as well: one
scars al-Tahtawi by inscribing loss in his heart while the other
fantasmatically brings him back to himself and to Egypt. This
reading of al-Tahtawi's relation to modernity moves us beyond
the monolithic "modern" as a site of exchange and translation
between Europe and the Ottoman world. Al-Tahtawi's body,
which is reflected in the mirrors, is at the center of this modern
experience full of anxiety and ambivalence.

WEATHERING PARIS

Whereas the café in Marseille frames al-Tahtawi's unsettling
encounter with European urbanity, Paris exposes this encounter's
violence even further. Paris is "the necessary setting for imagistic
renderings of those moments of existence that Baudelaire did not
so much experience as endure, or 'suffer' (leiden)."[59] The suffering involved in this encounter is best represented in al-Tahtawi's
experience of the weather in Paris, echoing in this regard his
experience of the stormy weather aboard the French battleship. In
the long title of Takhlis's third essay, al-Tahtawi alleges that this
is the section "he will perfect the most" as it involves a description of Paris and of its dwellers. He elaborates on the etymology
of the word "Paris" and discusses the city's geography, time zone,
and climate. Bemoaning its grey and gloomy weather, al-Tahtawi
claims that in Paris the sun rarely appears, as if "it had died for
the night to live" (my translation).[60] Identifying with the Parisian
sun, veiled by thick clouds, he interrupts his discussion of the

weather and quotes a series of poems that betray feelings of anxiety through a recurrent metaphor of sexual impotence.

In the first poem by al-Shihab al-Hijazi (790–875), the poet suggests that the sun "attempts to tear apart the resisting clouds like an impotent man attempting to tear the hymen of a virgin"[61] (*tuḥāwilu fatqa ghaymin wa-huwa yaʾbā, ka-ʿinnīnin yuḥāwilu fatqa bikrin*).[62] By comparing it to an impotent man, the poet personifies the sun, accentuating its struggle to penetrate the clouds in order to shine. The verse "it is like an impotent man attempting to tear the hymen of a virgin" is repeated verbatim in the second anonymous poem, always in the context of the sun trying to pierce through thick clouds. The third poetic fragment, by ʿAbd al-Rahman al-Safti (d. 1848), introduces Egypt as an object of desire; while Egypt is personified as the virgin fleeing her castrated suitor, he pursues her to "pierce her hymen, like an impotent man attempting to tear the hymen of a virgin"[63] (*ka-ʿinnīnin yuḥāwilu fatqa bikrin*]).[64] The verse in question reappears in a fourth anonymous poem about a man trying to conquer the city of Acre, though failing to deflower it as he would a virgin. This is no doubt a reference to Napoleon's unsuccessful attempt to take Acre in 1799. In the last poem, al-Tahtawi introduces Muhammad ʿAli and claims that "the patron," or, more literally, "the master of livelihoods" (*waliyy al-niʿam*), deflowered Acre and pierced its hymen, and "it was assumed that he would be impotent before it; however, he is strong and capable of piercing the seal of all cities of Syria and beyond"[65] (*fa-kāna man ẓannā annahu ʿinnīn bi-l-nisba ilayhā huwa shadīd qawiyy ʿalā faḍḍ al-khitām li-jamīʿ mudun al-Shām wa-ghayr al-Shām*).[66] Al-Tahtawi thus concludes by invoking Muhammad ʿAli as the virile penetrator and conqueror of cities.

While the mirrors in Marseille disorient al-Tahtawi by fragmenting his reflection, Parisian weather blinds him completely and further exposes his impotence and castration. In order to obliterate this experience, he conjures up Muhammad ʿAli as the conqueror who, like a *deus ex machina*, erupts in al-Tahtawi's poetic association and breaks the cycle of sexual anxiety. The reference to Muhammad ʿAli's taking of Acre in the last poem interrupts the recurrence of sexual impotence.[67] These poetic fragments, which accentuate al-Tahtawi's suffering, introdue two heroic functions: the heroic poet and subject of experience, and the heroic ruler who is conjured up as a savior in al-Tahtawi's fantasy. The heroic function, in this context, arises in between these two figures: one defined by Benjamin's reading of Baudelaire as the modern hero subjected to Paris's weather and urbanity, and the other embodied in the figure of the ruler and patron whose sheer virility and force conquer cities and break their hymens.[68] Similar to al-Tahtawi's trials aboard the ship, forms of struggle and confrontation, embodied in physical collapse and narrative dissonance, take shape at the intersection of these heroic functions, staging in the process the interplay between the aesthetic and the political in *Takhlis*.

Al-Tahtawi frames his relation to the weather in Paris by conjuring up Muhammad ʿAli as the virile conqueror whose protection he seeks in order to overcome his experience of fragmentation. The embodiment of the modern in this encounter moves Muhammad ʿAli from a historical figure (sacker of Acre) to a literary one (virile hero). The poetic fragments enact through their repetition both the archaic power of the sovereign and his heroic function as a literary figure in al-Tahtawi's fantasy. Through his complaint to Muhammad ʿAli, which is coupled with praise, al-Tahtawi introduces in this scene a poetic function that redefines heroism by situating it at the *heart* of the modern experience.

The violence al-Tahtawi endures as a result of the ruler's desire for technological modernity is expressed in the poetic repetition as an encounter that involves both the seeker of European knowledge (al-Tahtawi) and the one who desires it at the same time, i.e, Muhammad ʿAli himself. In this scene, al-Tahtawi presents Muhammad ʿAli as the heroic figure who both exposes al-Tahtawi's fragmentation and withstands it alongside him. *Takhlis*'s poetic association fantasmatically refigures questions of political power and legitimacy in the nineteenth-century encounter with Europe. The disturbance al-Tahtawi stages and the anxiety he endures as a result of Paris's weather are embodied in the literary invocation of the ruler to whom *madḥ* (praise poetry) is traditionally addressed, either as a savior in the encounter with the weather, or as the patron of poets and learned men in the encounter with the ship. Literary fantasy emerges as a site of embodiment and a space of negotiation between the anxiety of the young *'ālim* encountering modernity and that of the ruler desiring it. However, as the narrative evolves, al-Tahtawi's own desire for modernity, thus far contained or displaced onto that of the ruler, becomes intertwined with Muhammad 'Ali's desire. This fantasmatic intertwinement is the key site for the transformation of the Azharite scholar into state bureaucrat and modernizer of the educational system in Egypt under Muhammad 'Ali.

FATHER AND LOVER

Muhammad 'Ali kept a close watch over the mission's progress. Al-Tahtawi describes how he and his colleagues took periodic exams, administered by Jomard and other French instructors, who would then inform Muhammad 'Ali of the results. Al-Tahtawi mentions a letter by Muhammad 'Ali in the form of a *fermān* (decree), in which he encourages them to learn yet admonishes them for their procrastination. Like a firm and disciplining father, Muhammad 'Ali promises yet withholds the students recognition, constantly reminding them of the task at hand. In his commentary on the document, al-Tahtawi equates the fulfillment of Muhammad 'Ali's *gharaḍ* (his desire for military technology) with the performance of a filial duty.[69] Al-Tahtawi expresses the ways in which he and his colleagues perceive their task in France as bringing about Egypt's modernization. Gradually, al-Tahtawi conjures up Muhammad 'Ali as the military conqueror who reverses the imam's impotence, and as Egypt's modern ruler who becomes aware of his desire reflected and refigured in *Takhlis*'s literary spaces. The articulation of the modern lies in this interplay, which systematically decenters the desire for European modernity and stages its trials in various incidents, encounters, and ruptures in between the ruler and the imam, France and Egypt, and nineteenth-century travelogues and pre-Islamic poetry.

Following his encounter with Paris's weather, al-Tahtawi discusses French arts, sciences, and politics, describing in great detail the painstaking acquisition of European knowledge as "the arts required" (*al-funūn al-maṭlūba*)[70] by Muhammad ʿAli. Abandoning the metaphors of impotence and castration, al-Tahtawi deploys metaphors of sexual gratification in order to express his fulfillment of the pasha's desire.

> Wa-min hādhih al-maqāla tafham anna taʿallum al-funūn laysa sahl, wa-annahu lā bud li-ṭālib al-maʿārif min iqtiḥām al-akhṭār li-bulūgh al-awṭār fī tilk al-aqṭār.[71]

> [From this essay you will understand that the study of the arts is not an easy thing and that those seeking knowledge must defy dangers in order to attain their goals in those countries.][72]

Al-Tahtawi addresses the reader directly with the second-person pronoun (masculine), inviting him to appreciate the difficulty of his task as a seeker (*ṭālib*, student) of European knowledge. The imagery of sexual conquest, previously restricted to the expression of Muhammad ʿAli's desire, characterizes in this context al-Tahtawi's task.[73] As his acquisition of knowledge necessitates a dangerous act of penetration (*iqtiḥām*), al-Tahtawi overcomes the castration and impotence experienced in his encounters with the ship, the café in Marseille, and Paris's weather. Addressing the reader in this way, al-Tahtawi asks him to witness his pains and trials yet acknowledge his willingness to acquire Muhammad ʿAli's *gharaḍ* at the cost of his own life. In a direct interpellation of the reader, al-Tahtawi interrupts his discussion of the process of acquiring European knowledge and quotes the following poetic fragments:

> Daʿīnī anālu mā lā yunālu mina l-ʿulā
> fa-sahlu l-ʿulā fī-l-ṣaʿbi wa-l-ṣaʿbu fī-l-sahli
> Turīdīnā idrāka l-maʿālī rakhīṣatan
> wa-lā budda dūna l-shahdi min ibari l-naḥli.[74]

[Let me attain the heights that are unattainable
for its ease lies in hardship, and in ease lies hardship
You wish to attain higher things at a cheap price
but before the honey must come the bee stings.] [75]

Inna l-faḍāʾila bi-l-akhṭāri mūlaʿatun
fa-bghā l-faḍāʾila wa-bdhul juhdaka l-thamana
Wa-in arāka l-hawā minhu l-hawāna fa-qul
ḥukmu l-maniyyati fī ḥubbi l-ḥabībi munā.[76]

[Virtues are passionate about dangers
desire virtues and waste no effort in acquiring them
And if love makes you experience torment
trust that the verdict of death, for the lover's sake, is my wish.] (my
  translation)

Al-Tahtawi presents lovemaking and sexual penetration as metaphors for the acquisition of European knowledge within the context of Muhammad ʿAli's desire. In the first poem by al-Mutanabbi
(915–965),[77] the quintessential master of *madḥ* (praise poetry),
the poet conveys to his beloved (a woman, given the feminine
pronoun *anti* [you]) the difficulty in acquiring the knowledge she
desires. Reminding his beloved of the difficult task at hand, he
exposes her expectation of a facile acquisition (*idrāka l-maʿālī
rakhīṣatan*).[78] The beloved, in this case, is unaware of the requirements of her demand and of its painful repercussions on the poet
and seeker of knowledge (*ṭālib*). In the second poem, al-Tahtawi
claims that the fulfillment of the addressee's desire is not only
painful (as in the "bee stings" in the first poem) but also brings
about the *ṭālib*'s encounter with death (*maniyya*). Asking death
to be his judge in the second poem, the *ṭālib* willingly acquiesces
to the coercive desire of his beloved by choosing to encounter the
dangers entailed in its fulfillment.

Since al-Tahtawi states that in this section he describes the
process of acquiring Muhammad ʿAli's object of desire (*gharaḍ
waliyy al-niʿam*), then these poems conjure up the pasha himself, the desirer of European knowledge and the mission's patron.
As he feminizes Muhammad ʿAli in the first poem, al-Tahtawi

presents him as the insatiable lover, unaware of his desire's implications. Although this acquisition involves a dangerous penetration (*iqtiḥām*), al-Tahtawi, the student-lover (*ṭālib al-ʿilm*), is will-
ing to risk his life in the process. Driven by the promise of sexual
gratification—his and that of Muhammad ʿAli—given the metaphor of honey or royal jelly (*shahd*), al-Tahtawi overcomes the
impotence experienced in his early encounters with French culture and technology and enters into a fantasmatic relation with
Muhammad ʿAli. However, this fantasized sexual encounter is
grounded in the logic of immediate gratification, involving "bee
stings," and pertaining to the acquisition of Muhammad ʿAli's
gharaḍ within the mission's confines. The second poem, however,
and through its staging of an encounter with death, pertains to a
more comprehensive and thus dangerous encounter with modernity beyond the mission's circumscribed goals and aims.

While in the first poem al-Tahtawi addresses a capricious
lover, unaware of the difficulty and pain involved in her sexual
fulfillment, the addressee's desire in the second poem incurs al-
Tahtawi's confrontation with death. In the progression from the
first to the second poem, al-Tahtawi transforms the desire of the
beloved from one involving immediate gratification to a desire
for virtues, which he sets out to fulfill at the expense of his own
life. Whereas in the encounter with Paris's weather, the conquer-
ing hero who faces death on the battlefield is none other than
Muhammad ʿAli, in this set of verses it is al-Tahtawi himself
who fights for his ruler and risks death for his sake. This reversal
anchors the experience of the modern again at the intersection of
two heroic functions: the ruler and the *ʿālim*. From al-Tahtawi's
impotence and Muhammad ʿAli's virility in the encounter with
the weather, we move in this section to a virile and death-con-
quering al-Tahtawi on the one hand, and a feminized Muhammad ʿAli, damsel-like on the other. The poet's willingness to die
for his beloved (Muhammad ʿAli) in the second poem thus transforms and redirects the beloved's desire.

In these poetic fragments, al-Tahtawi appropriates the praise
genre or *madḥ* in order to introduce a modern experience, which

is not only about pain and hardship as in the first poem by al-Mutanabbi, but involves an encounter with death as well. Al-Tahtawi's poetic association as a site of the modern intervenes in the genre of *madḥ* itself as a way of recasting the ruler's desire. As Samer Ali argues, "[in] praise hymns the patron relied on the poet to corroborate and enhance his public appearance as the cosmic hero. The poet could then pressure him to prove his nobility with a sign of generosity."[79] Specifically, Ali notes that "in the *Rusafiyya* ode the poet symbolically forgoes the romantic feminine beloved for the political beloved in the person of al-Mutawakkil."[80] The substitution of the beloved by the ruler, the invocation of his power, and the encounter with death in his name and within the framework of his desire serve to position al-Tahtawi's text at the juncture of various literary and cultural contexts. The experience of modernity thus does not simply situate *Takhlis* in a modern travel genre but also involves a return in various directions and at various levels to the structuring tropes of the Arabic tradition. Al-Tahtawi conjures up Muhammad 'Ali as the ruler yet intervenes in his desire by occupying the position of the modern poet who endures a deadly encounter for his sake. This establishes a new structure of patronage between the Azharite and Egypt's pasha, fantasmatically transforming their roles into those of the new bureaucrat and the modern ruler. This double transformation, gradually taking shape in al-Tahtawi's literary fantasies, leads us to identify a narrative within a narrative, a level of articulation of the relation between power and knowledge, crucial to understanding *Takhlis* and the *Nahda* problematic which it stages. This transformation takes shape in the literary embodiment of al-Tahtawi's modern experience in between Egypt and France. Questions of borrowing from the West, return to tradition, and resistance to modernity as a clear and recognizable "Western project" are unsettled in this new approach to analyzing the unconscious or fantasmatic spaces of this early *Nahda* text.

Tahtawi's transition from Azharite *'alim* to bureaucrat are coextensive with a modern experience that redefines both the

literary and the political in *Takhlis*. The modern experience and
its relation to genre and to the transformation of the *ʿālim* into
a bureaucrat and the pasha into a modern ruler appropriates the
madḥ genre in a variety of ways. In al-Tahtawi's work, this genre
relies on the use of poetry and allegory for shaping the ruler's
desire, obtaining privilege, yet bringing it into the modern. This
process aligns the role of the court poet (al-Mutanabbi) with
the modern poet encountering death in Benjamin's sense. This
allows us to reread al-Mutanabbi's poetry in light of Benjamin's
understanding of poetic modernity and to align Adonis's reading of modernity with Benjamin's, and the Abbasid period with
the nineteenth century. It also serves to deconstruct the interpretation of Ibn Jahm's poem. Given Ali's reading, the ruler asks
Ibn Jahm to immerse himself in Baghdad's urban environment in
order to produce a modern poem. Analyzing the appropriation
of *madḥ* in *Takhlis* given Benjamin's reading of modernity, one
could argue that it is in fact poetry itself—the *Rusafiyya* ode—
that makes both the poet and the ruler modern. In this context,
modernity no longer consists in material acquisition or artifacts
or social structures imported from the West, but characterizes
instead the experience involved in fulfilling the ruler's desire or
demand. Like Ibn al-Jahm, al-Tahtawi's fulfillment of a modern
desire—his and that of Muhammad ʿAli—conditions the modernity of the ruler and of *Takhlis* as well.

SITTING WITH KINGS

Throughout *Takhlis*, al-Tahtawi intervenes in the desire of power
through poetic and literary associations, which arise from experiences of rupture and collapse embodied in the text.[81] In these
moments of staging, al-Tahtawi experiences modernity by casting
himself in the role of the wise advisor to the modern ruler. This
structure is alluded to at the end of his description of the encounter with the ship. Al-Tahtawi's discussion of French culture is
systematically interrupted by poetic associations as well as anecdotes about al-Farabi (870–950) and Sayf al-Dawla al-Hamadani

(reigned 944–967), Nuʿman ibn al-Mundhir (reigned 582–613) and Kisra Khosrow Parvez (reigned 590–628), and ʿUmar ibn al-Khattab (reigned 634–644) and ʿAmr ibn al-ʿAs (573–664). In these embedded narratives about Arab rulers, al-Tahtawi extols their virtue, courage, generosity, and patronage of arts and culture. One could argue that these anecdotes arise from moments of translationality, comparatively framing al-Tahtawi's juxtaposition of French culture with Arab-Islamic cultural history. However, what appears as a process of familiarization, discussed in Salama-Carr's article about language, for instance, in fact arises from a modern experience that ends up unsettling the function of familiarization and marking its collapse. This collapse theoretically moves the debate from questions of cross-cultural representation, translation, and exchange to embodiment, affect, and experience.

In his anecdote about Sayf al-Dawla al-Hamadani, the fabled ruler of Aleppo and patron of poets and scholars, and al-Farabi, the great Muslim scholar and scientist, al-Tahtawi brings the modern experience in all its epistemological and material violence to Muhammad ʿAli's court.[82] Al-Tahtawi starts by comparing Silvestre de Sacy to al-Farabi, claiming that in order to understand de Sacy's importance for the French, it's important to consider al-Farabi's importance in the Arab-Islamic context. As he makes a philosophical observation about the nature of communication, al-Tahtawi praises the work of de Sacy, the "eminent scholar" (*ḥabr*) at the École des Langues Orientales in Paris. Al-Tahtawi then claims that this *ḥabr*'s erudition and prestige allow the reader to imagine what al-Farabi was like during his time. Then, interrupting this explanation, al-Tahtawi tells an anecdote in which he fantasmatically casts de Sacy, al-Farabi, and himself in the role of the wise scholar, and Sayf al-Dawla and Muhammad ʿAli in that of the modern ruler and patron of scholars and poets. This staging is fictionalized in a violent confrontation between Sayf al-Dawla and al-Farabi.

Al-Tahtawi narrates al-Farabi's encounter with Sayf al-Dawla while attending a gathering of the finest scholars at his court in

Aleppo. When al-Farabi first enters, the ruler orders him to take a seat. Responding to the ruler's order, al-Farabi asks: "Where I am or where you are?" (*haythu anā aw haythu ant*). "Where you are" (*haythu ant*), replies the prince.[83] Al-Farabi then makes his way toward Sayf al-Dawla, displaces him from his pillow, and takes his seat. Alarmed and angered at this behavior, the prince consults his personal guards about the old man's insolence. Listening to the conversation between Sayf al-Dawla and the guards, "speaking in a mysterious language that only they understood" (*lisān . . . qalla an ya'rifuh ahad*),[84] al-Farabi asks Sayf al-Dawla to be patient. Impressed by his linguistic abilities, Sayf al-Dawla holds a private audience with al-Farabi, who then converses with the court's erudite scholars, impressing them with his knowledge and argumentation. Al-Farabi also assembles and plays a musical instrument, leading his audience to tears at one point, and to laughter at another. Like Socrates at the end of Plato's *Symposium*, al-Farabi *tarakahum niyām wa-kharaj* (left them asleep and departed).[85]

In al-Tahtawi's anecdote, Sayf al-Dawla appears as the paragon of the enlightened prince, surrounded by poets and scholars. Despite al-Farabi's violent displacement of the ruler from his seat, his boldness and erudition earn him admiration and respect. Al-Tahtawi ends his anecdote by imagining al-Farabi in an idyllic, pastoral setting, benefitting from Sayf al-Dawla's generosity: "[Al-Farabi] enjoys being alone in the outdoors, in a park, where he mingles with water, trees, and fruits, writing his books. As he sleeps on the grass, the wind transports the leaves along with al-Farabi's papers from one place to another. Sayf al-Dawla provides al-Farabi with a generous allowance" (my translation).[86] While the wind transports al-Farabi's writings as he sleeps in the park, another wind, nine centuries later, transports al-Tahtawi from Egypt to France in order to seek European knowledge, fulfill his ruler's desire, and benefit from his generosity. The anecdote thus embodies the relation between the ruler and the *'ālim* in a new age. To this ideal relation between al-Farabi and Sayf al-Dawla, between power and knowledge, al-Tahtawi implicitly juxtaposes his relation to his patron, Muhammad ʿAli, the ruler desiring technological modernity. This structure moves al-Tahtawi from the position of the anxious, impotent *ṭālib*, castrated by the desire of power, to that of the scholar whose learning commands respect and admiration, displacing power from its seat. Thus, power shifts in this anecdote from its association with a penetrating and archaic force associated with Muhammad ʿAli, to learnedness's hypnotic effects in the context of a new experience and knowledge. Al-Tahtawi's anecdote transforms learning itself into a power that subdues rulers in their own courts, surrounded by their guards and advisors.

While al-Tahtawi concludes his description of his experience aboard the battleship with a cautioning about the danger in "sitting in the company of kings without knowledge," in this scene al-Tahtawi overcompensates, in some sense, not only by acquiring the necessary knowledge to "sit in the company of kings" but one that allows him to displace them from their seat. The violent displacement, which could also be read as a colonial foreshadowing similar to the one evoked aboard the battleship, derives its power from al-Tahtawi's modern experience in France. The anecdote thus involves a process of "becoming modern" both in terms of acquisition of new knowledge in Europe, and in terms of the violent encounter with modernity endured by al-Tahtawi. Just as Sayf al-Dawla recognizes al-Farabi's learnedness and offers him an allowance at the end, Muhammad ʿAli is fantasmatically presented in al-Tahtawi's anecdote as the generous patron. This new form of patronage as the condition of Muhammad ʿAli's modernity thus consists in the pasha's acknowledgment of al-Tahtawi's new knowledge, and the pain and danger incurred in its acquisition as well. This acknowledgment fantasmatically stages al-Tahtawi's own transformation into a modern scholar who will eventually found upon his return Madrasat al-Alsun (School of Languages) and thus help lay the foundation of a modern educational system through this and other key posts, and by publishing such works as *Manahij al-Albab al-Misriyya fi Mabahij al-Adab al-ʿAsriyya* (The paths of Egyptian hearts in the joys of contemporary letters) (1869) and *Kitab al-Murshid al-Amin li-l-Banat wa-l-Banin* (Honest guide on the education of boys and girls) (1872).

CONCLUSION

Investigating the question of modernity in al-Tahtawi's work requires a close examination of its poetic associations. As debates about modernity in *Nahda* travel narratives or the "Arab rediscovery of Europe" genre center on the descriptive levels of texts, they ignore poetic associations, affects, and modes of embodiment. Focusing on the literary aspect of *Takhlis* and reading it as the *unconscious* of the *Nahda* narrative, this chapter has argued that it is in the literary staging of the relation between the ruler and the ʿālim that one could identify the site of negotiation and trials of Arab modernity in the nineteenth century. Given the structure of patronage within which al-Tahtawi operates in *Takhlis*, it is at the text's fantasmatic and experiential level that one ought to read his relation to power in a new age. Al-Tahtawi's modernity takes shape as a staging of the encounter with European modernity, involving both the ruler and the student/traveler at the same time. In this deployment of various roles and encounters across genres and cultural frameworks, al-Tahtawi draws Muhammad ʿAli into a violent encounter with European modernity—as he was drawn to it himself—in order to fulfill a modern desire. Instead of focusing on what al-Tahtawi observes and discusses in the main narrative, it is crucial to examine the ways in which a new relation to power unfolds in *Takhlis*'s moments of rupture and collapse, fantasy and anxiety.[87] Experiencing modernity and becoming modern oneself thus could be read in al-Tahtawi's trials and tribulations, which also operate as modes of rehearsal for new positions within an economy of patronage that draws on *madḥ* as a structure of a modern desire. In these multiple transformations and manipulations of both al-Tahtawi's and Muhammad ʿAli's positions, staged in the literary associations interspersed throughout *Takhlis*, one could identify the interplay of the aesthetic and the political in this early *Nahda* text.

Moreover, in this chapter I have argued that the relation to European modernity and the deployment of the Arab-Islamic tradition and models of learning can be investigated as a *repoussoir*, a by-product of the experience of the modern embodied in *Takhlis*. This *repoussoir*, which, according to Benjamin, allows the poet to fathom the collapse in the mechanism of consciousness, produces the idealized past as in Baudelaire's poem "Invitation au voyage," in which he claims: "Là, tout n'est qu'ordre et beauté, luxe, calme, et volupté" (There, all is order and beauty, luxury, peace, and bliss).[88] This idyllic state, the product of the modern, aligns Baudelaire's musing with al-Tahtawi's description of al-Farabi's pastoral setting at the end of the anecdote about his encounter with Sayf al-Dawla. Muhsin al-Musawi argues that the "*Nahdah* discourse [is] usually described as the awakening discourse, which is so called for its association with the European model of modernity and its desire to court a possible retention of a glorious past."[89] In light of my reading of al-Tahtawi, the past is not retrieved through the process of mimicry or a dialectical engagement with or resistance to European discourse on civilization and culture as it is often assumed. The return to the past in *Takhlis* is the outcome of trials and ruptures incurred through a modern experience. Al-Tahtawi's confrontation with modernity leads him to retrieve and appropriate but also deconstruct and refigure the Arabic tradition and its alleged "golden age." This complex work of subversion and appropriation, often violent and unconscious, unsettles "tradition" as a fixed and monolithic category. Tradition is by no means a site of authenticity that is preserved in the past and could be accessed in the present as whole and one with itself. An examination of al-Tahtawi's affects and associations thus exposes a disciplinary and scholarly fantasy that draws on "tradition" to resist or counter an equally reified notion of "modernity," imagined as unchanging and one with itself. Tradition, I argue, is always already modern in al-Tahtawi's literary text. In fact, it is precisely his appropriation of

the so-called "tradition"—anecdotes, *rihla*, and *madh*—that sets
the stage for his own modernity and that of Muhammad ʿAli.
This reading moves us beyond tradition/modernity as a set of
distinct and homogeneous categories that maintain their characteristics and attributes in the "Arab rediscovery of Europe" narratives. The processes of confrontation and embodiment I identified in *Takhlis* demonstrate that modernity and tradition are
always already intertwined through movement (of individuals,
ideas, affects) and distance that connect yet separate them. This
series of movements, ruptures, and incidents express the way
Arab modernity is staged, tried out, rehearsed, fantasized, and
imagined in the texts I examine in this book.

Takhlis's literary spaces constitute sites of embodiment of
forms of collapse and dissonance, which refigure genres and
social and political relations. Reading this *other* text opens up
the *Nahda* to multiple interpretations that allow us to challenge
the linear or genealogical readings of Arab modernity as starting
either in the Abbasid period or in the eighteenth or nineteenth
century. The modern needs to be read at a dynamic textual level,
in the interstices of time periods and genres. This reading of al-
Tahtawi allows us to situate play, incidents, and transformations, which are constitutive of this body of works, in between
the Abbasid and the contemporary period, European and Arabic literature and philosophy. The theoretical and comparative
emphasis on intertextuality across literary and cultural frameworks serves to debunk accepted notions of culture and civilization in the Arab and European contexts. In the next chapter, I
explore the way al-Shidyaq's experience of modernity, expressed
in modes of embodiment, satire, and linguistic play, unsettles
the discourse on civilization in Europe. A close attention to al-
Shidyaq's deconstructive strategy serves to interrogate the way
European civilization and the Arab-Islamic tradition are imagined and produced in the second half of the nineteenth century.

CHAPTER THREE

Aversion to Civilization

I have been assured by a very knowing American of my acquaintance in London, that a young healthy child well nursed is at a year old a most delicious, nourishing, and wholesome food, whether stewed, roasted, baked, or boiled; and I make no doubt that it will equally serve in a fricassee or a ragout.

—JONATHAN SWIFT, "A Modest Proposal" (1729)

Thus it happens that *nausea*, an impulse to free oneself of food through the shortest way out of the esophagus (to vomit), has been allotted to the human being as such a strong vital sensation, for this intimate taking in can be dangerous to the animal.

—IMMANUEL KANT, *Anthropology from a Pragmatic Point of View* (1798)

Of all the questions that preoccupied Arab intellectuals in the nineteenth century, civilization was the most important. Arab thinkers engaged European theories of development, which examined the role of religion and social and political institutions in preventing or bringing about civilization. From despotic government and religion in Montesquieu (1689–1755) and Holbach (1723–1789), to Volney's (1757–1820) ignorance of the natural law and Chateaubriand's (1768–1848) exhaustion of cultural genius, many Arab intellectuals engaged these orientalist models either by reclaiming an Islamic golden age or by charting trajectories for achieving civilization as defined by their European counterparts. In this context, some turned to Ibn Khaldun's (1332–1406) work, drawing on his notion of 'umrān (civilization). For instance, 'Abd al-Rahman al-Jabarti (1753–1825) suggested that the decadence of the Ottomans and of the Mamluks in the nineteenth century was due to the disappearance of their tribal bonds or *'aṣabiyya* (group solidarity), *'umrān*'s necessary requirement.[1]

Whereas the understanding of civilization as *'umrān* emphasizes the process of "building" and depends on the *'aṣabiyya* of a racially homogeneous group, al-Tahtawi's first translation of civilization as *tamaddun* ın *Takhlīs* emphasizes development within an urban cultural and social context. Given the root of the word *madīna* (city), *tamaddun* thus involves the values and practices of a modern city dweller. Going back and forth between Ibn Khaldun's work and Montesquieu's *Considérations sur les causes de la grandeur des Romains et de leur décadence* (1734), al-Tahtawi claims that the achievement of civilization leads to the elimination of war and poverty. *Tamaddun* also consists in regulating economics, politics, social order, and technological and material development in accordance with an Islamic set of beliefs and ethical standards.[2] Arab thinkers' engagement with European thought through intellectual exchange and extended stays in Europe needs to be examined in light of debates about civilization and modernity simultaneously. Just as al-Tahtawi brought modernity as an embodied experience into the court of Muhammad 'Ali, thereby redefining the structure of power and refiguring the role of the *'ālim* in a new age, the *Nahda* travelers and thinkers I examine in this book embody the modern through narratives of anxiety and collapse, which operate at the intersection of personal accounts and fictional narratives. Reading the traveler's or main character's body as the crucible for the modern serves to frame questions of power, writing, and experience between Europe and the Arab world in new ways.

Ahmad Faris al-Shidyaq (1804–1886), an exiled Arab thinker, proceeds through his embodiment of the experience of modernity to critique and deconstruct the epistemological structure through which European civilization is produced. Al-Shidyaq is a modernizer of Arabic language, accomplished fiction writer and satirist, and editor of a series of cultural and political journals. Published in Tunis after al-Shidyaq's nine-year stay in England and France,

Kashf al-Mukhabba' 'an Funun Urubba (Revealing the hidden in the arts of Europe), or *Kashf al-Mukhabba' 'an Tamaddun Urubba* (Revealing the hidden in European civilization) (1863, henceforth: *Kashf*),[3] is a travelogue containing detailed discussion of French and British customs, hygiene, crime, history, urban planning, and political institutions. In *Kashf*, al-Shidyaq praises European people and development yet systematically undermines their definition of civilization and their association of civilization with modernity in order to explain cultural superiority and justify colonialism. Pondering its true meaning and engaging it from different angles, al-Shidyaq exposes civilization's inconsistencies and inherent contradictions. In the process, he identifies and unveils its violent mode of production through the binaries of race, class, dress, and eating habits. For instance, al-Shidyaq is unable to understand how England's dull and unhealthy cuisine is compatible with the notion of civilization. From quoting Cicero (106–43 BCE) on British meat-eating habits to discussing the types of food available in cities and villages, al-Shidyaq's struggle to explain why the British eat what they eat exposes the vagueness and inconsistency of the definition of civilization.

In this chapter, I argue that al-Shidyaq's linguistic and literary modernization coincides with a radical unveiling (*kashf*) of the European experience and understanding of civilization in the nineteenth century. Drawing on theories of embodiment in the work of Louis Marin, Gilles Deleuze, and Félix Guattari, and focusing on al-Shidyaq's trials in England, I argue that the body of the Arab traveler is staged as a site of ingestion and expulsion, incorporation and rejection of European food and ideological models.[4] In this light, I investigate al-Shidyaq's ailments, fainting, and physical collapse as he moves back and forth between London and the countryside, upper and working class, thereby situating his deconstruction of civilization in visceral reactions to customs and culinary practices specifically. In narrativizing the trials that constrain and poison him—food tastings, accidents, and anxiety attacks—al-Shidyaq diagnoses civilization's violence to the body. I argue that al-Shidyaq stages his physical collapse

due to bad food as a symptom of civilization in England. This
in turn unsettles civilization's exclusionary and reductive binary
oppositions of civilized/barbarian, superior/inferior, and East/
West.

LIFE IN EXILE

Al-Shidyaq was born in the Mount Lebanon area, in 1804, to a
family of Maronite scribes and notables.[5] As a result of political
feuds, the family was forced to leave its ancestral home in 'Ashqut
and take up residence in Damascus, before returning to settle in
the Lebanese Mountain town of Hadath. Having lost his father
at an early age, and having experienced, along with his brother
As'ad, persecution for working with Protestant missionaries in
Lebanon, the young al-Shidyaq left for Cairo in 1825.[6] In Cairo,
he studied at al-Azhar, succeeded al-Tahtawi as the editor of the
journal *Al-Waqa'i' al-Misriyya*, and met his future wife. His
brother As'ad's imprisonment and death in the Maronite Patriarch's dungeons in 1830 sealed al-Shidyaq's life in exile. Following Cairo, al-Shidyaq headed to Malta, where he spent the next
fourteen years working for American missionaries and the British administration on the island before finally moving to England
with his family in 1848. In England, al-Shidyaq collaborated with
Reverend Samuel Lee (1783–1852), the Arabist at Cambridge, on
the translation of the Bible into Arabic.[7] Unable to obtain a teaching position, he moved to France in 1855. In Paris, al-Shidyaq
met a number of intellectuals and thinkers and became the first
to translate "socialism" into Arabic (*al-ṭarīqa al-ishtirākiyya*).[8]
In 1857, he moved to Tunis, converted to Islam, and gained the
favor of the Ottoman sultan, who then invited him to Istanbul.
Al-Shidyaq arrived in the Ottoman capital in 1860. In 1861, he
founded the journal *Al-Jawa'ib*, which he edited until 1884.[9]
Upon his death in 1887, al-Shidyaq's body was repatriated to
Lebanon. A struggle ensued between various communities in
order to determine the burial site of this man who was born a
Maronite and had converted to Protestantism and then to Islam.

Al-Shidyaq's body, through travel and in death, enters a transactional economy that involves movement across locales, ethnic and religious identities, and cultural spaces. This embodiment, which takes shape biographically and textually, during his life and following his death, is a strategic site for investigating al-Shidyaq's work.

Al-Shidyaq is the author of travelogues, social and political essays, and language and educational manuals. His best-known work is an experimental text entitled *Al-Saq 'ala al-Saq fi ma Huwa al-Faryaq* (*Leg over Leg*) (1855, henceforth: *Saq*).[10] This fictional account about a character named Faryaq is a complex and composite text, part satirical novel and part travel narrative.[11] Its title, which suggests a libertine posture and attitude, sarcastically subverts notions of *adab* (manners, respectability, but also literature). In fact, al-Shidyaq presents Faryaq's sexual ambivalence by destabilizing his gender identity and speculating that he is perhaps a genie, or that he was mutated (*musikh*) a few days after his birth, or that he admired women and praised womanhood so much that God turned him into one.[12] This breakdown of sex and gender fixity takes shape through linguistic innovation and word play, collapsing reality and fiction, Shidyaq and Faryaq, "Faris" and "Shidyaq." Alluding to al-Shidyaq's European exile, Kamran Rastegar argues that *Saq*'s linguistic deconstruction and sexual innuendoes betray "something of the anxieties of the colonized male subject within the colonial metropolis. His displacement of this anxiety into satire, and into a self-conscious performance of a mastery of Arabic, is one way he seeks to reconstitute a masculine subjectivity within the colonial encounter."[13] This important observation aligns the cultural and political context with experiences of anxiety and literary modernization arising from the encounter with European cities in the nineteenth century. Forms of embodiment at work in *Saq* also take shape in al-Shidyaq's travelogue *Kashf*. Furthermore, the narrativizing of the self in *Saq* through the transformation of al-Shidyaq into a character named Faryaq is echoed in the sarcastic production of the subject of experience in *Kashf*. This suggests that the travel narrative could only be interpreted in relation to the fictional account *Saq*, considered by many recent critics as the first Arabic novel and modern autobiography.[14]

Nadia al-Bagdadi argues that *Saq*'s innovation lies in its language use and deconstructive play, irony and libertinism, but also in its conceptualization of individual rights (*ḥuqūq al-raʿiyya*).[15] Al-Shidyaq presents the individual both as an autonomous social and political entity, and a subject of desire. This conceptualization frames the work's modernity at the cultural, aesthetic, and linguistic levels. In fact, Radwa Ashour argues that *Saq* marks the true beginning of the Arab Renaissance, or *Nahda*.[16] Ashour suggests that al-Shidyaq's innovation and modernity (*ḥadātha mumkina*, possible modernity) subvert the colonialist and orientalist paradigm that Arab thinkers and authors reproduced in various ways from the nineteenth century onward. Ashour argues that al-Shidyaq's text involves dynamic negotiation at the intersection of European and Arabic genres and historical contexts. In this light, al-Shidyaq's modernity could not be reduced to a European literary and cultural model. Al-Shidyaq's modernity, or, as I argue, the trials of Arab modernity in al-Shidyaq's text, needs to be explored through a close reading and a thorough analysis of a different kind of modernity with which al-Shidyaq's work is increasingly associated.[17] The important question to raise is thus the following: How is it possible to fully engage this alternative modernity or *other* modernity without fixing al-Shidyaq's text as yet another literary and cultural origin, similar to Haykal's *Zaynab* (1913), "the first Arabic novel"? In order to avoid such epistemological closure and therefore liberate critical approaches from the confinement of genre and the demands of origin, it is necessary to engage modernity in al-Shidyaq's text as a process that manifests itself through a series of *aḥdāth* (accidents), thereby generating its *ḥadātha mumkina* (possible or alternative modernity).

KASHF, OR REVEALING THE HIDDEN

Full of anecdotes and encounters followed by reflections and analyses, *Kashf* has a satirical and ethnographic style that could be compared to the tenth-century *riḥla* of Ibn Fadlan, ambassador of the Abbasid Caliph al-Muqtadir to the Turks, Russians, and the Volga Vikings. Employing registers of parody and aversion, Ibn Fadlan vacillates between mockery and anxiety as he describes the traditions and practices of the different ethnic groups he encounters. For instance, he refers to the Turks' custom of plucking beards to make goatees, claiming that one could not distinguish Turkish men from bucks.[18] In the case of the Vikings, however, Ibn Fadlan expresses great thrill and anxiety—which permeates his language and style—in describing a sati-like funerary rite that involves burning a concubine alive with her dead master following an orgiastic celebration.[19] Disgusted at the Vikings' eating habits and washing rituals, he relates, in great detail, how a water bucket is passed on from one guest to another in order to wash hands and faces following a meal. Ibn Fadlan remarks that they also spit and blow their noses in the same bucket, and, finally, dip their combs in it in order to brush their hair.[20] He mentions their love for alcohol as well, claiming that they hold on to the goblet even in their death.[21]

From Ibn Fadlan's travelogue to Montesquieu's *Lettres Persanes* (1725) and Voltaire's *Lettres philosophiques* (1778), disgust and mockery, expressed in anecdotes and "sociological" analyses in both fictional and ethnographic texts, serve to situate al-Shidyaq's work at the intersection of a series of Arabic and European literary traditions spanning eight centuries.[22] In *Kashf*, for instance, al-Shidyaq frequently refers to Voltaire (1684–1778), echoing his sarcastic and shrewd observations as well as his philosophical reflections on English society and beliefs. In this context, al-Shidyaq offers detailed descriptions of British snobbery, superstition, hygiene, eating habits, laws, aesthetics, and prostitution. He notes that a handful of families own all the land in Britain, and critiques the priests' complicity in oppressing the poor. He also describes the theater and acting, traces them to Greek tragedies, and laments the fact that the Arabs only settled for the philosophical writings of the Greeks. Furthermore, as a result of his collaboration with Cambridge professor Rev. Samuel Lee, al-Shidyaq offers a unique and rare Arab view of the British academy in the nineteenth century. Al-Shidyaq considers both shocking and comical the fact that British scholars of Arabic and Islam cover up their lack of knowledge by quoting one another and by listing their undeserved and exaggerated titles and fields of expertise on the covers of their various publications. Identifying and diagnosing the self-referential structure of epistemological production, al-Shidyaq's critique echoes what Edward Said terms "the restorative citation of antecedent authority," through which orientalist knowledge—and thus, the Orient itself—is imagined and reproduced.[23] Critiquing the culture of expertise at Cambridge and Oxford, al-Shidyaq claims that British teachers of Arabic do not know the language well enough because "they don't learn languages from native speakers."[24] This leads these scholars, according to al-Shidyaq, to make countless intentional and unintentional mistakes as they teach and translate Arabic texts, and the Quran especially. He finally mentions that teachers of Hebrew earn ten times more than those who teach Arabic at these institutions.

Al-Shidyaq's description of the British varies from praise to criticism. He praises them, then criticizes them, then praises them again for the same practice throughout the text. As soon as he makes an observation or offers a coherent account of a social phenomenon, he immediately reworks and reformulates his explanation, mixing registers and contexts. Discussing British snobbery, for instance, al-Shidyaq breaks it down in terms of class, gender, and urban development, justifying it in one respect and disproving it in others. In this way, al-Shidyaq exposes through systematic interrogation of practices and concepts the inconsistency of clearly defined social and epistemological models. Through linguistic play and repetition, Socratic questioning and mockery, he dismantles foreclosed and static structures of meaning. Homi

Bhabha argues that an "important feature of colonial discourse is its dependence on the concept of 'fixity' in the ideological construction of otherness."[25] This "fixity," according to Bhabha, is racial, cultural, and historical. Al-Shidyaq pushes the limit of knowledge about the "other," and, in so doing, dismantles the binary through which the "one" and the "other" are produced as being fundamentally opposed along racial or cultural lines. Al-Shidyaq moves from engaging meaning and knowledge as being fixed and as having recognizable essences and signifieds, to meaning and knowledge as the outcome of dialectical and ideological production. A sophisticated theory of meaning and signification emerges from *Kashf*, requiring further investigation and study.

The critique of European civilization is a recurrent theme in al-Shidyaq's work. Defining it in relation to good taste and manners (*adab, ta'addub*) at one point, and situating it in relation to European industrialization and material development on the other, al-Shidyaq stresses the confusing and frustrating vagueness of what is meant by "civilization." He tries out different definitions, from French aesthetics and joie de vivre, which the French spread everywhere, according to al-Shidyaq, to British superior work ethics and administration.[26] Ultimately, al-Shidyaq observes that lacking a clear essence or inherent characteristics, civilization only gains meaning through the dialectics of *tamaddun/hamajiyya* (civilization/barbarism). In his later writing, he goes further by asserting that European civilization means "forcing other people to dress and eat in a certain manner and to oppress them, forcing them to do what they don't intend to do."[27] Specifically, al-Shidyaq denounces European colonial practices in Algeria, both in *Kashf* and in *Al-Jawa'ib*'s various articles. According to him, civilization's dialectical structure gets activated in a hegemonic opposition to what is outside of itself, thereby leading to the oppression of other nations. In this model, notions of discipline, order, and social organization operate as "essential" characteristics that confer upon Europe its supremacy and identity. While living in Istanbul, al-Shidyaq critiques the Ottomans' consumerist interpretation of civilization, which for them meant owning "something made in France, Britain, a precious stone from India and Ceylon, Chinese pottery, Persian rugs, Moroccan leather and so on."[28]

Norbert Elias points out that the concept of civilization includes all that a society thinks and produces, believes in and practices, from technology and science "to the way in which food is prepared."[29] This concept, which emerges in the modern age from the French and British contexts specifically, became synonymous with Europe's "self-consciousness" or awareness of its own superiority in relation to other nations. Through *Kashf's* deconstructive play and modes of embodiment, al-Shidyaq exposes this ideological production. Instead of engaging the European discourse of civilization dialectically by claiming that "we" (Ottomans or Arabs) are more civilized than or as civilized as "you" (British or French), or that "we" will eventually catch up and attain civilization, or that "we" are civilized and could just point to "our" past in order to prove it, al-Shidyaq first claims that "you" are barbarians (*hamaj*), xenophobes, unjust, rude, and have bad hygiene. He thus starts with the reversal: "You are what you think we are, i.e., inferior." Then, he contextualizes this reversal by providing alternative examples only to claim, at the end, that "we are like you and you are like us, both human," and that there are no inherent or essential differences between us. Al-Shidyaq's deconstruction reverses the hierarchy by shifting its levels, moving from the generalizing, power-knowledge relation to the context-specific one. This strategy allows him to undermine civilization's ideological binary opposition and to break down its model of epistemological closure. Specifically, mocking civilization and exposing its contradictions and inconsistencies, al-Shidyaq argues that perhaps there is nothing *mukhabba'* (concealed, hidden)—as in signified, essence, or secret—in European civilization (*tamaddun*), and that the *mukhabba'* is that which arises from movement and the body's reaction to food, weather, and other external stimuli. In order to identify civilization's *mukhabba'*, al-Shidyaq thus undertakes in *Kashf* a diagnosis of ingestion and indigestion, posture and movement, and aversion and collapse.

Al-Shidyaq's title brilliantly captures his deconstructive strategy. The phrase *kashf al-mukhabba' 'an funūn Ūrūbbā*—as opposed to *kashf funūn Ūrūbbā*—involves a satirical wordplay and a structure of ambiguity reproduced throughout the work. The notion of *kashf* depicts a process of "revealing, unveiling, and examining."[30] *Kashf*, the noun, also means "record, bill, and account." *Kashf* thus implies "exposing ill intent" (*kashf al-amr*), and, more importantly, "bill of health" (*kashf ṭubbī*). The title introduces yet mitigates the process of *kashf*, going back and forth between understanding and explaining European arts and civilization on the one hand, and diagnosing the ailments they cause on the other. The body, which is at the same time textual, social, and material, is both the site and object of this *kashf*. In order to unveil the *mukhabba'* of European civilization, al-Shidyaq examines its physical manifestations on his own body. Similarly to *Saq*, which mixes nudity with critique and diagnosis, *kashf* operates as a form of *ta'riya* (stripping naked). Revealing what European civilization conceals thus involves multiple levels of observation, analysis, and self-examination, which emerge from al-Shidyaq's language, gestures, collapses, and ills. It is thus necessary to read al-Shidyaq's body in various environments and in relation to other bodies and objects, thereby treating it as a sign, a narrative, and a site of inscription for external stimuli and new meaning.

"DROWNING AND FIRE" IN LONDON CITY

Al-Shidyaq's alignment of the unveiling of civilization in England with his own fear of physical violence and poisoning is best represented in his account of London's business district—the City. He vividly describes its streets, buildings, locomotives, middlemen, and traders. His description reproduces the dizzying circulation of people and capital in the text itself. The City, engine of modernity and industrialization, emerges in al-Shidyaq's description as the source of commercial and literary production, capitalism and modern writing.

The British's hustle to ride the City line, whether they are traders
or clerks, is like the Copts' vying for jobs in Egypt's Citadel. I have
previously mentioned that all coaches have the name of the bank
written on them, as they all head to that destination except on rare
occasions. Thus you can imagine the ensuing hustle and bustle.
Verily, these vehicles' roaring sound drives one's patience away.
No one in the City can concentrate on anything else but the work
they're doing. It is in this unhealthy place [*mawrid wakhīm*] that I
was destined to write this book. Not in Italy's green meadows or in
Damascus's elegant gardens. So I imagine [*akhāl*] smoke arising and
darkness intensifying in between its words. Every time I went out
in the street, I would fear [*ūjas*] that some ill might befall me, due to
crowds and animals, or the bad food served in the City restaurants.
When I return to my room, I feel like I just survived drowning
or fire. However, whoever leaves this prison and heads to "Regent
Street," it is as if he was leaving London for Paris because there
people walk slowly, enjoy what's around them, smoke their pipes,
talk, laugh, or smile. The sound of musical instruments makes one
think that there is also time for pleasure and enjoyment. The City,
on the other hand, God created it just for work and hardship. Work
for work's sake. Work work. This is the religion of this people. They
don't get tired of it unless it gets tired of them. This is not to men-
tion that in one institution alone, one could find up to 500 traders and 1000 brokers. And despite the fact that the City line, with
its narrow streets and shabby buildings, is below all other lines in
London, it is the most revered one among the British, so much so
that when they take it heading north, they say "we are going down
to such and such place." One can't find in the City a place for rec-
reation or promenade or anything else that could comfort the soul.
You see nothing but grim faces and a hustle of wheels, coaches, carriages, and bicycles coming and going, as well as narrow and muddy
streets and soot-covered walls and pathways crowded with people.[31]

This passage at the end of *Kashf* embodies al-Shidyaq's experience of modernity in England. The City district emerges as the
site of a decaying modernity; its decay is manifest and arresting, taking place in the here and now. He describes alleyways
and cramped buildings covered in soot as collectively constitut-
ing a *mawrid wakhīm* (unhealthy place),[32] infernal, filthy, and

overcrowded. Devoid of any distraction or pleasure, this environment prevents people from focusing on anything but the task at
hand. This absence of concentration except on work, according
to al-Shidyaq, precludes enjoyment and relaxation, and aesthetics
and contemplative thought as well. In this constant succession of
bodies and machines, the distinction between various elements—
human, animal, and mechanical—collapses in a new framework
of decay and speed. This collapse generates modes of permeability, interchangeability, immediacy, and reversals that fundamentally challenge fixed meaning and representation in al-Shidyaq's
text.

Al-Shidyaq observes that this mechanical ritual of work has a
distorting effect on bodies and language. For instance, he mentions that although the City is at the bottom of the map, those
who head there say, "we're going up to the City" when they in
fact go down, and down to other parts of London when they in
fact go up. This distorting effect denotes a subversion of order
and signification. Substituting "up" for "down," the City defies
gravity and alters hierarchies within language. Power shifts in
this scene from meaning and signification as fixed and static categories, intertwined with recognizable and determined linguistic and epistemological structures, to movement and circulation,
which are generated in a new space of competition and production, embodied in al-Shidyaq's text.

Al-Shidyaq reproduces the City rush in his writing. Reflecting on himself as an Arab author in Europe, but also as a body
negotiating crowded streets, averting being run over by speeding
carriages, he anchors his text in the intervals and interstices of
modernity. The embodiment of speed and movement appears in
the text's various alliterations ('awājil wa-ḥawāfil wa-maḥāmil
[wheels, coaches, and carriages] and masālik ghāṣṣa bi-l-nās
[pathways crowded with people]), repetitions (al-'amal al-'amal
[work work]), and other narrative devices.[33] The modern Arabic text mirrors and echoes the sights and sounds of commercial
and industrial production, which arises from a mawrid wakhīm,
full of hazards to body and mind, language and meaning. The

urban movement outside takes shape in the text itself, rendering it permeable to mechanical sounds and smoke and darkness, now emerging in between its words and through its alliterations. Modernity's rhythm conditions this text by inscribing it with danger, pollution, and unpredictability. According to al-Shidyaq, to write in the City and to write the City entail risking death by "drowning and fire." Thus, the modern text arises from this experience of competition, confrontation, and survival.

Comparing and contrasting the French and the British, and England, Italy, and Syria, al-Shidyaq *regrets* that God did not will for him to write his book in the green pastures of Italy or in Damascus's elegant gardens. With smoke and darkness intensifying between its words, al-Shidyaq's text arises from a *mawrid wakhīm*—London's business district—rather than from an idyllic setting wherein reflection and contemplation are the fundamental requirements for writing and aesthetics. This *mawrid*, a hellish prison and new source of literary and commercial production, engenders the constantly fleeting arche of modern writing. This writing operates as an Orphean procession that engulfs the text with its flames and smoke. The appropriation of this modernist trope, which one finds in T. S. Eliot's work[34] and, in the Arabic context, in Adonis's poetry and Tayeb Salih's novels (the subject of my next chapter), frames al-Shidyaq's modernity in a new and hitherto unexplored fashion. In the midst of this urban space, the condition of new writing is different from the meditative solitude of the author amid lush meadows and parks. The industrial world replaces the pastoral one, thereby marking a shift from melancholic sensibility to instantaneity.

Moreover, surviving "drowning and fire" and comparing Londoners' rush in the City to that of the Copts working in Cairo's Citadel—where al-Shidyaq had previously worked while living in Egypt—betray a satirical tone, used pervasively in describing his experience and encounters in England. The image of al-Shidyaq in the City as if going to hell and back, running and then taking shelter in his room, is thus a satirical one as well. Therefore, his satirical description of the Arab traveler's encounters in

Europe transforms the subject of lived experience into a fictional character going in and out of the text. The modern hero's body, imprisoned in the hellish City, is sarcastically staged as the site of inscription and resistance to modernity's material and discursive articulations in England. Focusing on the body of the *damned* traveler and modern hero who satirizes surviving hell in the European metropolis brings the travel narrative closer to the fictional account—*Kashf* closer to *Saq*. Staging the body as the site of physical trials and signification, al-Shidyaq experiences modernity by trying it on like a piece of clothing, mocking it, and tasting and taking it in like a food item.

The embodiment of speed and commercial production coincides in al-Shidyaq's text with the ingestion of bad food and the inhalation of poisonous fumes. The *mawrid wakhīm*, the unhealthy site of literary and commercial production, is a source of pollution and indigestion. As the body runs and hides, inhales and exhales, ingests and expulses, it unsettles literary genres and ideological projects. Tracing this body's posture and movement, reverberation and indigestion, and disgust and collapse, serves to identify the ways in which the modern emerges from al-Shidyaq's text. From London to the countryside, al-Shidyaq's physical reactions and susceptibility to various hazards shape *Kashf*'s narrative. In this context, ingesting and expulsing food are thus important functions that allow us to trace the body's actions and movements, and identify in the process the centrality of affects in producing the modern Arabic text and in shaping its processes of *kashf*—unveiling, diagnosis, critique.

IN THE VILLAGE OF THE DAMNED

Al-Shidyaq describes the village by Cambridge where he first resides as *qarya mash'ūma* (forsaken village). He laments the absence of proper roads, means of transportation, cafés, and other social and public forums for distraction.[35] Just like London's business district, this wretched place that imprisons and oppresses him lacks the food quality and variety necessary for someone who has lived and traveled across the Mediterranean. In this way, he identifies bad food, confinement, and the absence of distraction as the staples of village life. While in the City al-Shidyaq struggles to avoid being run over by speeding carriages, in the forsaken village he struggles to obtain adequate nourishment.

> You might find in the village a store that sells the worst kind [*nifaya*] of candles, soap, sugar, coffee, and tea, and a shabby [*ḥaqīr*] house that sells out of a small window some onions, potatoes, bad sweets, and tasteless apples. If you were to buy all these things combined it wouldn't cost you fifty pennies. And during winter, one cannot even step outside to breathe some fresh air due to the excess of mud on the road. One could spend days trapped in one's house. One cannot find in the village any horses, donkeys, mules or carriages so that one's shoes become the only mode of transportation. Some of the more affluent folks might have a bicycle to ride from one village to another, and some might have a little cart pulled by a small horse for this vehicle is tax exempt. As for regular carriages and horses, they need to be reported for tax purposes, as I will discuss later. Every time I needed to buy provisions, I was forced to go on foot to the nearby town. Once I had to ride in a dirt box [*tābūt*], though it was empty. Even if a wealthy person lives in one of these villages he will be unable to enjoy his wealth for he can only acquire what is available to the poor folks, unless, that is, he purchases his provisions from London or elsewhere. God knows that during my stay in this forsaken village [*qarya mash'ūma*], my only concern was to provide for myself and acquire the bare means of sustenance by taking the train to buy legumes from Cambridge and nuts from Royston and beer from London. When I realized how expensive this was getting, I rationed, which caused me to feel weakness in my stomach and knees the like of which I have never experienced in my life. This was due to the village's bad beer, which tastes like medicine yet has no nutritional value. So I fainted once as I was translating at the house of Dr. Lee, who then ordered his maid to fetch me a piece of toast [*qiṭʿat khubz mashwiyya*].[36]

Al-Shidyaq frames his experience in the village through registers of confinement and damnation, malnutrition and the quest for sustenance. Whereas he returns to his room in London for a momentary respite from street danger, the village's muddy roads and lack of adequate transportation confine him to it. The absence of distraction, healthy food, and freedom of movement thus characterize the *qarya mash'ūma* as well. Al-Shidyaq emphasizes that even those who could afford to buy different varieties of food are unable to do so, having to settle instead for basic and rather unhealthy kinds. Thus, regardless of economic means and social status, village folks have nothing else to eat but some "meat, butter mixed with carrots, bread mixed with potatoes, cheese, sour cream, eggs, and cabbage."[37] Moreover, while words like *nifāya* (garbage) capture his disgust with British cooking more generally, and the produce found in the village store specifically, the *tābūt* (dirt box)[38] that al-Shidyaq had to ride in evokes animal feces. Laying or crouching in the empty box marks the interchangeability of al-Shidyaq's body and animal excrement turned soil-fertilizer. Staging the body as a site of ingestion and expulsion, running and crouching, he collapses nutrients with waste through the registers of garbage and manure, food and excrement, and animal and human.

Al-Shidyaq's physical reactions in *Kashf* characterize a series of trials and accidents (*aḥdāth*) arising in between the body of the traveler and the text he produces, and between the body and that which confines and gives it shape—be it the room that shelters him or the dirt box that transports him. The text's modernity emerges through the body's reaction to external stimuli that cause it to experience danger, confinement, malnutrition, and collapse. Consumed by the need to secure nutritious food and access basic transportation in England, al-Shidyaq sarcastically laments being reduced to an early stage of human development, struggling for survival. Moving back and forth between London and the countryside, the room and the street, al-Shidyaq's narrative unsettles the binary opposition of urban/rural and modern/premodern through which civilization and modernity are associated with progress, material development, and nutritious and abundant food.

Al-Shidyaq's state of malnutrition and impoverishment in the village brings about his physical collapse at Reverend Lee's house.

An unprecedented weakness in the stomach and knees over-
whelms al-Shidyaq, leading him to faint. This collapse marks the
body's inability to internalize, digest, and benefit from what it
takes in. It also puts in question the relation between food and
nourishment on the one hand, and exposes, on the other, the ideological construction of the Eucharist-like piece of toast (qiṭ'at
khubz mashwiyya) that the maid fetches in order to revive him.[39]
The critique of civilization is extended in this sarcastic framework to the piece of toast, which nourishes spiritually and ideo-
logically yet in no way fulfills al-Shidyaq's need for nutritious and
fresh food and drink. In this light, the sarcastic tone, always per-
meating Kashf, is deployed to describe his physical collapse while
translating the Bible into Arabic.

The spread of the Bible beyond England's borders as a result of
translation and Protestant missionary work is interrupted in this
scene. Through its collapse, the body viscerally reacts to indigestible and unhealthy food and culinary practices on the one hand,
and to ideological and political projects and personal trauma
on the other. Ussama Makdisi argues that al-Shidyaq's brother,
Asʿad, who died in captivity in the Maronite patriarch's dungeon,
was an inadvertent victim and "the first martyr" of Protestant
missionary work in the Arab East.[40] The young student of theology whom the missionaries had employed and converted, found
himself at the center of a struggle for cultural, religious, and
political supremacy in nineteenth-century Lebanon. Al-Shidyaq's collapse in this scene thus needs to be read in relation to the
allegedly murdered brother, whose work al-Shidyaq continues in
England.[41] In this context, al-Shidyaq's collapse due to unhealthy
food and drink could be read as embodied interruption and con-
testation, which align the indigestible with the untranslatable.
This collapse is nonetheless staged and satirized through fainting
and revival, bad beer and the piece of toast. This process transforms the text from an objective account of al-Shidyaq's encounters in Europe to a complex and fictionalized narrative, full of
possibilities of subversion through mimicry, wordplay, and textual disruption.

"THE FABULOUS ANIMAL"

In his discussion of Port Royal's codification of French language in the seventeenth century, Louis Marin analyzes Jean de la Fontaine's (1621–1695) fable "Life of Aesop," about a mute servant accused of eating his master's figs. Marin argues that, for his defense, the servant succeeds in turning his body into a site of subversion of a master narrative invested with the power of meaning and representation. Engaging de la Fontaine's text, Marin claims that Aesop is first introduced as a deformed creature, lacking speech: "He is an animal, or almost one. He grunts and stammers."[42] Reduced to unintelligible utterances and gestures, Aesop, according to Marin, is excluded from language. When the beautiful and articulate Agathopus—the treacherous butler in the story—consumes along with his friends a basket of figs belonging to the master, he accuses Aesop, thinking that the latter will be unable to defend himself. Brought to the master as a supplicant risking death, Aesop raises his hand to defer the impending punishment, gain time, and "open up a space of possibility within the moment of urgency."[43] Marin suggests that "Aesop's raised hand sets the stage for a counter-discourse, which will not be spoken," but rather embodied in acts and gestures.[44] When the master grants him a deferral, Aesop fetches lukewarm water, drinks some, and takes his finger to his tongue in order to make himself vomit. Marin argues that Aesop's staged action triggers bodily symptoms that in turn affect meaning, power relations, and the development of the narrative. Having expelled only water, Aesop gestures that Agathopus should mimic his action. Unable to refuse, the butler drinks the water and makes himself vomit the figs. Having been devoured rather than eaten, the figs come out of Agothopus's stomach almost whole, in a sign of his greed and gluttony.

From the monstrous-looking Aesop to the beautiful yet beastly-acting Agathopus, the subversion of the dominant narrative—Agathopus's accusation—is staged through the body's crouching and pointing, fetching and drinking, and ingesting and expulsing. The counternarrative arises from this interplay between various actions and performances, and from the space and time in between the accusation and the punishment, life and death, and the body of the master and that of the servants. We witness in Aesop's tale "the production of a body that tells a story, and in so doing, the body inverts the effects of representational discourse."[45] Through forms of embodiment and mimicry, Aesop "deconstructs the verbal story that explicitly claims to be true."[46] Unable to argue against Agathopus by engaging his narrative dialectically, Aesop stages his body in order to expose the falsehood of Agathopus's narrative and dismantle the structure of power underlying its system of signification. Aesop thus turns his body into a site of subversion that "allows the weak to displace and reverse the power contained in the discourse of the strong."[47] This embodied intervention, which unfolds through a series of events (*aḥdāth*), staged and narrativized in the "here and now," disrupts and repositions language, discourse, and the text. By exposing the violence of the dominant narrative, this form of embodiment "opens up a space of possibility" for an alternative language and an alternative modernity (*ḥadātha mumkina*, possible modernity). This staging enacts a *kashf* of that which is concealed in Agathopus's belly. This *mukhabba'* (hidden, concealed) that comes out in the form of vomit is intimately tied to the *mukhabba'* in the master narrative—the lie endowed with the ideological power of representation.

The strategic staging of the body in *Kashf* operates similarly to that of Aesop. Al-Shidyaq describes himself as animal-like, deformed through his fez and exotic clothing, chased by kids and drunks as he walks around London.[48] Unable to provide for himself in the village or find adequate transportation, he is reduced to a state of confinement and deprivation. In both cases, the text arises from the staging of the body in the here and now, escaping speeding coaches in the City and collapsing due to bad village food and beer. The body is thus the site of experience and of a counterdiscourse that interrogates the epistemological coherence of such "distinct" notions as city and countryside, and civilization and barbarism. Al-Shidyaq's *staging* of experiences of aversion, anxiety, and indigestibility unsettles civilization's association with fixed historical narratives and models of truth and knowledge. Specifically, al-Shidyaq's counterdiscourse dismantles, in the "here and now," the master narrative of European civilization and models of representation, which exclude and reify the unfamiliar and Aesop-like "other" racially, culturally, and historically. Through affects and embodiment, this counterdiscourse bypasses the dialectical engagement with European models of cultural difference to which many Arab intellectuals succumbed. Al-Shidyaq thus produces the "other text," full of affects and possibilities, arising in between the literary text and the body of the traveler narrating his encounters in England.

Al-Shidyaq stages his body in moments of rupture and material and literary collapse on the streets of London and in the text itself. If being civilized means to eat and dress and act in a particular manner, then how come adopting such manners leads al-Shidyaq to aversion and disgust, ailment and ill health, both in London and in the countryside? In this context, one could read al-Shidyaq's collapsing body as a site of trial and trying out, ingesting and expulsing, which expose the coercive violence of civilization itself. The body thus enacts and reproduces the discrepancy within the discourse of civilization by mitigating its correspondence to specific cultural practices (eating habits, dress, and doing business) and models of representation (progress, health, and development). The body's inhaling and exhaling, running and fainting, ingesting and expulsing unsettle civilization as fixed and self-evident. The trials of Arab modernity arise from these events (*aḥdāth*), which stage the collapse of notions of "modernity," "civilization," and the "West," and, conversely, notions of "premodern," "barbarity," and the "East," as fixed, absolute, essential, and one with themselves. By deconstructing this ideological structure, al-Shidyaq creates the possibility of trial and experimentation—a dynamic *mawrid* (source) of Arab modernity.

THE LEWD CARRION

Expressions of anxiety and disgust in England shape al-Shidyaq's systematic dismantling of the notion of civilization. In a section devoted to British cooking and eating habits, he extends his aversion to food to the lack of culinary sophistication in an upper class setting in London. Moving beyond the village/city or lower-class/upper-class binary oppositions,[49] al-Shidyaq exclaims how the British, despite their industrialization and enlightenment, lack basic culinary know-how. He notes that they settle for grilled meat and boiled herbs with vegetables on the side.[50] He also claims that such food cannot fulfill someone who is "accustomed to a wide range of cuisines."[51] He blames London's restaurateurs and innkeepers for this culinary ignorance, "which one fails to see even in the poorest households of the Arab East (afqar al-nās fī al-bilād al-mashriqiyya)."[52] Reiterating, obsessively, British ignorance of basic culinary practices like frying eggs with gee and cooking beans, al-Shidyaq describes how the British strangle rabbit and deer, letting them sit for days before consuming them.

> What is most strange is that eating rotten meat doesn't disgust them. They only eat deer and rabbit thirty days after having strangled them. I was invited repeatedly to the homes of the wealthy serving rabbit, while I could still detect the smell of rot [jakhr][53] exuding from its orifice, thus the poem I composed:
>
> They serve the rabbit whole and flat as if it was just dug up
>   with its tail and teeth and nails and wide open mouth
> Its raised tail and naked [taʿarrā] butt in the face of all the guests
>   for God, in God, by God, I unmistakably smelled its rot.
>
> And so is the case for chicken and bird, which they only eat after they strangle and let sit for days; they claim that this makes their meat tender and tasty.[54]

While bad food and drink in the village lead al-Shidyaq to faint, the food in London shocks and disgusts him. Visual and olfactory affects, centered on the dead rabbit and the imagined smell exuding from its orifice, erupt in a narrative discontinuity. Instead of him collapsing, the collapse in this scene occurs in the text, which digresses from the descriptive narrative to the poem, capturing al-Shidyaq's aversion. Just like smoke and darkness arise from his text in the City, this scene's visual and olfactory stimuli penetrate his nostrils and permeate his prose. Al-Shidyaq's smelling of the rabbit's inner rot while it lies naked on the plate, in between life and death, is embodied in the poem. Through sexual allusions to orifices and nudity, the poem presents *kashf* (revealing) as a form of *ta'riya* (stripping naked) for all the readers to see. *Kashf al-mukhabba'* (revealing the hidden) thus consists in exposing a disgusting spectacle of decay—the unveiled secret or lie of European civilization. Moreover, while the rabbit's smell triggers disgust, its visual display emphasizes the absence of ritual slaughter or the strangling of animals and letting them sit for days before eating them mixed with fat and blood.

In *Civilization and Its Discontents* (1930), Freud suggests that the advent of civilization marks the transition from the primacy of the sense of smell to the primacy of vision. He argues that when humans adopted erect positions, genitals as sites of olfactory fixation gave way to visual, sexual stimulation.[55] This transition to the visual and the aim-inhibited love thus situates the olfactory in an early stage that was transcended. Whereas the olfactory is an archaic sense, linked to desire, the visual, marked in Lacan's mirror stage as the access to the Symbolic or language (discussed in chapter 2), is coextensive with civilization and the formation of subjectivity. In this context, Julia Kristeva argues that the encounter with the abject ushers in a relation between subject and object that threatens the boundaries of the ego.[56] The abject's suspended state between inside and outside, life and death, and form and formlessness, stages the eruption of the imaginary or pre-oedipal into the Symbolic.

This psychoanalytic reading emphasizes the eruption of the archaic in al-Shidyaq's staging of the critique of civilization throughout *Kashf*. However, and as a result of this staging, his visceral reaction to rotten meat and disgusting food could not be reduced to a collapse in the ego. Al-Shidyaq's encounter with and

unveiling of forms of decay in England require a wider comparative engagement with other philosophical and literary discussions
of decay, disgust, and modernity in the nineteenth century. The
expression of disgust in al-Shidyaq's text could thus be situated
in relation to literary and poetic modernity as theorized by Benjamin and addressed in the previous chapter, for instance. The
cadaver as a literary site of disgust and aversion toward civilization is a recurrent motif in nineteenth-century European literature. Baudelaire captures this motif in his poem, "Une Charogne"
(Carrion).

> Legs in the air, like a lewd woman, scorching and sweating poisons,
> reeking belly split open nonchalantly, cynically.
> The sun beat down on that rotten meat, as if to be sure it was well
>   done, and
> to render unto Mother Nature a hundredfold all she had joined
>   together.
> And the sky watched that superb carcass blossom like a flower, the
>   stench
> so strong you thought you might fall in a faint on the grass.[57]

In Baudelaire's poem—a selection from which I quote here—
the poet is shocked and titillated by an arresting and disgusting
spectacle: the cadaver of a she-dog, decomposing in broad daylight. Both in al-Shidyaq and Baudelaire, the sexualized and lewd
corpse denotes a decaying modernity that underlies the European
metropolis. Poisonous smells exuding from a spectacle of decomposition aligned with food preparation and consumption expose
the decay as a fundamental process occurring in the here and
now, on the street and on the dinner table—for all to see. The
decay in both poems permeates the text with smells and fumes.
In both cases, this dynamic decay is a source (*mawrid*) of both
disgust and perverse erotic fascination. Thus, the decay is never
fully repressed but is rather constitutive of that which is seen and
experienced in the European city. This leads Winfried Menninghaus, who reads decay in nineteenth-century texts (including
Baudelaire's poem) to claim that decay does not simply represent
the underbelly of modernity or the putrefying world below, but

offers instead "an image of the above-ground state of civilization itself."[58] In this sense, Baudelaire's carrion and al-Shidyaq's rabbit are *living* cadavers, exuding poisonous smells and adopting sexual positions in the here and now, above ground, *shamelessly*. Nudity and shamelessness are woven into al-Shidyaq's narrative through a medical discourse of *kashf* as in "bill of health" (*kashf ṭubbī*) in order to expose the *shameless* contradictions, ailments, and symptoms of European civilization as he encounters it in England.

The *mukhabba'* takes shape in al-Shidyaq's text as unveiled decay, which appears and disappears, poisons the body, makes it collapse, deprives it of fresh air, and suffocates and strangles it. Decay and rot are apparent in the City streets and buildings, in the produce at the village store, in the dead animals and food served in restaurants and at the homes of the wealthy, and even in the coffee mixed behind closed doors at cafés. This decay lies also in the way European civilization is organized through categories of work and knowledge as a way of determining its relation to the "other"—who "lacks" work ethics and organization.[59] *Kashf* thus operates as a diagnosis of the ideological production of civilization on the one hand, and as an identification of symptoms and traces, smells and fumes on the other. The *mukhabba'* as ill and decay arises from a *mawrid wakhīm*, which produces indigestion, capitalism, and modern writing. The hidden in Europe's arts (*funūn*), which al-Shidyaq seeks to diagnose, is the hidden in *funūn al-ṭahī* (culinary arts) as well. This hidden, exuding as a poisonous smell from the rabbit's orifice yet naked for all to see in al-Shidyaq's poem, exposes modernity as a disgusting work of art (*fan, funūn*), disgusting dish, and a disgusting "modern" text that reeks and smokes.

Discussing the development of attitudes toward meat-eating habits in Europe from the Middle Ages onward, Norbert Elias attributes the disappearance of the spectacle of slaughter and the veiling of food preparation to the "civilizing process." Elias writes: "It will be seen again and again how characteristic of the whole process that we call civilization is this movement of segregation, this hiding 'behind the scene' of what has become distasteful."[60] Modernity and civilization in al-Shidyaq's text are exposed to their constitutive distastefulness. *Kashf*'s deconstructive play and modes of embodiment unveil what's "behind the scene"—which is also flagrant—revealing a spectacle of decay and exposing a polluted and failing modernity, right on the surface. Al-Shidyaq diagnoses the decay of industrial modernity in England and interrogates its association with civilization as consisting in superior eating habits, education, and healthy living conditions. His modern encounter, which permeates his text with smoke and smells, unsettles modernity itself as a fixed and recognizable project. This encounter also disrupts the process of contemplative writing, which requires relaxation, good weather, and good food—true markers of the *old* civilization, from Pompeii to Granada. Through a violent process of disruption, penetration, and permeation, modernity calls attention to its own rottenness and smells in *Kashf*. Fermentation, smoke, decomposition, and decay are dynamic processes at work in al-Shidyaq's text; they infuse it with life and movement, pungent and overwhelming smells, and lewd spectacles. In this *mawrid wakhīm*—a disgusting and unhealthy place—al-Shidyaq decenters modernity and civilization as fixed and coherent narratives and produces his thoroughly modern text.

AVERSION AND DETERRITORIALIZATION

Forced to try different food and experience various environments, al-Shidyaq frets and worries, mocks and interrogates throughout the narrative. His *Kashf* aims at what modernity claims to veil and suppress as a condition of its functionality, meaning, and operation. This "concealed element," or *mukhabba'*, takes shape through smells and fumes that arise from al-Shidyaq's anecdotes and accidents (*aḥdāth*) as he runs and collapses in the City and the village, inside and outside. Just like Aesop narrativizes his body in order to subvert Agathopus's lie and saves his life, al-Shidyaq "tries" and "tries on" British food and culture insofar as he is able to strip, expulse, and spit them out. This enables him to break apart the epistemological framework through which the notion of civilization—with its "invisible" signified or secret—is constituted and produce a modern text, full of possibilities.

Kashf's narrative of aversion and disgust, malnutrition and collapse, could be understood in light of Deleuze and Guattari's notion of "deterritorialization." The physical collapse, gutturality, aversion, and the form of writing that Deleuze and Guattari identify in Kafka's work help frame the modern embodiment and the dismantling of civilization in al-Shidyaq's text. In *Kafka: Towards a Minor Literature* (1975), Deleuze and Guattari analyze the political and aesthetic dimensions of the register of animal voices and actions, encounters and transformations, in Kafka's writing.

> To become animal is to participate in movement, to stake out the path of escape in all its positivity, to cross a threshold, to reach a continuum of intensities that are valuable only in themselves, to find a world of pure intensities where all forms come undone, as do all the significations, signifiers, and signifieds, to the benefit of an unformed matter of deterritorialized flux, of nonsignifying signs. Kafka's animals never refer to a mythology or to archetypes but correspond solely to new levels, zones of liberated intensities where contents free themselves of their forms as well as from their expressions, from the signifier that formalized them. There is no longer anything but movements, vibrations, thresholds in a deserted matter: animals, mice, dogs, apes, cockroaches are distinguished only by this or that threshold, this or that vibration, by the particular underground tunnel in the rhizome or the burrow. Because these tunnels are underground intensities.[61]

Deleuze and Guattari argue that "becoming animal" in Kafka charts a trajectory of avoidance and going around. These rhizomatic tricks and trials subvert and overcome the dialectics of the psychoanalytic discourse invested in identifying oedipal manifestations in Kafka's *Metamorphosis* (1915) and diaries. The father/son relation expressed in models of weakness and strength, castration and desire, are displaced and substituted in Deleuze and

Guattari's reading by forces and intensities, rhythms and vibrations, which liberate and give rise to forms of deterritorialization and becoming.

> Rich or poor, each language always implies a deterritorialization of the mouth, the tongue, and the teeth. The mouth, tongue, and teeth find their primitive territoriality in food. In giving themselves over to the articulation of sounds, the mouth, tongue, and teeth deterritorialize. Thus, there is a certain disjunction between eating and speaking, and even more, despite all appearances, between eating and writing. Undoubtedly, one can write while eating more easily than one can speak while eating, but writing goes further in transforming words into things capable of competing with food. Disjunction between content and expression. To speak, and above all to write, is to fast. Kafka manifests a permanent obsession with food, and with that form of food *par excellence*, in other words, the animal or meat—an obsession with the mouth and with teeth and with large, unhealthy, or gold-capped teeth.[62]

According to Deleuze and Guattari, Kafka's deterritorialized language, which has broken with the figurative and the representational and their corresponding master narratives and structures of power, is a site of affects and embodiment. This language also characterizes al-Shidyaq's Arabic, which he inflects with guttural sounds, repetitions, alliterations, and wordplay. Al-Shidyaq's work stages the condition of the modern in language itself. This sets in motion the disjointed trajectory of Arab modernity's trials—digging in the burrows, crisscrossing the streets of London and other European capitals, attempting to understand and explain, assimilate and expulse. Al-Shidyaq's experience and linguistic innovation generate the modern through embodiment, vibration, and speed, pushing the limits of language. In this context, Aziz al-Azmeh and Fawwaz Trabulsi claim that "al-Shidyaq stripped Arabic language" (*'arrā al-Shidyaq al-lugha al-'Arabiyya*).[63] This *ta'riya* (stripping naked) needs to be read as a form of deterritorialization or *kashf*, an exploration of the body and of the cultural and political forces affected by its movement and postures. This *ta'riya* coincides with a breakdown of the ideological narrative of progress and civilization, which takes shape through the binaries of race, culture, and aesthetics. Given Deleuze and Guattari's understanding, to deterritorialize is to unfix and decenter by accentuating movement, energy, and intensity. Deterritorializing in al-Shidyaq's text consists in revealing (*kashf*) European civilization's stink and violence, contradiction and inconsistency. This process takes shape in the Arabic text, in the Arabic language—the stage of a modern *t'ariya*. The *mukhabba'* is thus unveiled as disgusting smells and poisonous fumes that exude from orifices and exhaust pipes, both in the homes of wealthy Londoners and in the City streets. These fumes and smells penetrate the text and make its author and main character choke, cough, and vomit as in Aesop's tale. Deterritorialization, according to Deleuze and Guattari, exposes Agathopus's narrative—and the narrative of civilization—as a poisonous ideological lie. Countering this lie does not consist in contesting its modes of representation (orientalism) or reimagining and drawing on an Arab-Islamic tradition but rather in exposing and dismantling its binary opposition. Al-Shidyaq's modern text dismantles and unfixes the master narrative of European modernity and civilization. Modernity in this context is no longer singular, opposed to tradition, or identifiable with the West. The debates and critical approaches that engage it as such bypass *other* possible modernities, which arise from a series of events, movements, and peformances in between the city and the village, the street and the text, and the literary and the political.

Al-Shidyaq launches a final assault against civilization as a coherent and fixed structure, homogeneous and one with itself. In a diatribe at the end of his book, he addresses London dwellers on the one hand, and *Kashf*'s reader on the other, calling the latter to witness the injustice inherent in this so-called "civilization." Infusing sarcasm with anger in order to denounce civilization's contradiction, al-Shidyaq describes British social ills, pollution, and poor weather, repeatedly lamenting the absence of good restaurants in London. He claims that it is shameful (*'ār*) for Londoners (the assumption here is that they are "shameless," like the cadavers discussed above), who are some of the wealthiest and most industrious and powerful people in the world, to lack the necessary know-how to make and sell quality foods and drinks; they even failed to consider licensing this commerce to a foreigner who does. "Could this be explained," continues al-Shidyaq, "in any other way but that you, Londoners, are but foolish, stupid, cheats, or frauds? . . . As for their cafés, they are mostly filled with riffraff, just lying around, drunk, or dirty. When you order coffee they mix it without you seeing with milk and sugar and serve it in this fashion so you can't tell what's in it."[64] He also mentions how people buy food and eat it standing up as if they are performing some strange ritual; how they butcher sick animals and serve their meats drenched in pepper to cover up their stench; how they have ruined and contaminated the very idea of food, failing to learn anything from the French, the Italian, and the Eastern Mediterraneans. These failures and misdeeds lead al-Shidyaq to accuse Londoners and the British more generally of being misguided and accursed, despite their wealth and power. He continues that if these practices are the result of civilization, then he prefers *jahl* (ignorance, barbarity).[65] Returning obsessively to the absence of culinary sophistication, al-Shidyaq asks sarcastically: "*Alā taʿjab ayyuhā al-qāriʾ* (aren't you surprised, oh reader), that these people who have more than 5000 ships . . . , 2000 newspapers . . . , and they still don't know how to cook and eat properly."[66]

This section's style and rhythm could be compared to al-Shidyaq's encounter in the City. Both encounters operate as sites of production of the modern text itself. In this scene, al-Shidyaq shames and attacks the British, rejecting and spewing out all that he was forced to ingest and that had poisoned or disgusted him. This passage is the site (*mawrid*, source) of convulsions, seizures, and invectives. Al-Shidyaq is fuming, so to speak, as if he's expulsing in this very moment—in the here and now—all the fumes he inhaled. Through these affects, al-Shidyaq enacts a violent purging of the body from its ailment. His anger, which comes through in his obsessive return to the site of disgust and contradiction—namely food—rids al-Shidyaq from the ill and shakes off the ache with which he struggled throughout. Thus, this diatribe operates as a dismantling and a fragmentation of the epistemological model that associates civilization with superior eating habits and social practices. Through this performative catharsis, he dismantles the model of civilization that confuses and disgusts him, thereby rejecting its reductive binary opposition and refusing to believe its secret.

This *kashf*, which I trace in al-Shidyaq's encounter from the City to the forsaken village, frames the trials of the Arab traveler in Europe as *aḥdāth* (events, accidents, anecdotes). *Nahda*'s practices and trials—and *ḥadātha* (modernity) as such—arise from this series of accidents and events. Thus, this passage captures the chapter's thesis, which consists in establishing that these trials of modernity fundamentally unsettle prevailing discursive models that limit and fix meaning through the logic of origin and binary opposition, both in the colonial and orientalist settings (East/West), but also at the scholarly level (modernity/tradition or modernity as complicity with the West). In so doing, al-Shidyaq tries out Arab modernity and charts its trials through linguistic experimentation, travel, anecdotes, mockery, and argumentation.

CONCLUSION

Like Robinson Crusoe, Jonah, and Hayy ibn Yaqzan, al-Shidyaq goes in and out of his room (*ḥujra*)—also animal hole (*juḥr*)—dangerously venturing out in the City streets and treading the muddy roads of the accursed village. The modern takes shape in this interplay between his genuine and dramatized fear of death, his capriciousness about food and his aversion to it. The modern is embodied in al-Shidyaq's running away from speeding carts, his anxiety about crossing the City streets, and from his fear of asphyxiation due to toxic fumes and smells. This body in motion, in and outside the text, characterizes both physical movement and the movement of signifiers, words, and rhythms. It exposes in the process modes of industrial and ideological violence within the British context

(rural/urban, upper class/lower class) and in the relation between
Europe and its "others"—other cultures, races, and languages.

The *mukhabba'* al-Shidyaq sets out to explore is both a category of concealment applied to himself—hiding in his room yet
venturing out—but also to civilization as something shameful
and shameless at the same time. The *mukhabba'* is thus the time
the meat has been sitting out; the absence of ritual slaughter; the
ill al-Shidyaq might incur from consuming the rotten meat; and
the veiling of the act of mixing coffee with milk and sugar before
serving it at the café. The *mukhabba'*, which manifests itself in
Kashf through its smells, fumes, and nudity, characterizes the
process through which this civilizational model constitutes
and maintains itself. Al-Shidyaq thus suggests that "the king is
naked"—just like the rabbit—and that the system through which
civilization becomes meaningful has no signified or fixed essence
or secret. Rather, it functions through automation, sounds and
movements, smells and fumes, which permeate al-Shidyaq's text.
Kashf, the process and the book, *kashf ṭubbī* (bill of health,
medical examination) and *Kashf al-Mukhabba'*, is permanently
altered by that which it examines and diagnoses. The smells and
sounds the text reproduces, in between its words, are constitutive
of its literary modernity.

That said, it is important to explore the alternative to the concept of civilization in al-Shidyaq's text. While one would imagine
a return to authenticity or tradition in moments of crisis, anger,
and confrontation with modernity, al-Shidyaq presents an exilic
identity that transcends national and linguistic boundaries. Al-
Shidyaq claims a culinary and cultural sophistication by drawing
on an alternative discourse to that of civilization in England. The
community imagined in this moment of crisis includes itinerant
thinkers speaking and writing Arabic, French, Turkish, and Italian, moving back and forth between Syria and Egypt, Malta and
Tunis, Marseille and Istanbul. A constant flow of writers com-
posing letters and poetic fragments, and narrating anecdotes (as
opposed to treatises on culture and civilization) and episodes of
collapse and aversion across the Mediterranean, introduced new

aesthetic sensitivities and shaped Arabic culture and language in fundamental ways. Al-Shidyaq's writing thus constitutes an important framework for investigating modern Arabic literature and thought, which has produced the likes of Jabra Ibrahim Jabra (1919–1994), 'Abd al-Rahman al-Munif (1933–2004), Mahmoud Darwish (1941–2008), Edward Said (1935–2003), and countless others moving back and forth between Arab and European or American cities. As they map out cultural positions and domains, express anxieties and frustration at airports and border crossings, these authors interrogate cultural essentialism and homogeneity. This body of writing, which takes shape in al-Shidyaq's work as a dismantling of civilization and of the new categories imposed on the Ottoman intellectual in the nineteenth century, connects different coasts and cities, languages and cultures, and provides the intertextual possibilities that allow the critic to read *historically* across historical contexts—from this *Nahda* text to contemporary writing—an intertextuality of *aḥdāth*.

Narrativizing exile and displacement through forms of collapse and embodiment, al-Shidyaq resists the disciplining of the body according to the model of civilization, which eventually mediates European colonialism, as Timothy Mitchell argues in *Colonising Egypt* (1991), for instance. Al-Shidyaq rebels against confinement, both physical and cultural, and exposes in the process its violent eradication of identity as composite, complex, and multicultural. Al-Shidyaq's work could thus be read as a response to colonialism's homogenizing and hegemonic practices. Edouard Glissant argues that colonization is a power of disorder as it disrupts the native culture and creates the dilemma of modernity and authenticity.[67] In this light, it is important to read al-Shidyaq in dialogue with Glissant, Said, Fanon, and other critics of the colonial episteme and its imagined binary oppositions. In a reference to Deleuze and Guattari's work, Muhsin al-Musawi argues that this dialogue, and "the issue of minority literature" specifically, "may lead us to a reading of Arabic culture in its relation to the imperial legacy."[68]

Exile, in Edward Said's words, "is strangely compelling to think about but terrible to experience."[69] It generates the critical distance that provides the author with the ability to analyze, discuss, and reimagine questions of literature, culture, identity, and politics from the position of a painful experience. From Karl Marx (1818–1883) and Sigmund Freud (1856–1939) to Theodor Adorno (1903–1969) and Max Horkheimer (1895–1973), countless authors embodied in their texts displacement and persecution. Himself an exile, out of place in the West and the East, yet at home in both, Said emphasizes the productive ambiguity of this liminal state. In al-Shidyaq's case, al-Azmeh and Trabulsi claim that "this exiled man had only his language,"[70] emphasizing his text's exilic nature. *Kashf* could thus be read in relation to that of Adorno, Edward Said, and others. Be it Said's critique of Orientalism or Adorno's and Horkheimer's critique of the Enlightenment,[71] these texts involve what Deleuze and Guattari characterize as a powerful and transformative erring in language and thought that expose structures of violence: "Writing like a dog digging a hole, a rat digging its burrow. And to do that, finding his own point of underdevelopment, his own *patois*, his own third world, his own desert."[72] Said, Adorno, Horkheimer, and al-Shidyaq all interrogate the canon and unsettle its episteme. Theirs is a writing that disrupts and disperses only to reconstitute, assemble, and generate. Just as Kafka does with German, al-Shidyaq makes Arabic "vibrate with intensity,"[73] taking it— letting it take him—to new and different horizons, from the nineteenth century to the present, from *Kashf* and *Saq* to Ahmad Alaidy's *An Takun ʿAbbas al-ʿAbd* (*Being Abbas al-Abd*) (2003) (subject of chapter 6).[74]

In the next chapter, I move from al-Shidyaq to Tayeb Salih, from the *Nahda* travel narrative to its postcolonial articulation, in order to investigate the way poetry, haunting, and fragmentation stage in Salih's work the encounter with European colonialism. In a similar vein, I argue that the emphasis on the linearity of colonialism and its underlying binary opposition and unilateral and teleological movement from North to South (West to East) stifles theoretical frameworks by reducing debates to the politics of representation and the binaries of tradition and modernity.

Exploring modes of ambivalence in Salih's text highlights different embodiments of conflict and anxiety in between Europe and North Africa, the novel and poetry, and Arabic and English. While *Kashf* stages the traveler's body as the site of subversion and collapse of the model of European civilization and its underlying hierarchy, the poetic association and allegorical staging in *Mawsim al-Hijra ila al-Shamal* (*Season of Migration to the North*) (1966) operate as sites of collapse that align Arabic mythology with English poetry, colonial wars in the Sudan with World War I. This exploration of the work's narratives of absence and fragmentation serves to reframe the relation between the literary and the political and tie in the *Nahda* narrative to the postcolonial novel and beyond.

CHAPTER FOUR

Staging the Colonial Encounter

I fear, my son, that the West might take you away from us. What I fear most is that a European woman might captivate and lure you into her web, which will break your poor mother's heart. Nahida is awaiting your return, my son; I see it in her eyes every time she visits. I sense her longing for you every time your name comes up, though she tries to hide it, and you know how shy she is. Even if you don't want Nahida, there is always Ni'mat and Thurayya and your cousin, Hadba'. There are plenty of girls here. Come back, my son, and I will marry you off to the most beautiful girl, pure and chaste. (my translation)

—SUHAYL IDRIS, "The Latin Quarter" (1953)

You were manipulating her to the point of tears, which made you desire her even further. You would reject her to the point of desperation, and, suddenly, you would assail her and burn her with passion, quench her thirst and make her lose consciousness. When she awakens, she looks at you with gratitude and drowns you in kisses. Everything went as planned: You married Chris and got the Green Card, and then the American citizenship. (my translation)

—ALAA AL ASWANY, *Chicago* (2007)

Literary representations of the Arab encounter with modernity in the "late *Nahda* period"[1] often depicts the transformative experience of a male Arab student studying in France or England. This long and well-established genre includes Tawfiq al-Hakim's (1898–1987) *'Usfur min al-Sharq* (*Bird from the East*) (1938), Yahya Haqqi's (1905–1992) *Qindil Umm Hashim* (*The Lamp of Umm Hashim*) (1944), and Suhayl Idris's (1923–2008)

Al-Hayy al-Latini (The Latin Quarter) (1953). Often mediated through amorous and sexual affairs, these encounters are read through the tradition/modernity and spirituality/materialism binary oppositions. "Desire for the north," as Waïl Hassan suggests, "becomes the desire for the European woman."[2] In Idris's work, for instance, a relationship with a French woman unsettles the Lebanese student studying in Paris. This relationship tears him apart and forces him to choose between duty toward his family and country, and his own desire. Existentialist philosophy permeates the fictionalization of the Arab experience of modernity in the twentieth century through narratives of individual and political fulfillment.[3]

Published on the eve of the *Naksa*—the catastrophic Arab defeat of June 1967—Tayeb Salih's (1929–2009) *Mawsim al-Hijra ila al-Shamal* (*Season of Migration to the North*) (henceforth: *Mawsim*), a novel written by a Sudanese person who himself studied and lived in England, stages the Arab-African encounter with colonialism and European modernity in instances of sexual conquest, haunting, and intoxication. Salih fictionalizes this encounter through the figure of Mustafa Saʿid, a Sudanese man who moves to England following World War I, and returns to an independent Sudan after thirty years of trials and tribulations. The nameless narrator, a young Sudanese literary critic who has lived and studied in England as well, interprets Mustafa's narrative by recognizing a trajectory of loss, embodied in postures and utterances, smells and accents. The narrator accompanies Mustafa into colonial gravesites. Answering the call of the dead and mirroring the loss of those grieving for them, Mustafa descends into hell like an Orphean character seeking to recover his lost object—an irretrievable moment of origin, constantly displaced between Europe and Africa. From Muhammad ʿAli's *fuḥūla* (virility) and identification with Sayf al-Dawla in al-Tahtawi's fantasy discussed in chapter 2, and al-Shidyaq's going to hell and back in the City in order to produce the modern text discussed in chapter 3, this chapter investigates Mustafa's association with Othello and Tariq ibn Ziyad,[4] the ghoul and the *afreet* (evil

spirit). Examining echoes, reflections, and smells, I identify in
Salih's novel the stage or the "theater" of the Arab-African experience of European modernity in the colonial context.[5] Expressed
in violent confrontation and physical collapse in *Nahda* texts,
this experience turns to murder and destruction in *Mawsim,*

Salih scholarship often reduces the novel's significance to Mustafa's sexual exploits in England, interpreted at face value as a
coherent narrative of anticolonial retribution. Instead, I focus on
the narrator's interpretation of Mustafa's narrative as he experiences those affects that "split the narrative open" and lead the
narrator to uncover (*kashf*) Mustafa's anxiety. In this context,
the trials of Arab modernity arise from the staging of the colonized subject's encounters in Europe and in Africa on the one
hand, and from the narrator's interpretation and unveiling of this
staging in a postindependence historical and literary context. In
the absence of an actual or possible return to a specific experience of loss, colonial trauma could only be staged and embodied
in texts.[6] I argue that this fictionalization unsettles the identification of a personal experience that is linked to a recognizable
encounter, situating it instead in spectacles of disaster between
Europe and Africa. In this light, the encounter with modernity
could be accessed only through a dramatic production that simultaneously produces the modern Arabic text—as I argued in the
previous chapters—and conditions the return to and reinvention
of tradition.

COLONIAL GRAVESITES

Roger Allen characterizes Salih's novel as a bildungsroman that
explores the transformative effects of the East/West encounter
in the 1960s and beyond.[7] Often compared to Joseph Conrad's
(1857–1924) *Heart of Darkness* (1902), *Mawsim* was translated
into English in 1969, and into other languages soon after. The
work has been widely taught and studied in the American academic context, becoming, in some respect, the quintessential
postcolonial Arabic novel and Third World literature text. This

positions Salih's novel in relation to such works as Assia Djebar's (b. 1936) *L'Amour, la fantasia* (*Fantasia: An Algerian Caval-cade*) (1985) and Jamal Mahjoub's (b. 1960) *In the Hour of Signs* (1996). Like *Mawsim*, these works deal with colonial trauma, memory, and the question of modernity. The modes of staging and the trajectories of return deployed in these works need to be addressed as one investigates the interplay of affects in the Arab postcolonial context.

Djebar's works, from *Femmes d'Alger dans leurs apparte-ments* (*Women of Algiers in Their Apartments*) (1980) to *Blanc d'Algérie* (*Algerian White*) (1996), involve processes of revisit-ing colonial gravesites and tracing an intertextuality of loss and fascination through a dangerous negotiation between languages and cultural registers, French school memories and tales about murdered ancestors.[8] In her novel *L'Amour, la fantasia*, Djebar describes the extermination of the Oulad Riah tribe in Alge-ria in 1845. Adopting the genre of the French official report, which betrays the event's horror, Djebar infiltrates the text of Pélissier, the French officer overseeing the massacre, in order to descend into a cave in the Atlas Mountains and excavate the burned bodies of cattle and children, women and men: "When the body is not embalmed by ritual lamentations, it is like a scarecrow decked in rags and tatters. The battle cries of our ancestors, unhorsed in long-forgotten combats, re-echo across the years."[9] Cadavers of victims of colonial genocide fester in the literary text a century and half after the first French boat appeared in the port of Algiers. Similarly, these cadavers per-meate the text through a process of literary *kashf* (revealing). This *kashf* consists in tracing smells and recognizing muffled utterances, battle cries, and wailing. It also consists in identify-ing the literary staging of spectacles of disaster and fascination: French perfumes and poetry, and official reports permeated by the smoke from the Oulad Riah burning bodies. Revisiting the colonial encounter in Djebar's work could only be fictionalized and staged through a descent guided by smells and sensitiv-ity to smoke, claustrophobia and sensitivity to darkness. The descending body, according to Djebar, has to fit into narrow spaces, lose itself in the dark, in order to access the subterranean galleries where other bodies lie on the ground, decomposing, burned. This speleological journey, critical and investigative, deploys the literary sensorium, embodied in various utterances and smells that lead the critic in the dark, beyond the linearity of history and its cultural master narratives.

Assailed by the cries of those who perished, the author fictionalizes the historical account by recognizing the cries of murdered ancestors and confronting them in the text. Djebar's colonial scene is one of extermination wherein no one survives to tell the story. Through hearing and smelling, the author stages these encounters in the absence of an actual origin. Infiltrating official colonial reports and appropriating their language, the text seeks out, gropes for, and approximates an irretrievable experience. Writing enacts haunting and exorcism at the same time, emancipating yet torturing the author turned medium and gravedigger. In *Mawsim*, the narrator-critic mediates these processes by following Mustafa into the subterranean galleries, which open up to the narrator—who is in pursuit of smells, sounds, and shadows— like gateways into other dimensions.

THE BOOK OF MIGRATION

Narrated in the Arabic genre of the *hakawāti* (storyteller), *Mawsim*'s opening lines describe the narrator's return to his native village in the Sudan after seven years in England, where he studied "the life of an obscure English poet."[10] Upon his return, he states that missing home or the "warmth of the tribe" was the most painful aspect of his life in Europe.[11] When some villagers asked him whether the British lived in sin instead of marrying, the narrator answers "that Europeans were, with minor differences, exactly like them, marrying and bringing up their children in accordance with principles and tradition, that they have good morals and were in general good people."[12] The narrator then meets Mustafa, a conspicuous stranger who had settled in the village. Intrigued, the narrator pursues him and forces him to reveal his true identity. When Mustafa starts telling his story, the narrative shifts from the primary frame, which includes the narrator and Mustafa, to Mustafa's embedded tale.

Mustafa describes his birth in 1898[13] to a dead father and a melancholic mother. Attending colonial schools in Khartoum and then Cairo, Mustafa, a child prodigy, moves to England by the end of the Great War. The first Sudanese to study and teach at Oxford, he becomes an economist who denounces capitalism and its imperialist repercussions. However, "in England, he realizes that no amount of schooling would make him one of 'them,' that fundamentally and culturally he was the Other, one of the colonized, a dark shadow in the land of 'light.'"[14] This description, which draws on Frantz Fanon's analysis of the black man who tries yet fails to pass as white in the European metropolis, is coupled with a deep-seated resentment on Mustafa's part.[15] The latter insists on inscribing his otherness, especially in relation to British women, through self-exoticizing gestures and decorum. In England, Mustafa presents himself as the savage black man who saddles his camel and goes to war in his love den, seducing his victims with incense, perfumes, and lies.[16] Through this staged sexual warfare, he performs the role of an archaic hunter and creature of hell, waging a war of retribution against British colonization. His exploits, worthy of a pre-Islamic panegyric, disavow a fictionalization of the encounter with England in *Mawsim*. In this context, Muhsin al-Musawi suggests that Mustafa's sexual war serves "to make known what has been silenced, marginalized, and distorted."[17]

The critical attention to sexuality in Salih's novel is perhaps due to its explicit sexual scenes and the fact that it was censored in most Arab countries when it was first published. This attention to sex is coupled in the critical tradition with emphases on Mustafa's psychosexual development, which is shaped by his relation to his mother and to Mrs. Robinson, the British woman who cares for him as a teenager in Cairo.[18] These critics treat Mustafa's acts of physical and emotional violence as symptomatic expressions of the colonized man's pain and frustration, resentment and humiliation. While Joseph John and Yosif Tarawneh read the novel through a series of Freudian concepts such as "incest taboo," "masochism," and "theory of the drives,"[19] Muhammad Siddiq undertakes a Jungian reading of Mustafa's oedipal complex in the novel.[20] Siddiq argues that he is stranded between a failed relation with the mother and relentless attempts at overcompensation through various projections and associations—the mother likened to such archetypes as the sea, the city, and the West. Offering a different perspective, Saree Makdisi emphasizes the novel's ambivalence and confounding of literature and history, East and West.

> *Season of Migration* sprawls not only between the past, the present, and the future; it fans out, through and across the different registers of textuality, narrative, form, chronology, and history, none of which remain stable, and each of which is wrapped up in a series of endless and constantly expanding contradictions. . . . [*Season*] presents itself as the narrative of a vast puzzle of which it is also one small part, and its reader another; it is therefore a narrative that necessarily will be incomplete . . . that it is itself composed of these contradictions. . . . [*Season*] leaves us floating uneasily in the present, waiting for a resolution that does not come.[21]

Makdisi points to the text's ideological and narrative instability, which engulfs the reader and leaves him/her in a state of critical anxiety. This anxiety consumes the narrator in the novel as well, who interprets Mustafa's tale by drawing on multiple textual and cultural registers. More specifically, the narrator operates as an investigator of some sort, following traces, interpreting whispers and postures as he seeks to reconstitute Mustafa's story. Trained as a literary critic in England, the narrator thus becomes a reader of the body of his main character—Mustafa—the scarred and scarring body of the colonized man at the intersection of multiple disasters and cultural contexts, from the colonial wars to World War I, the Sudan to England.

The narrator engages Mustafa as a text that mediates and reflects the loss expressed in the lingering gaze of "women with dead faces," "women with masks," and "troops returning, filled with terror, from the war of trenches."[22] These images and voices come to Mustafa when he encounters the narrator in the village. Through the narrator's critical perspective, the reader is led to complicate the dialectics of loss and retribution in the novel and unsettle "the Arab encounter with modernity" as a process of self-fulfillment in the vein of al-Hakim, Haqqi, and Idris. The emphasis on the narrator's perspective allows the reader to identify and trace a structure of loss often suppressed by the critical tradition that considers this novel as an instance of an anticolonial Reconquista. In this sense, Salih's strategic recourse to the narrator sheds light on the fictionalization and staging of the Arab-African encounter with modernity as a way of undermining its imagined fixity. In *Mawsim*, this encounter is always already fictionalized from the position of a modern reader and critic within the novel itself. The narrator reads Mustafa's tale by recognizing its affects and tracing them to colonial trauma. The trials of Arab modernity arise from the narrator's recognizing symptoms and signs, interpreting and misreading, and eventually rejecting Mustafa's narrative.

THE VOICE FROM HELL

Mustafa, who triumphantly justifies his seduction and manipulation of British women, suppresses his trials and tribulations in England upon his return to the Sudan. His tale reveals that after thirty years in England, which ended in his imprisonment for the murder of his wife, Jean Morris, and following a nomadic wandering across three continents, he returns to the Sudan. He settles down in a small village by the Nile and marries a local girl, Hosna.[23] However, when the narrator returns to his native village and meets Mustafa, the stranger's suppressed past erupts when he recites, in perfect English, a poem at a friend's house. As the men start drinking, the host insists that Mustafa drink as well. Resisting then relenting to the call of the spirits, Mustafa, intoxicated, lies in the position of the dead and recites a poem about "the women of Flanders," waiting for those who never returned from the trenches of the Great War.

> Mustafa sank down [*dafana nafsah*] into the chair, stretched out his legs, and grasped the glass in both hands; his eyes gave me the impression of wandering in far-away horizons. Then, suddenly, I heard him reciting English poetry in a clear voice and with an impeccable accent. It was a poem which I later found in an anthology of poetry about the First World War and which goes as follows:

> *Those women of Flanders*
> *Await the lost,*
> *Await the lost who never will leave the harbour*
> *They await the lost whom the train never will bring.*
> *To the embrace of those women with dead faces,*
> *They await the lost, who lie dead in the trenches,*
> *The barricade and the mud,*
> *In the darkness of the night,*
> *This is Charing Cross Station, the hour's past one,*
> *There was a faint light,*
> *There was a great pain.*

> After that he gave a deep sigh, still holding the glass between his hands, his eyes wandering off into the horizon within himself. I tell you that had the ground suddenly split open and revealed an afreet standing before me, his eyes shooting out flames, I would not have been more terrified. All of a sudden there came to me the ghastly, nightmarish feeling that we—the men grouped together in that room—were not a reality but merely some illusion. Leaping up, I stood above the man and shouted at him: "What's this you're saying?" . . . Pushing me violently aside, he jumped to his feet and went out of the room. . . . Mahjoub, busy laughing with the rest of the people in the gathering, did not notice what had occurred.[24]

Mustafa's experience in England, which has thus far been kept a secret from the villagers, erupts in this scene through a poem about loss, recited in perfect English. Sinking down in the chair, he mirrors an impossible burial. Medium-like, Mustafa encounters the faces of women awaiting their beloved who disappeared during World War I. Their faces reflect absence, which, in turn, leaves them silent and withdrawn. The poem conjures up a spectacle of absence that ties in British women with World War I, technological warfare, and the inability to mourn. The reference to the Great War specifically presents trauma as an impossible experience, or the experience of those who perished, now reflected on the faces of those who await them. Mustafa's eyes, wandering afar, become like those of the women in the poem. The eyes and the face are but a screen that bounces images and events that cannot be fully described, inscribed, but only called into presence through reflection, movement, and affect.

Of all the people present, only the narrator recognizes the language, the poem, and the significance of Mustafa's posture. Mustafa's performance thus interrupts the temporality of the scene, introducing another dimension, hellish and out of time. This break emphasizes the fictionalization of the process of remembering *as* return to the lost origin of trauma. This process takes shape as a temporal and linguistic break, which requires understanding a different language and recognizing a different voice arising from Mustafa's interiority yet coming from afar. Specifically, the voice that comes out of Mustafa coincides with the narrator's experience of what is more frightening than the opening of the ground and the apparition of an *afreet*, shooting flames. The splitting open that the narrator experiences as he observes Mustafa's posture and hears his poem also occurs in the narrative itself, in the Arabic text, from which emerges the English poem about irretrievable loss. This scene not only unfolds visually in front of the narrator, but physically arrests him as well. The narrator shouts while Mustafa jumps to his feet and "pushes him violently." The affects align experiencing and witnessing with the acts of reading and interpreting that which creates dissonance in the narrative, in the text itself. The narrator experiences Mustafa's performance (which he joins) as a violent shaking up that takes the narrative in different directions. Not only is the listener pushed violently and unsettled, but the speaker himself jumps in terror following his own trance.

The narrator experiences Mustafa's posture as that of someone going into a place of death. The expression *dafana nafsah* literally means, "buried himself" or "went into the grave." The poem, emerging from a state of intoxication, becomes part of a trajectory of loss that combines a posture (burial), an image (women's faces), and a text (the poem itself). The narrator points out that although it appears as if it is coming from afar, the poem as "the voice" emanates from the interiority of the Odyssean hero, "who identifies with this sense of loss."[25] This emphasizes the body, the state of intoxication, and a general interplay of affects expressed in shouting and jumping as the sensorial framework through which memory is accessed, narrative is constituted, and the experience of loss is recognized. Thus, Mustafa's encounter with modernity in the colonial context—as a child prodigy in the Sudan and as a Fanonian "inassimilable" black man in London—manifests itself not only in the poem about World War I— the text—but also in the way the poem erupts in this scene and becomes manifest, arresting and causing dissonance and interruption that only the narrator-critic could witness.

As it unfolds to the narrator alone (the other men did not even notice what happened), this scene provides clues for reading Salih's text. Mieke Bal argues that the focalizer or the agent of focalization is the one from whose perspective the novel's events are experienced and viewed.[26] The focalizer is "a specific agent of perception, the holder of the 'point of view.'"[27] She argues that what is seen transforms the seer both morally and politically. In *Mawsim*, only the narrator recognizes the trajectory of loss expressed in Mustafa's poem. Salih thus presents a didactic structure wherein the narrator, an agent of focalization, shapes the reader's perception of Mustafa's story at one level, and the reader's understanding of the novel within which the story is embedded at another. Listening to his story and experiencing its affects, the narrator reads loss in the association between scenes of disaster (colonial wars and World War I) and Mustafa's trials in England. This reading, which has direct repercussions on the novel's reception, traces colonial violence through a process of fictionalization and staging. What is lost in the colonial encounter is situated in between the Sudan and England and could not be traced to a personal experience locatable in a particular site. The trials of Arab modernity in this context thus need to be investigated in the narrator's modes of experience, recognition, and interpretation as he follows Mustafa's return to gravesites and scenes of disaster through a trajectory of smells, reflections, postures, and cries.

SPECTACLES OF DISASTER

In his 1917 essay "Mourning and Melancholia," Sigmund Freud differentiates between two modes of experiencing loss: Whereas mourning characterizes a process that liberates the subject from his/her attachment to the object of loss (a lover, a country), melancholia characterizes the inability to let go of the beloved. In melancholia, the lost object is transformed into a constitutive lack that the ego internalizes and with which it identifies. Freud argues that due to the subject's ambivalent relation to the object of loss, the ego, unable or unwilling to cede on the attachment, preserves loss through identification. Not knowing what it has lost in the death of the other, the ego internalizes loss. In this way, the melancholic subject experiences the emptiness brought about by the loss of the external object as a loss in the ego itself.[28] The distinction between mourning and melancholia in Freud, though useful as a starting point for engaging representation and modalities of loss, is not clear or conclusive. Suffice it to say at this point that the trajectory of loss operates through a process of reflecting absence, accentuating the unlocatability of the object of loss, and situating the process of interpretation in Salih's novel as the only way to simulate, trace, and approach it through modes of staging and fictionalization.

The question of loss is a fundamental trope in Arabic literature. Moneera al-Ghadeer traces melancholy to pre-Islamic elegies, marking the poetic temporality of the loss of home or the encampment, the loss of the tribe and the beloved. Through a comparative engagement with works by Freud, Derrida, and

Judith Butler, among others, and with the articulation of loss in the Arabic postcolonial context specifically, al-Ghadeer identifies melancholia as "the phantasm of being loyal to the lost object and establishing unending love, with all it entails, from a state of waiting, agony and pleasure."[29] The economy of loss and the melancholic desire identified in al-Ghadeer's work depict both a poetic discourse and a literary and philosophical framework involving Europe and the Arab world.

Elaborating on Freud's work and on his writing on World War I neuroses specifically, in which he diagnoses the experience of loss and the repetition of the traumatic event in patients' dreams and flashbacks, Cathy Caruth argues that victims of trauma are tormented by the memory of the indescribable event.

> The pathology consists, rather, solely in the *structure of its experience* or reception: the event is not assimilated or experienced fully at the time, but only belatedly, in its repeated *possession* of the one who experiences it. To be traumatized is precisely to be possessed by an image or event. . . . The traumatized, we might say, carry an impossible history within them, or they become themselves the symptom of a history that they cannot entirely possess.[30]

> The trauma is a repeated suffering of the event. But it is also a continual leaving of its site. The traumatic reexperiencing of the event thus carries with it what Dori Laub class the "collapse of witnessing," the impossibility of knowing that first constituted it.[31]

From the event as the site of generative ruptures and possibilities discussed in previous chapters, we move with Caruth's formulation to the traumatic event as the site of repetition, return, and haunting. This quest for an impossible origin or undoing of the traumatic experience traps the subject in a structure of reenactment with multiple articulations. The impossible telling or witnessing of the event unleashes symptoms that alter the course of personal and historical narratives. Identifying and tracing these *other* narratives, manifested in Salih's context through a trajectory of smells and sounds, cries and postures, provide access to the story that Mustafa "withholds" from the villagers in the novel. The narrator, in this context, is a reader of symptoms and interpreter of traces and signs that risk engulfing him as well.

Dore Laub's "collapse of witnessing" to which Caruth refers characterizes the experience of the women of Flanders mirroring disaster in Mustafa's poem. However, these women experience trauma only through the disappearance of the beloved at the scene of disaster—the battlefield of World War I. Their structure of loss could not be traced to an immediate experience, only inscribed on their faces and reproduced and reenacted by Mustafa as he recites the poem. His affects—posture, recitation, and accent— embody this irretrievable loss. However, this process needs to be juxtaposed with another site of loss in the novel, namely Mustafa's mother, whose face mirrors a catastrophic unfolding in the Sudan as well. This mirroring allows us to investigate loss in between the Sudan and England, complicating in this way the rigidity of the binary models through which Salih's text and postcolonial literature more generally are often read.

Complementing the narrator's critical work is Mustafa's portrayal of his mother as a voiceless creature, unable to express emotions or show love and attachment: "I see her clearly with her thin lips resolutely closed, with something on her face like a mask, I don't know—a thick mask, as though her face were the surface of the sea. Do you understand? It possessed not a single colour but a multitude, appearing and disappearing and intermingling."[32] In describing her face as that of the sea, constantly changing color, Mustafa points to its reflection of loss and mirroring of a scene of disaster happening elsewhere. The mother's face, like that of the women in the poem, reflects an absence tied to an indescribable event. His mother could be waiting for the departed husband who died right before Mustafa was born. This leads one to reconsider his birth year, 1898, which coincides with his father's disappearance and marks the British extermination of the Sudanese at the Battle of Omdurman. The inscription of loss on the faces of Mustafa's mother and the women of Flanders involves, therefore, the mirroring of two catastrophic events: the colonial war on the Sudan and World War I. The reflection and mirroring of loss align these spectacles of disaster, mitigating in the process questions of origin and personal experience. Accents, faces, and postures are the only sites through which this loss manifests itself in Mustafa's narrative.

While some critics point to Salih's reference to Omdurman and the Great War, few engage these allegories of disaster or ground them in the economy of affects that mediates Mustafa's trials and tribulations in England. The scene of modern carnage at Omdurman on September 2, 1898, described in Jamal Mahjoub's novel *In the Hour of Signs* (1996),[33] should be juxtaposed to the one that takes place sixteen years later on the European continent itself. In this context, the colonization of the Sudan through the elimination of all forms of resistance to British rule at the end of the nineteenth century is part of a modern and technological mode of violence that engulfs Europe as well. In this context, the dead of Omdurman and of World War I are inscribed on the faces of African and British women who, in turn, seek out Mustafa and the narrator, the focalizer of his tale. Visual reflection and mirroring, simulation of burial and a perfect yet uncanny English accent, refigure death from colonial violence and war through a literary staging of historical disaster. This, I argue, characterizes the embodiment of the encounter with Europe as it takes shape in the novels of Djebar, Mahjoub, Salih, and others. These works can approach the disaster only through modes of fictionalization, alignment, and embodiment. In this light, the emphasis shifts from the experience of trauma (Omdurman, Oulad Riah massacre) discussed by Caruth and Laub, to the narrator's experience of Mustafa's story and his transferential relation to the women in the novel, which are staged through body postures, accents, and other affects.

The structure of loss, which arises from the narrator's reaction to Mustafa's tale, complicates our understanding of the Arab-African encounter with modernity in the novel. In this encounter, modernity (associated with England, technology, the English language) is confronted with its own ghosts and victims across two continents. Salih's text situates the experience of war and violence in between multiple sites of disaster involving Sudanese and British people, soldiers and civilians, the women of Flanders and Mustafa's mother. In this context, models of instability and ambivalence challenge conventional readings of East/West binary opposition. The colonial encounter should thus be read in the narrative staging that exposes and complicates modernity's homogeneity. Embodying the quest for an irretrievable origin, the literary text stages the experience of modernity as a condition of not knowing what was lost. The trials of Arab modernity arise in Salih's work from the simultaneity of this comparative reading that constantly juxtaposes and moves in between multiple registers and sites, situated beyond East and West. Thus, Mustafa's "exploits" in England could not be traced to a specific experience or relation to the parents, for instance, as the strict psychoanalytic reading would entail (failed identification with the father, melancholic mother). However, despite the absence of a clear and causal relation between the traumatic event (Omdurman) and Mustafa's experience, one is unable to understand his trials in England without aligning these spectacles of disaster.

It has become impossible, since Halbwachs, to disentangle collective from individual memory in the context of historical and catastrophic events.[34] The trials of Arab modernity in Salih's text are mediated through the narrator's interpretation of Mustafa's tale by moving from the catastrophic moment of the colonial encounter to an independent Sudan. This interpretation and transition seek to heal and reinvent Arab subjectivity beyond the causal dialectics of loss and trauma on the one hand, and the performance of a hypermasculine sexuality as a veiling of this trauma on the other. Engaging this process of interpretation involves displacing modernity in between Europe and the Sudan, London and the village where two British-educated Sudanese meet. These trials also involve a literary remapping and refiguring of the encounter with technological modernity in the colonial context through the deployment of Arabic interpretive models,

which draw on a variety of mythic structures and cultural anxieties. In staging and moving beyond Mustafa's archaic retribution
against modernity's traumatic war machine, the causal relation
between British colonization of the Sudan and his sexual retribution against English women collapses. The demise of this causal
relation serves to reframe the *Nahda* dialectics of the disoriented
Arab male student or intellectual—Idris and al-Hakim—and
unsettle the encounter with modernity as the *Nahda* condition
of self-fulfillment.

MUSTAFA UNDEAD

Mustafa's encounter with England allows us to read postcolonial literature in the Arab context especially as consisting in a
series of trials and embodied attempts to mourn and confront
catastrophic loss and fragmentation. *Mawsim*'s narrator experiences Mustafa's affects in order to interpret his tale. This critical
vantage point into the novel guides and shapes our understanding of Salih's work. In this context, Mustafa's disappearance in
the flood at the end, embodied in the wailing heard in his house,
is followed by the narrator's explanation that Mustafa failed to
return from the flooded fields.[35] The wailing in this scene mirrors
the affects (posture, accent, and recitation) through which Mustafa betrays his identity in a state of intoxication at the beginning. Moreover, his disappearance replicates that of the soldiers
who fail to return from the battlefield of World War I. After
his alleged drowning in the flood, Mustafa becomes the absent
one (*ghāʾib*)—a Derridean specter present through his absence
(*ghiyāb*)—that sees the narrator without being seen by him.[36]
When the narrator enters Mustafa's room at the end, he gazes at
the portraits of his departed lovers. The narrator claims that it is
in the portrait of Jean Morris, Mustafa's murdered wife, that he
recognizes Mustafa's spectral presence, looking at him through
Jean's eyes. The narrator-critic becomes, just like Mustafa in the
beginning of the novel, overcome by the reflection of absence,
which he constantly seeks to trace, anchor, and situate. This leads

him to read Mustafa's encounter with Jean Morris as a staged confrontation from which arises the text itself. This confrontation could be characterized as a site of collapse, fragmentation, and fictionalization that allows the modern subject, the narrator in this context, to move beyond modernity as a homogeneous and fixed project. Reading the modern encounter through modes of evanescence, ambivalence, and embodiment, the narrator identifies the narrative intertwinement between haunting and loss on the one hand, and the sexual and amorous affects of Mustafa's encounters in England on the other. The narrative of sexual exploits as a fixed anticolonial narrative theorized psychoanalytically gives way to a reading of tremors, haziness, and smells. Identifying and engaging a postcolonial sensorium in Salih's novel, I argue, serves to remove sex as a fixed ideological terrain through which the colonized subject mounts a coherent critique of colonialism. Such reading of Mustafa's sexuality not only fixes East/West in simple and unreflexive categories, but also presents women, and British women especially, as a legitimate target of the colonized man's emancipation.

JEAN MORRIS OR THE MOORISH JINN

As he describes his sexual escapades to the narrator, Mustafa boasts about his prowess and seduction, appearing triumphantly manipulative and intentionally deceitful. He explains that he had turned his bedroom in England into a "theatre of war," infused with incense and decorated with colored lights and other exotic paraphernalia.[37] Focusing on the transformation of his love den into a battlefield against colonialism[38] and following to the letter his justification, critics reduce Mustafa's actions to anticolonial retribution,[39] thereby ignoring the staging of the bedroom as "theatre," which assumes a drama, a performance, an interplay of affects, a reenactment, and an audience. In this context, the bedroom, likened to an archaic battlefield, is a modernist trope that frames Mustafa's encounter with Jean Morris—an element of fire and creature of hell. Describing his first encounter with

Jean while he was intoxicated at a party in London, Mustafa says: "She opened the door and lingered; she appeared to my gaze under the faint lamplight like a mirage shimmering in a desert."[40] He compares Jean to a "mirage," a "cloud," a "shooting star," turning his bed into "a patch of hell" when he finally marries her.[41] As the story progresses, Jean becomes the "demon," appearing and disappearing in front of his eyes.[42] These descriptions frame Mustafa's own staging of his encounter with British women through which he becomes an archaic and hellish creature, waging a war of retribution.

Jean's name mirrors the ambiguity of her character and emphasizes her liminal state between human and nonhuman, presence and absence.[43] While Jean is akin to "Jeannie," as in "jinn," Morris could be understood in association with "Moorish." Jean Morris could thus be read as the "Moorish Jinn." Bearing in mind Mustafa's repeated references to Shakespeare's *Othello* and his identification with the Moor as he tells his story to the narrator, one could imagine Jean as being both Othello and Desdemona at the same time.[44] Jean, the site of catastrophe according to Mustafa, the siren calling him to the shore of disaster, is in fact a Moorish jinn, an ethereal creature from both East and West. Jean's position through Shakespeare's *Othello* and the historical context of the play (Battle of Lepanto, Venice and the Ottoman Empire, the Moor as the racialized other in sixteenth-century Europe)[45] thus complicates the model of the amorous encounter between the Arab-African man and the European woman in Salih's novel. Given the encounter with Jean, whose Europeanness is unsettled and displaced, the bedroom as a "theatre of war" and as a "patch of hell" operates as a stage for the reenactment of an impossible experience. Through this staging, which the narrator-critic experiences and deciphers, Mustafa's descent to hell—in search of trauma's origin—and his encounter with hell's creature are aligned as part of the same evanescent and violent "modern encounter" taking place both in the village in the Sudan and in England, across European and Arab-African literary, political, and cultural registers.

Jean's ambiguous position is emphasized through her depiction as the inevitable site of disaster, thereby mirroring Omdurman and the trenches of World War I. In a declarative sentence repeated throughout his narrative, Mustafa announces the catastrophic unfolding of his encounter with Jean: "The train carried me to Victoria Station and to the world of Jean Morris."[46] The repetition of this statement operates as a foreshadowing of a great disaster. Furthermore, it introduces technological modernity in the context of the European war machine as that which binds South to North, the Sudan to England, from the train station in Cairo to London's Victoria Station. While the train precipitates the movement westward or northward and, in this way, the moment of disaster, it describes a necessary return, material and literary, historical and cultural. This highlights a departure (*hijra*, migration) qua return, a back-and-forth that could not be located in a fixed site or attributed to a unidirectional framework. As "geography and history are amongst the novel's protagonists, performing roles as fact and figure,"[47] the train also represents the railroad Kitchener built to invade the Sudan, thereby collapsing travel to Europe with colonial violence and describing multiple literary, political, and military trajectories in the process. Through the registers of disaster, myth, and technology, Salih aligns colonial trauma and its irretrievable origin with Mustafa's encounter with Jean. This shifts the debate from anticolonial retribution to questions of intertextuality and affects in the novel.

Depicting Jean Morris as Mustafa's true foe refigures the triumphalist representation of his encounter with British women as a form of Reconquista. The narrator, experiencing and reading Mustafa's tale, exclaims upon seeing Jean's portrait in Mustafa's room at the end: "Was this then the phoenix [*'anqā'*] that had ravished the *ghoul*?"[48] Likened to the *'anqā*—a mythic creature in Arab and Middle Eastern sources—Jean ravishes and devours the ghoul. Mustafa, compared to a mythic killer (the ghoul but also the *faḥl* [virile one]) who performs conquest in his "theatre of war," or bedroom, is mocked and defeated in meeting Jean. The narrator, expert on European literature and poetry, aligns a

structure of anxiety in Arabic sources with Shakespeare, Omdurman, and World War I in order to interpret Mustafa's trials in
England. As Waïl Hassan notes, Salih uses the narrator "to ridi-
cule the vanity and preposterousness of these characters,"[49] but
also to unsettle the interpretation of his actions as anticolonial
retribution.

The ʿanqāʾ is the phoenix, the mythical bird that dies and
rises from its ashes, thereby representing rebirth and repetition of a catastrophic unfolding. The medieval lexicologist Ibn
Manzur describes the ʿanqāʾ as "the long necked one," "the
one with the exposed neck" (ʿunq), or "the one whose neck is
white."[50] Though never seen, the ʿanqāʾ is a large bird that carries its victims into the setting sun, earning in this way the attri-
bute mughribu as in ʿanqāʾ mughribu (westerly phoenix). Known
yet not seen, the ʿanqāʾ is also the dāhiya (catastrophe), which is
linked to an impossible seeing or awareness. Furthermore, the
idea of tughribu or mugribu (flying west) is associated with the
notion of tagharrub (become of the West) in the medieval source.
Though the meaning of ghurba—which also means "alienation
in the West" or "diaspora"—varies in Ibn Manzur's lexicon, it is
associated in at least one instance with possession by the jinn.[51]
In this sense, Jean, the Moorish jinn and the ʿanqāʾ, carries her
victim to the scene of disaster—the "icy battlefield"—Omdurman and World War I.[52]

According to the narrator's interpretation, Mustafa's encounter with the ʿanqāʾ is rooted in a cultural anxiety that operates
both at the psychological level (fear of death and fragmentation),
and at the political and cultural one as well (al-gharb [the West]
as the site of disaster or the unknown to which the ʿanqāʾ takes
her victims). The train that carries Mustafa to Jean Morris, the
ʿanqāʾ, who anchors the West as the site of disaster, is also the
train that carries Kitchener's soldiers to Omdurman. The train
thus denotes the movement of technology and myth, the ʿanqāʾ
and the soldiers, precipitating in both cases the moment of catastrophe as a crash across historical and literary contexts. However, the train that takes Mustafa west to Victoria Station and to

Jean Morris is the same train that brings him back to the Sudan wherein he *joins* the soldiers in the trenches of World War I and Omdurman following his disappearance in the flood at the end. This interplay between the historical, the literary, and the mythological anchors the fictionalization of the modern encounter with Europe in the constant displacement of colonial trauma and its object of loss. Reading Mustafa's relation to Europe through the analogy of the *ʿanqāʾ* and the ghoul, the narrator interprets Mustafa's narrative—the text within the text—by tracing its affects and thus shaping the reader's understanding of the novel. The narrator exposes yet turns away from Mustafa's experience. In choosing life at the end,[53] the narrator, unlike the soldiers of World War I, the Oulad Riah tribe in Djebar's novel, and the Sudanese who perished at Omdurman, returns from the brink of disaster to tell the story.

CONCLUSION

Musa al-Halool draws on the notion of the "uncanny" in Freud to analyze the relation between Mustafa and the narrator, reading one as the other's double, endowed with frightening familiarity that emerges from an extreme form of narcissism.[54] Saree Makdisi's reading of Salih's work emphasizes the fragmentation of the narrative and calls attention to the interplay between the reader and the author as sites of both meaning and instability within the framework of debates about modernity and tradition. Benita Parry critiques Makdisi's thesis, noting that "rather than valorize a zone between cultures, the novel questions its very possibility within a situation poisoned by colonialism."[55] I agree with Parry, who situates the novel in a historical and political context wherein "the memories of imperial dominion embedded in the novel are at their keenest in the recollection of colonialist violence in Sudan."[56] Though she locates the novel at the center of the encounter with the colonial crime, Parry stops short of recognizing and confronting the novel's trajectory of loss.

In reading *Mawsim*, one notices a constant displacement of the traditional scenes of identification and a disruption of mirroring. Salih's work offers a complex psychic disturbance, creating a different time of fusion, often indescribable. In the novel, there is a constant shifting of the classic setting of psychoanalysis and its model of causality. The embodiment of the colonial catastrophe risks consuming the author's text as it requires coexisting with colonial language and returning to the scene of genocide. In reading the novel, one identifies a radical fragmentation, both narrative and structural, that eludes the critic and sends him/her foraging across texts, time periods, and cultural references. It is this kind of fragmentation, recognized and described both here and in other chapters, which stages the modern encounter examined in this book. These moments of fragmentation, both literary and physical, enable one to understand contemporary Arabic texts as sites of reading and refiguring of modernity as something never fixed, stable, or clearly circumscribed.[57]

The novel's didactic element, as I showed by emphasizing the role of the narrator as critic and reader embedded in Salih's narrative, offers its own theoretical framework. The emphasis on experience and loss serves to depict a critical relation to the text, a recognition of the proliferation of affects—posture, accent, wailing—that could not be reduced to a simple representation of colonial dynamics belonging to fixed narratives and ideologies. Recognizing the tremor and the evanescent image in Salih's text characterizes a literary approach that complicates what is clearly articulated and expressed even by the main character himself when he identifies as an Othello-like conqueror of the West, avenging the plight of his fellow Sudanese, victims of colonial violence. Reading the modern encounter in the text allows us to rethink the very notion of reading. The encounter with England, as I have demonstrated in this chapter, does not make the Arabic text modern in a causal or historical sense, through its engagement with the historical metanarrative that is. On the contrary, it's the modernity of the encounter and its production through the literary-critical gaze of the narrator following traces, experiencing affects, and struggling to interpret signs and gestures that exposes the ways in which Arabic and European texts are tied in together, in dialogue across literary and cultural contexts.

Mawsim's modernity also operates in the way in which different traditions (from the *'anqā'* to *Othello*) are deployed to stage and disseminate the various encounters. This reflects the kinds of perspectives through which Arabic literature's modernity is examined, taught, and imagined. This modernity does not consist in copying Western genres (the novel) or adopting European ideas (the individual) and social and political models (secularism). Instead, modernity arises in this context from the *aḥdāth* (events) of the encounter with European colonialism, cities, and texts on the one hand, and the embodiment of this encounter and its constant displacement from West to East and East to West on the other.

Moreover, generating multiple registers of modernity, the modern encounter staged in the novel occurs in the Sudan as well, where the narrator meets Mustafa in the village and deciphers his narrative about Europe. Recognizing and deconstructing Mustafa's narrative, and framing the latter's retribution as a melodramatic and stylized performance, the narrator suggests that modernity is not a catastrophe or a benediction but rather an inevitable occurrence, a constant tremor and dissonance, which is constitutive of both the political and the literary. Modernity as "foreign" to the East or Africa—a site of technological development and absence of spirituality especially—is thus a myth, like the *'anqā'*, which is mocked and exposed in the narrator's analysis. This myth, like the "lie" with which Mustafa associates Othello ("[I'm] no Othello. Othello was a lie"),[58] operates as a narrative staging that requires close reading and interpretation. According to the narrator, the African-Arab subject will reclaim colonial schools and hospitals and will not experience guilt or anxiety by speaking the colonizer's language.[59] Thus, the modern is no longer located in England nor is it equivalent to its culture and history but in the *aḥdāth* unfolding in between England and the Sudan, in London and in the village by the Nile.

The fictionalization of the modern, which we see from al-Tahtawi to Alaidy, coincides with the production and reinvention of Arabic tradition. In Salih's novel, it arises in the village from a conversation between two "modern" subjects, so to speak. This rural site in the Sudan is already traversed and changed by modernity and could not therefore be claimed as the repository of tradition. The production of this encounter in the village retrospectively imagines and produces it as violent and tumultuous. Mustafa's tale, in this context, is as much a modern production—a theater piece—as it is the product of the colonial subject's experience. Consequently, the notion of the Arab-African man or the Eastern Man (*rajul sharqī*) in Europe is always already staged and fictionalized. In this context, the return to Arab cultural history is the product of the dialectic that produces modernity and tradition simultaneously. In Salih's case, the retrieval of the *'anqā'*/ghoul analogy is both a return to the Arab anxiety about Europe, and a fictional structure or a literary model that heuristically engages and refigures the encounter with British women, and England more generally. The *'anqā'* and the ghoul unsettle the fixity of the Arabic tradition as well. The narrator, expert on British poetry, could only mediate and read Mustafa's encounter through these modernist tropes.

The literary embodiment of the encounter with modernity activates new modes of critique and refigures the conventional reading of East/West in modern Arabic literature. Specifically, Mustafa's encounters between England and the Sudan are a stage for deconstructing and recognizing the modus operandi of fictionalization. This reading allows us to consider the fact that "modernity" and the "East" are in fact the product of an unstable dialectic. Staging and analyzing this dialectic exposes the trials of Arab modernity, which involve fantasmatic projection, mourning, and comparative literary analysis. The trials are not reduced to Mustafa's trials in England; instead, "trials" need to be understood as the complex work of fictionalizing and deconstructing the encounter with modernity in the literary text. These trials consist in creating the possibility for multiple readings of modernity that systematically resist circumscription and epistemological closure. The investigation of affects offers a terrain of inquiry that moves us away from the historical and critical metanarrative through which these texts (postcolonial fiction) and encounters (East/West) have been read and disseminated. The instability of these epistemological models "split open" the narrative, allowing different voices to be heard and different texts to be read, written, and deciphered. The state of intoxication from which the narrative emerges and gets repeated in the encounter with Jean is thus a site of a modern narrative production, like the city in al-Shidyaq, the stage of *aḥdāth*, a series of events that unravels.

Moreover, problematizing questions of race and colonial violence, *Mawsim* emerges from yet unsettles the so-called *Nahda* dialectics of the encounter with Europe, as Waïl Hassan correctly notes,[60] anchoring it instead in colonial trauma. The novel bridges the gap between the "Arab rediscovery of Europe"—with which al-Tahtawi's and al-Shidyaq's works are generally associated—and the post-1967 literature of the Defeat and current Arabic literary production. In the next chapter, I analyze performances of gender and sexual identity in works by Hanan al-Shaykh and Hamdi Abu Golayyel. I argue that the trials of Arab modernity in these works arise from encounters in London, Cairo, and Beirut. The articulation of Arab sexuality in these contemporary novels is not the outcome of borrowing from the West or of colonial violence alone, as some critics argue, but emerge instead from complex networks of intertextuality, evanescence, and rupture. Just like the clue to Salih's novel lies in aligning the mythological with the technological, Omdurman with World War I, understanding modern Arabic literature's embodiment of homosexuality in al-Shaykh's and Abu Golayyel's texts requires an engagement with sexuality and madness—both in its Foucauldian articulation and through forms of disguise (*takhaffī*), awaiting their unveiling (*kashf*).

CHAPTER FIVE

Majnun Strikes Back

What is madness?

It appears to be a mysterious condition, much like life and death. You can learn a lot about it if you look at it from the outside, as for its interior—its core—it's a reprehensible secret. (my translation)

—NAGUIB MAHFOUZ, *Whisper of Madness* (1938)

I use "queer" to refer to a range of dissident and non-heteronormative practices and desires that may very well be incommensurate with the identity categories of "gay" and "lesbian."

—GAYATRI GOPINATH, *Impossible Desires: Queer Diasporas and South Asian Public Cultures* (2005)

Lesbian is such an ugly word to me. It makes me cringe—especially the French version that is more often used in Lebanon "Lesbienne" (with an elongated "ieeeen"). Ugh. Even worse was the word "dyke." But it's still all good compared to "sou7aqiyyeh." That one really makes me want to vomit. . . . I find it intriguing how people form certain images to go with words, how they give absolute meanings to words. When they say the word "lesbian," it represents a single image in their heads. They have no idea what different and diverse people the word "lesbian" can represent.

—ANONYMOUS, *Bareed Mista3jil: True Stories* (2009)

Bareed Mista3jil: True Stories (Express mail) (2009) is an anonymously published collection of autobiographical writings by queer Lebanese women. In these essays, sexuality is at the core of identity formation, individuality, family struggle, and a slew of social and political forces cutting across class and religious backgrounds. In the powerful interrogation of the word "lesbian" quoted above, from Arabic to English to French, the author identifies the cultural spaces at the intersection of which takes shape a constantly

negotiated sexuality. Going back and forth between different into-
nations, affects, and connotations, the author contests the monolithic nature of the word "lesbian," insisting on its complexity in
terms of type (butch, femme), sexual identification (gay, bi, trans),
culture (Arab, American, French), and sound ("ieeeen"). "Lesbian" is thus a multilayered word that triggers different reactions
and cannot be reduced to a binary opposition that operates neatly
along Western or Eastern sexual models. "Homosexual" and
"homosexuality" are equally complex concepts, operating across
cultural contexts and registers. These forms of negotiation frame
representations and investigations of a queer Arab sexuality in contemporary literature and cultural production.[1]

Recent critical attention to articulations of homosexuality in
the Arab world such as Joseph Massad's *Desiring Arabs* (2007)
examines questions of Western hegemony and the Eurocentric
framework of Arab modernity's legal, cultural, and political
apparatus. In *Women with Mustaches and Men without Beards:
Gender and Sexual Anxieties of Iranian Modernity* (2005),
Afsaneh Najmabadi argues that modernity in nineteenth-century Iran, for instance, involved processes of normalization of
sex and gender. Others, such as Dror Ze'evi's *Producing Desire:
Changing Sexual Discourse in the Ottoman Middle East, 1500–
1900* (2006) and Khaled el-Rouayheb's *Before Homosexuality
in the Arab-Islamic World 1500–1800* (2005), engage with the
Arabic and Ottoman literary and cultural models of same-sex
love and practices. In *Crossing Borders: Love between Women
in French and Arabic Medieval Literatures* (2008), Sahar Amer
reads articulations of homosexual love and desire at the intersection of Arabic and European literary, linguistic, and cultural
models. Kathryn Babayan and Afsaneh Najmabadi's anthology,
*Islamicate Sexualities: Translations across Temporal Geogra-
phies of Desire* (2008), consists of a series of theoretical inter-
ventions that engage queer theory and sexuality studies, "putting into play a dialogue—sometimes comfortable, sometimes
tense—between contemporary Euro-American lesbian/gay/queer
studies and Middle Eastern/Islamicate studies."[2]

Engaging Michel Foucault's historical and epistemological models of "modern" and "premodern" in such works as *History of Sexuality, Volume 1: An Introduction* (1976), *Discipline and Punish* (1975), and *Madness and Civilization* (1961), I argue that a critical dialogue with and a critique of Foucault's reading of modernity serve to complicate clearly demarcated sexual models belonging to distinct cultural traditions. Critiquing Foucault while acknowledging the inability to dismiss his project's cultural and historical framework, I examine a series of sexual *aḥdāth* that stage the production of queer Arab sexuality, which resists codification by a fixed set of social and political discourses. Focusing on crossings of madness and homosexuality in works by Hanan al-Shaykh (b. 1945) and Hamdi Abu Golayyel (b. 1967), this chapter examines affect and performativity in order to unsettle emphases on East/West and modern/premodern binaries taken for granted in debates about Arab sexuality. I argue that al-Shaykh's *Innaha London ya ʿAzizi* (*Only in London*) (2000, henceforth: *Innaha London*) articulates homosexuality through antisocial acts of madness across cultural and linguistic registers and literary traditions. In *Lusus Mutaqaʿidun* (*Thieves in Retirement*) (2002, henceforth: *Lusus*), Hamdi Abu Golayyel's association of homosexuality with madness serves to identify a new site of resistance to social and political violence. In both novels, the homosexual and Majnun-like character resists the codification of his sexuality and social behavior, whether in Beirut, London, or Cairo, systematically unsettling the distinction between sane and insane, modern and premodern, and East and West. This embodied resistance ushers in a new configuration of Majnun: a homosexual rebel and impassioned lover, disrupting social norms and exposing structures of violence. He swears, cross-dresses, accosts people in the street, jumps, and collapses. Though confused and combated, he expresses his desire through gestures and obsessive behavior, which produce new articulations of sexual practices and identities in contemporary literature.

My comparative reading of the queer Majnun in al-Shaykh's and Abu Golayyel's works anchors current debates about Arab homosexuality in the performative, the bodily, and the affective. From fragmentation and disorientation in confronting European modernity in al-Shidyaq, al-Tahtawi, and Salih examined in chapters 2, 3, and 4 respectively, we move in chapter 5 to contemporary fiction's treatment of homosexuality as madness, performance, and rebellion. Thus, this chapter explores the ways in which the sexual practices and fantasies of the *Nahda* student in al-Tahtawi and of the colonized subject in Salih are transformed in al-Shaykh's and Abu Golayyel's novels into sites of subversion and critique of social and political normativity across cultural and linguistic spaces. The trials of Arab modernity in between London, Beirut, and Cairo are expressed in affects, gestures, and subversive acts, further accentuating the theoretical urgency to analyze contemporary texts in light of *Nahda* and postcolonial texts. The trials of Arab modernity in these novels emerge from a series of *aḥdāth* (events, accidents)—sexual encounters, fits of madness, and acting out. These sites unsettle the prevalent dichotomy between Euro-American gay and lesbian identities and "traditional" Arab social and sexual practices, thereby giving rise to new models of subjectivity and sites of investigation.

QUEER CONTEXTS

Representations of homosexuality and homoeroticism in modern Arabic literature span a wide range of texts and cultural and historical registers. In his 1947 novel *Zuqaq al-Midaq* (*Midaq Alley*), Naguib Mahfouz presents the homosexual as a married man, a marginal figure of the Cairene *ḥāra* (neighborhood). In *Hajar al-Dahk* (*The Stone of Laughter*) (1990), Hoda Barakat portrays the struggles of her main character, Khalil, with homosexuality in a social context shaped by the Lebanese civil war (1975–90). In *Tuqus al-Isharat wa-l-Tahawwulat* (Rituals of signs and transformations) (1994), Syrian playwright Saadallah Wannous offers a complex view of the interplay of same-sex love and models of masculinity in nineteenth-century Damascus. Seba al-Herz, Saudi author of *Al-Akharun* (*The Others*) (2006), produces a languorous narrative about a woman's desire for other women. Hatim Rashid, the homosexual character in Alaa Al Aswany's 'Amarit Ya'qubyan (The Yacoubian Building) (2002), though killed at the end, is strong and assertive, dismissive of any attempt to shame him.

Analyzing representations of homosexuality in modern Arabic literature, Frédéric Lagrange argues that during the Arab encounter with modernity in the nineteenth century, European values and practices challenged Arab models of desire through discourses on civilization and cultural development. Taking Lagrange's thesis further, Joseph Massad provides a critique of colonial and orientalist discursive practices that have systematically produced knowledge about sexuality in the Arab world. From the role of non-governmental organizations to the reactions of local governments accused of violating homosexual rights, Massad identifies a set of political and cultural forces that contribute to the discursive production of Euro-American notions of gay and lesbian identities in the Arab world.[3] Massad's drawing on the rich legacy of Islamicate sexualities, and, for instance, on the work of Khaled el-Rouayheb, which situates these representations within an Arab-Islamic historical and cultural context, makes possible further investigations of the intertwinement of Arabic and European cultural models.

Recognizing the importance of the critique of orientalism, I interrogate both the reading of modernity as a coherent project imposed by colonial violence and NGOs, and recent critical appropriation of Arab cultural history as a repository of authentic sexualities suppressed by this project. Reclaiming Arab-Islamic tradition as a site of resistance to Western hegemony depicts an impossible return to something that is always already imagined, reconstituted, or reconstructed. Only a comparative analysis across contemporary and classical texts, and Arabic and European cultural contexts, could produce a complex understanding of the development of sexual and gender models in Arabic literature and culture. Specifically, investigating a series of queer aḥdāth in al-Shaykh's and Abu Golayyel's narratives serves to recover the experience from the totalizing and abstraction of the modernity/ tradition binary. Engaging Foucault's work in this context characterizes a return to European cultural and theoretical models *en guise* of creating a necessary dialogue that acknowledges yet critiques the importance of the encounter with European cities and social and political practices for Arab modernity's articulation in various literary and cultural contexts.

In volume 1 of *History of Sexuality,* Michel Foucault argues that the nineteenth century in Europe witnessed the birth of the homosexual. Identifying the word "homosexual" in Westphal's essay from 1870, Foucault demonstrates that homosexuality was discursively produced through the psychiatric and legal systems that sought to classify, categorize, treat, and contain it: "The nineteenth-century homosexual became a personage, a past, a case history, and a childhood, in addition to being a type of life, a life form, and a morphology, with an indiscreet anatomy and possibly a mysterious physiology. Nothing that went into his total composition was unaffected by his sexuality. It was everywhere present in him. . . . The sodomite had been a temporary aberration; the homosexual was now a species."[4] Foucault establishes a temporal and development distinction between the modern and the premodern, reading the "now" as the stage for the discursive production of homosexuality as an identity through a *scientia sexualis* that turns the homosexual into a historical subject, distinct from the premodern or non-Western sodomite. The homosexual as "species" becomes recognizable through a particular physical configuration that gives him shape and makes him visible. The categories of "homosexual" and "sodomite" in this context allow Foucault to expose the deployment of new forms of power invested with political and scientific authority. He distinguishes Western modernity's production of homosexuality through a system of scientific and juridical truth from an Eastern and premodern *ars erotica*, within which sexuality evolved through an economy of pleasure.[5] Foucault's distinction of modern and premodern, *scientia sexualis* and *ars erotica*, is by no means ontological, but rather instrumental; it is necessary for his theoretical topos that seeks to trace modernity's discursive production of subjectivity in the nineteenth century. Nonetheless, Foucault's formulation and its critical appropriation often preclude disciplinary crossings, treating the modern Western narrative as being distinct both from its premodern counterpart in the West, and from that which is imagined as being outside of the West altogether. For Foucault, argues Dina al-Kassim, "the premodern and the Eastern are thereby always defined by an opposition that secures their uniqueness by saving them from modern disciplinary projections."[6] Engaging and critiquing Foucault's model serve to complicate both his model and its appropriation by recent critical investigations of homosexuality in modern Arabic literature and culture.

Foucault fails to acknowledge the correlation between the modern and the premodern, East and West, which is systematically staged in contemporary Arabic literature and in the long and constantly evolving intellectual and cultural relation between Arabic and European texts and cultures. Sahar Amer argues that Foucault's understanding of homosexuality stifles the recognition of other gay- and lesbian-like identities pervasive in Arabic and European texts and cultures. Reading homosexuality in French and Arabic medieval writings, Amer identifies a queer intertext with hybrid linguistic registers, motifs, and metaphors. This queer textuality undermines the association between sexuality and cultural purity and between modernity and tradition. Framing it within a historical context that is equally determined by cultural exchange as it is by conflict and resistance, the intertextuality Amer identifies represents a strategic site for the investigation of homosexuality in contemporary Arabic literature at the intersection of Arab-Islamic and European cultural traditions and theoretical contexts.

BUT IT'S LONDON, DARLING!

In *The Translation Zone: A New Comparative Literature* (2006), Emily Apter analyzes the state of texts and the relation of

languages to sites of power. She defines "translation zone" as "a
site 'in-translation,' that is to say, belonging to no single, discrete
language or single medium of communication . . . [that] applies to
diasporic language communities, print and media public spheres
[and] theaters of war."[7] Apter's notion cuts across physical borders by imagining complex spaces of interaction and negotiation.
Queering these spaces, Gayatri Gopinath reads desire in between
articulations of home and diaspora, thereby situating it in processes of negotiation across cultural and linguistic registers. In
this context, Gopinath notes, "the radical disruption of the hierarchies between nation and diaspora, heterosexuality and homosexuality, original and copy, that queer diasporic texts enact
hinges on the question of translation."[8] This translation, however, is not merely a mode of communication across languages
and cultural contexts, but also involves models of performativity that inscribe meaning in the body and refigure in the process
emphases on questions of representation, cultural exchange, and
borrowing.

Thinking through the categories and frameworks developed
by Apter and Gopinath, I focus on *Innaha London*'s depiction
of homosexuality in between London and Beirut, examining
the ways in which queer desire challenges social norms both in
Europe and in the Arab world. The queer character's transgressive expression of sexuality takes shape at the intersection of
Arab-Islamic literature and language, home and diaspora, and
American and European pop culture and discourses on sex and
civilization. Al-Shaykh appropriates yet complicates homosexuality association with a clearly identifiable and culturally circumscribed modern project. In al-Shaykh's text, queer Arab sexuality takes shape as a position of dissidence and rebellion against
the normative structures of homo/hetero and ideological constructions of authentic Arab-Islamic sexual practices opposed to
homosexuality's discursive production in the West.

Al-Shaykh's humorous narrative starts on a plane going through
turbulence, transporting the four main characters from Dubai to
London. The plane's hurling "up and down like a yo-yo"[9] depicts

the characters' cultural and psychological states and introduces dissonance and affects as a strategic framework for narrative development. The turbulence and the reference to Dubai, the global city par excellence, disrupt the spatial and cultural boundaries of East and West, strategically destabilizing fixed models of desire, identity, and language.[10] Amira, a Moroccan prostitute, is returning home from a disappointing "business" trip; Lamis, a recently divorced Iraqi woman who also lives in London, is returning from a failed attempt to settle down in Dubai; Nicholas, a British expert on Islamic art, is returning from a trip to Oman; and, finally, Samir, a middle-aged Lebanese man, married with five children, and living in the United Arab Emirates, comes to London for the first time in quest of sexual freedom.

As the plot evolves, London emerges as a fantasized space of personal and sexual freedom. Lamis and Nicholas fall in love; she perceives him as the British man who will allow her to express her sexuality freely and he sees her as the beautiful yet fragile Arab woman in need of protection. The two lovers struggle to overcome their cultural projections, leading the relation to a standstill. Meanwhile, Amira, the one who brings everyone together in the narrative, decides to explore new professional horizons by pretending to be a Gulf princess in order to swindle wealthy Arab men in London. After a few successes, she gets caught and beaten in a humiliating and tragic scene. As for Samir, with no place to go, he moves in with Amira and becomes her most loyal companion. Accompanied by his pet monkey, Samir sets out to discover London, never wanting to return to his wife, kids, and the life he left behind.

Depicted as a "flamboyantly dressed man" wearing a Versace shirt and cowboy boots and looking like Klinger in *MASH*,[11] Samir's transvestism is transcultural. It is shaped by the worlds of fashion and television from Lebanon to Italy to Hollywood, blurring the lines between East and West, native and foreign. Going into first-class cabin in order to find a sedative for the pet monkey he is illegally transporting in a basket and that is threatening to expose him, Samir approaches Lamis: "Excuse me Mamselle.

Please [dakhīlik], have you got a sedative? My nerves [raḥ jinn] . .
."[12] Al-Shaykh's text emphasizes the imminent advent of madness
with the repetition of such expressions as dakhīlik (I implore you)
and raḥ jinn (I'm about to go mad, I will go mad).[13] Describing his
emotional breakdown, Samir's use of the word jinn, a colloquial
expression that could denote disbelief, frustration, and anger and
that is derived from the word jinn as in genie or spirit. Soon after
he gets his sedatives, Samir comes back for more. When Lamis
tells him that she had just given him some, Samir replies: "I know.
You gave me two. I'm not crazy even though I might look it."[14]
In this second instance, the word majnūn (crazy, mad) takes on a
new meaning, aligning Samir's emotional state with his appearance. This etymological play and confusion bring to mind yet
another Lebanese colloquialism, majnūna or majnūneh (crazy or
mad woman, also khawta), which is similar to the French colloquial word folle (queen, fairy). Samir thus goes back and forth
between junūn as a mental disorder and junūn as the expression
of a flamboyant homosexual desire recognizable in dress and
actions. In both cases, the question of sexuality and its articulation on the plane—and, later, in London —is framed through
movement, shaking up, and breaking down. These somatic states
constitute the framework through which sexuality takes shape in
the novel.

HISTORIES OF MADNESS

In *Madness and Civilization: A History of Insanity in the Age
of Reason*, Michel Foucault argues that while madness in the
European Middle Ages was associated with the mystical and the
supernatural, the seventeenth and eighteenth centuries conse-
crate madness as the antithesis of reason (*déraison*, unreason).
The nineteenth century gradually produces madness as a mental
illness through medical and psychiatric discourse. The mad person is incarcerated and forced to confess in the European asy-
lums into the twentieth century. However, this break with the
premodern in Foucault's model is not complete. In fact, madness

as a state of possession by the spirits haunts the psychiatric production of madness. In the novels I examine, madness takes shape
at the intersection of the psychiatric clinic and the supernatural
world.

In the Arab-Islamic context, advances in sciences in the Middle Ages had, early on, produced madness as a treatable mental illness. The eleventh-century physician Ibn Sina (Avicenna)
(980–1037) devotes a section of his *Qanun fi al-Tibb* (*Canon of
Medicine*) to mental illnesses. During that time, Islamic psychiatric clinics abounded in Egypt, Syria, and throughout the Islamic
world. This demonstrates that some form of psychiatric institution, treating madness as a curable illness, coexisted with madness as a state of possession. Furthermore, in *Khitab al-Junun
fi al-Thaqafa al-'Arabiyya* (The discourse on madness in Arab
culture) (1993), Syrian critic Muhammad Hayyan al-Samman
reads madness in the works of a series of thinkers, from al-Jahiz
(781–868) to Ibn Khaldun (1132–1406). Quoting al-Naysaburi
(d. 1016), al-Samman suggests that the mad challenge main-
stream beliefs, customs, and dress codes.[15] The *majnun* is thus
the rebel, the entertainer, and the prophetic figure. Al-Samman
further argues that the voice of madness in Islamic texts and historical narratives is that of the dissident speaking truth to power
by challenging social and political norms. Expressing the collective will of the oppressed and the marginalized, the mad one violently subverts social order in words and deeds.

Ibn Manzur (1233–1311) defines *junun* as a form of veiling (*sitr*) and withdrawal of reason (*'aql*).[16] This *junun* is often
associated in Arabic literature with a state of amorous possession. The most notable example could be found in the story of
Layla and Majnun, from the seventh century, recorded in al-
Isfahani's (897–972) tenth-century work *Kitab al-Aghani* (The
book of songs). In this narrative of 'Udhri, or unrequited love,
the inability of Majnun (his real name is Qays ibn al-Mulaw-
wah [d. 688]) to unite with his beloved drives him to madness
and death.[17] 'Udhri love poetry derives from the practices of a
Yemeni tribe, Banu 'Udhra, whose men were known for powerful

infatuation and unconsummated love that often led to death. In this context, madness depicts a state of being consumed by one's own desire, likened to invisible demons or jinn. Jamil (d. 701), from the ʿUdhra tribe as well, is another important example of an ʿUdhri poet whose public declaration of love (for Buthayna) brings about his debilitating obsession. Roger Allen notes that "the story of Jamil involves a breaking of the tribal code regarding contact between the sexes, in that he publicly revealed his feelings towards his beloved."[18] This characterization of the lover's *junūn*, caused by the beloved's disappearance, coincides with the public declaration of love and desire. *Junūn* thus not only characterizes the passion itself but also its public expression. In this light, Samir's *junūn* in *Innaha London* refers both to his mental state and to his veiled desire, embodied in transgressive acts and words in London. *Junūn* thus operates as an unveiling of desire—*kashf*—that shatters and destabilizes the social and cultural codes of love and sexuality. And just as Majnun, Layla's lover, befriends the animals on his maddening quest for his beloved, Samir and his Capuchin monkey set out on their *junūn*, a maddening pursuit of blond men in London.

The strategic association of Samir's sexuality with madness through *junūn*'s fluctuation across cultural registers (Arabic, British, French) gives rise to a new language of desire in the novel. Looking and acting mad, Samir transgresses cultural and social norms. The monkey in the basket, waiting to be set free in London, mirrors Samir's sexual desire.[19] Once Samir gets his sedatives from Lamis, he says: "I want to tell you a secret. Please swear you'll keep it to yourself. Swear you won't tell on me. . . . I've got a little monkey in this basket."[20] Samir "comes out" to Lamis as someone who is trafficking a monkey and needs sedatives to keep it asleep. Samir's announcement that he is going to go mad (*raḥ jinn*) thus implies that he is about to act like a monkey insofar as the monkey is a *majnūna* (*folle*, flamboyant homosexual) who will come out of its basket once the plane lands and the sedatives' effects dissipate. *Raḥ jinn*, in this context, is not simply a characterization of an unstable psychological state due to the plane's turbulence and Samir's fear of getting caught by British customs; it is also a statement of intent depicting a somatic condition, i.e., *raḥ jinn*, "I will go mad," once the plane lands and the monkey is set free. *Raḥ jinn* thus operates as a performative utterance, framing Samir's expression of desire in London as the advent of unrestrained acts of social and sexual transgression, monkey-like.[21] Coming out in London thus draws on modern articulations of homosexuality and sexual freedom in a European context, and on the Arab-Islamic treatment of *junūn* as a state of dissidence and subversion through dress, behavior, and expression of desire as well.

THE BROTHEL, THE CLINIC, AND THE ASYLUM

Samir fantasizes London as a paradise of normative homosexuality where "he'd see rows of English boys . . . walking hand in hand."[22] However, he struggles to interpret the world around him given his limited understanding of English. His experience of going—unknowingly—to an HIV clinic best exemplifies the articulation of *junūn* in London. While at a phone booth in SoHo, Samir notices an advertisement with a picture of two men kissing. Overwhelmed by his desire and unable or unwilling to understand the English text, he hails a taxi, shows him the ad, and asks him to drive to the designated location. Once there, he enters a neatly organized and sanitized space, unlike the "homosexual brothel" he'd imagined. A receptionist with a picture of a little girl on her desk welcomes him and hands him a form to fill out. Perplexed, Samir imagines that in England "everything is done according to laws and protocol, even you-know-what."[23] Though the space falls short of the fantasized brothel, Samir insists on sexualizing it nonetheless. Explaining to her that he is unable to fill out the form, the receptionist proceeds to ask him a series of personal questions, making him uncomfortable, and, soon enough, critical of the laws and codes that regulate sexuality in England. "Even the things that people think are going to be difficult are simple in our country . . . , there are no contracts

or forms to fill in. You can do it in graveyards, garages, at roadblocks."[24] In this statement, Samir critiques Foucault's *scientia
sexualis* as a model that subjects sex to the knowledge-power
law. In this sense, the woman at the clinic asks Samir the truth
about his sexuality, forcing him to confess by writing it down. As
Samir resists this codification of sexuality in London, he conjures
up war-torn Lebanon (with the reference to the "roadblocks,"
the Lebanese civil war's infamous signifiers) as the place of freedom. Consequently, the perception of England as the site of sexual liberation gives way to England as the site where a modern
legal and medical apparatus constrains desire and interrupts its
play. Samir's sexual dissidence thus aligns the collapse of social
and political order in Lebanon as a result of the civil war (also
referred to as *al-aḥdāth*, the events) with sexual freedom, critiquing in this way the codification of sexuality through the medical
institution represented by the HIV clinic.

After having asked him his age and medical history and
whether he had contracted any sexually transmitted diseases,
Samir becomes very angry and frustrated, refusing to become
what Foucault calls a "confessing animal."[25] Realizing that he
speaks Arabic, the receptionist calls up a colleague, James, who
had lived in Egypt and could communicate with him. While
Samir fantasizes about the "beautiful" James, currently unavail-
able, the receptionist suggests:

> "Shall we try together, then if you feel you really want James . . . ?"
> She wants to try with me, to convince me to give up my habit and
> start liking women. I understand now, he thought. You put pho-
> tos of children up so that men will decide they're longing to have a
> family. She was like his father's sister who used to hit him and say,
> "Walk straight. Like a soldier. Don't swing your hips." She was the
> one who'd arranged for him to be married off.[26]

Expecting sexual emancipation in London, Samir finds instead
the apparatus of his desire's containment. He interprets the little
girl's picture on the receptionist's desk and the invitation to "try
together" as acknowledgments of his homosexuality *en guise* of
suppressing it. The memory triggered in this encounter is that of

the aunt who had forced Samir into an arranged marriage. In this light, the modern institution of the clinic becomes complicit in Samir's eyes with family authority, both seeking to suppress his desire through acts of emotional and physical violence, constraining and regulating his sexuality within the confines of marriage and the medical establishment. Through Samir's visceral reaction to the image at the booth in SoHo and his miscommunication and misunderstanding throughout this scene, Beirut and London become interchangeable. When he heads to the clinic (or what he thinks is a brothel) in order to perform an act of *junūn* (madness)—having sex with men—Samir finds his desire curbed and stifled. This sets the stage for the articulation of a queer desire in opposition to, yet in between two, different forms of social and political authorities: the coercive Lebanese family and the British medical institution.

Samir's trip to the clinic conjures traumatic childhood experiences. The aunt's violent enforcement of social norms is tied to early encounters with madness. When Samir's parents caught him cross-dressing on the rooftop at the age of thirteen, they sent him to a mental institution. The narrator reveals that when Samir's mother saw him, "she called her husband . . . and edged away from her son, scared that he would throw himself off the rooftop if she went closer. Her crazy relative had jumped off a rooftop. Mad people hated anyone touching them when they were having one of their fits."[27] The son's dancing and cross-dressing align *majnūn* as mad with *majnūn* as *majnūna* (queen, fairy). In constructing an identifiable homosexual narrative of the teenager possibly attempting suicide, the narrator ties in Samir's actions with those of the mother's relative, another *majnūn* who had jumped to his death. Since Samir's fit on the rooftop is one of possession by the jinn that make one mad, the mother's distance from her son disavows both a fear of coming in touch with the possessed and a genuine concern for her son's safety.

Samir's homosexuality, even on this rooftop in Lebanon, takes shape at the intersection of cultural and linguistic frameworks that could not be reduced to Lebanon or Arab culture in any exclusive or authentic manner. Samir's homosexuality, likened to madness, involves models of gay teenage behavior and psychological development, 1950s and 1960s psychiatric "treatment" of homosexuality, and French and Lebanese colloquialism, to name a few. In this context, it's important to recognize the characterization of the psychiatric hospital in Lebanese colloquial as ʿasfūriyyeh (ʿasfūr, bird, i.e., the place of the birds or bird-like). This reference emphasizes the relation between sexuality and freedom, on the one hand, and the expression of desire and its institutional disciplining, on the other. The ʿasfūriyyeh to which Samir is sent seeks to clip his wings and prevent him from committing suicide by flying off the rooftop. In an attempt to cure his homosexuality, the asylum in Lebanon subjects Samir to electric-shock "therapy." In this light, references to the psychiatric hospital, the HIV clinic, and the brothel shape the articulation of Samir's queer desire in London. This desire is expressed through transgressive, compulsive, and flamboyant acts that require interpretation across linguistic and cultural registers and theoretical models from Arab-Islamic culture to Foucault. This queer sensorium, embodied in fits and shocks, compulsive behavior and visceral reactions, frames the articulation of homosexuality in the novel. The trials of Arab modernity arise from these sexual aḥdāth.

The play of affects and the intertwinement of various discursive practices and cultural forces in *Innaha London* complicate the Foucauldian model yet challenge its dismissal as a Eurocentric framework inapplicable to a non-Western context. Specifically, the liminal space Samir occupies in this diasporic setting interrogates the modern codification of desire identified by Foucault. From the family and the psychiatric hospital in Lebanon to the HIV clinic in London, the expression of Samir's desire unsettles the distinctness of modern and premodern cultural and medical models. Samir's *junūn*, which is psychological and sexual, social and political, refigures the reading of modernity as the site of social and sexual normativity that arises in Europe and is transplanted into the Arab world. Samir's desire arises from a network of interactions and exchanges that ties in Foucault's psychiatric clinic with possession by jinn, European modernity with family authority, verbal with nonverbal communication, and Beirut with London.

SOCIAL SUBVERSION

Samir transgresses social norms in London. Gripped by his inner demons—the unseen jinn that bring about his seizure or *junūn*—Samir seeks out his blond men by stopping people in the street, touching them, and chatting them up. In one instance, Samir accosts a young man from Bosnia.[28] Being Lebanese, Samir tries to establish a bond by bringing up their respective war experiences. When this seduction strategy fails, Samir insists that the young man try on the jacket that Samir was wearing and that the young man liked. Samir exploits the miscommunication to wrap the jacket around the man, violating social norms and physical boundaries. Monkey-like, Samir performs his desire through antisocial acts. His nonverbal communication, which directly brings forth the relation to the body through touching and gesturing, works in tandem with linguistic miscommunication. While his actions and clothing could be considered humorous, they in fact undermine social order in London.

Moreover, the narrator reveals that during Lebanon's civil war, Samir would cross-dress in boas and gowns and chat up and entertain militiamen in the streets.[29] The narrator explains that the war and the ensuing collapse of the rule of law emancipated Samir from the social restrictions that stifled his desire. In this way, al-Shaykh aligns London with war-torn Beirut, representing them as stages (as in theater) upon which Samir performs *junūn*. While in Lebanon his *junūn* is symptomatic of the state's collapse, in London his *junūn* unsettles the "overbearing" norms regulating desire and social interactions.

Samir's transgressive acts and flamboyant clothing and demeanor could be associated with Arab-Islamic representations of madness over centuries of literary and cultural development.

They could also be interpreted as camp, extensively discussed in queer theory.[30] Judith Butler argues that performativity, through actions and words, produces gender and sexuality as "essential" components of one's identity. In the act of performance, drag has the potential to displace categories of authenticity and imitation as well as normative constructions of gender and sexuality.[31] Crossing homosexuality and madness in the novel through references to Samir's *junūn* thus serves to present the flamboyant and outrageously dressed homosexual as a rebel against social and political codification of desire. Al-Shaykh's depiction of the mad and flamboyant homosexual, transgressor of social norms, highlights an intertextuality that connects the Arab-Islamic cultural contexts with contemporary theories of social and sexual subversion. It also identifies questions of encounter and affect as key sites for investigating the literary embodiment of Arab sexuality beyond the binary codification taken for granted in critical debates.

Furthermore, al-Shaykh's staging of Samir's *junūn* in *Innaha London* could be traced to her earlier novel, *Hikayat Zahra (The Story of Zahra)* (1980). Caught in warfare, Zahra is a depressed woman who is often described as mad. Escaping her oppressive father through a loveless marriage, she finds herself trapped in a relationship that drives her further into despair.[32] In both *Hikayat Zahra* and *Innaha London*, the civil war (Lebanon's *aḥdāth*) stages the advent of madness. Whereas fear and depression characterize the madness of Zahra, the heroine of the Lebanese war novel from the 1980s, a transgressive and flamboyant homosexuality characterizes that of Samir in al-Shaykh's later work. *Innaha London*'s mad figure ties in Zahra with the ʿUdhri poet Majnun, linking in this way literary developments in modern Arabic literature to articulations of madness and desire in the classical period. Mirroring both Zahra's fits and the ʿUdhri poet's obsessive quest for the elusive beloved, Samir pursues and falls in love with men in London who acknowledge yet fail to reciprocate his desire. Expressed through acts of transgression that systematically expose social and political violence, Samir's desire incorporates Majnun's tribulations and Zahra's anxieties.

The alignment of homosexuality with madness in *Innaha London* serves to identify multiple instances of miscommunication, resistance, and collapse. These queer events (*aḥdāth*) generate new configurations of Arab subjectivity, which need to be read in relation to *Takhlis*'s state bureaucrat, *Kashf*'s exiled intellectual, and *Mawsim*'s postcolonial subject, discussed respectively in chapters 2, 3, and 4. The disoriented *Nahda* traveler struggling with European modernity is queered in al-Shaykh's text. This queering unsettles the binaries of East and West, homo and hetero, and casts the trials of Arab modernity as a process that continues to unfold both in Europe and in the Arab world. The trials of Arab modernity arise from this dynamic negotiation and critique, which I locate throughout the book in modes of performativity in Arabic travel narratives, postcolonial novels, and new writing.

THIEVES IN RETIREMENT

Set in the working-class "fringe neighborhood"[33] of Manshiyyat Nasser in greater Cairo, Hamdi Abu Golayyel's *Lusus Mutaqaʿidun* (*Thieves in Retirement*) published by Dar Merit in 2002, appropriates the narrative structure of Mahfouz's *Awlad Haritna* (*Children of the Alley*) (1959), positioning the narrator as a stranger to yet a resident of the neighborhood, which is centered around Abu Gamal's *ʿamāra* (apartment complex). Whereas in Mahfouz's novel, the God-like Gabalawi is the undisputed patriarch who mediates between his various sons, the new Gabalawi (Abu Gamal) in Abu Golayyel's work is lacking in authority, forced to cover his weakness by oppressing the homosexual son. Sayf, Abu Gamal's assertive and defiant youngest son, gradually emerges as the rebellious figure in the novel. His family suppresses his overt sexual behavior by beating him, trying to kill him, incarcerating him in an asylum, and, finally, marrying him off. Similar to al-Shaykh's Samir, who is institutionalized and forced into an arranged marriage when signs of his homosexuality first appear, Abu Golayyel's Sayf is the target of familial violence as his homosexuality is acknowledged yet suppressed. Sayf's "condition" is referred to as *junūn*—a space of queerness that is systematically forced outside of the social.

The narrator describes Sayf as putting on makeup and lipstick and wearing tight clothes in order to accentuate his body parts.[34] This appearance conjures up Foucault's homosexual as a species with a visible morphology and physical characteristics. Adopting a peculiar mannerism in speech and acts, Sayf seduces men from outside and inside the neighborhood, including the narrator. It is also revealed that the eighteen-year-old Sayf repeatedly attempted suicide like gay teenagers sometimes do when they become aware of their difference and experience persecution. The narrator claims that society damns young men who act like women by denouncing them through all kinds of slurs, "the least burdensome of which is 'insane' (*junūn*)."[35] The narrator describes how the neighbors were all gossiping about Sayf's madness—speculating about his homosexuality.[36] *Junūn* applies to those whose demeanor and dress defy social and sexual norms. Sayf's nonconformity coincides with a type of madness that is discursively produced and circulated by the community. The neighbors' gossip produces homosexuality as an antisocial and subversive behavior. Like Samir in *Innaha London*, Sayf shocks the *ḥāra* (neighborhood) by flaunting his desire at a variety of levels. The mad person here resembles the homosexual in Foucault's sense but also the rebel discussed in al-Samman's reading of madness as a category of opposition to social authority in the Arab-Islamic cultural context.

Sayf is first mentioned in the novel when the narrator, a tenant in Abu Gamal's building, overhears Gamal blaming his father for failing to kill Sayf.[37] Sayf's homosexuality likened to madness is presented as the source of the family's shame. According to Gamal, the "cure" for Sayf's overt homosexuality is murder.[38] After mentioning this unfinished "honor crime," the narrator explains that while the real power struggle between Abu Gamal and his eldest son, the drug-dealing and socially mobile Gamal, is about control over the apartment complex, its apparent manifestation is centered on Sayf's homosexuality. The older son, Gamal, is the leader of the pack, fighting his father and insisting on the elimination of the *khawal* (effeminate gay man) in the family. This elimination allows Gamal to deflect the attention from his own corruption and salvage a patriarchal authority he seeks to appropriate. Countering the gossip about Sayf's *junūn* thus brings about Gamal's intervention, leading him to lock his brother up in an insane asylum. This act highlights the complicity of the modern institution—the psychiatric clinic—with the "traditional" *ḥāra*'s enforcement of social and sexual norms.

MAKING HOMOSEXUALITY DISAPPEAR

Gamal uses his "contacts" to have his brother incarcerated, expressing satisfaction at the latter's "disappearance" (*ikhtifāʾ*)[39] in the asylum without a psychiatric examination or assessment of his case. In this intervention, the modern institution is at the service of a violent and corrupt patriarchal power, which seeks to restore its legitimacy and counter ill repute by eliminating the mad, queer son. Abu Golayyel uses the word *ikhtifāʾ* as if the institutionalization is an act of hijacking perpetrated by some security apparatus against a political dissident. While *ikhtifāʾ* connotes a process of disappearing or an arrest conducted at night, the scene of Sayf's *ikhtifāʾ* occurs in broad daylight. Abu Golayyel describes the scene in which *ʿarabiyyat al-maganīn* (madmobile) stops in front of the *ʿamāra* in order to abduct Sayf.[40] This *ikhtifāʾ*, perpetrated against Sayf in front of the entire neighborhood, conjures up a spectacle of ritualized punishment akin to the one Foucault describes in *Discipline and Punish* as the site of deployment of the premodern power of the sovereign. According to Foucault, the rise of modernity through systems of incarceration and punishment coincides with the elimination of corporeal punishment and the abstraction of the operation of justice. Foucault argues that the modern system moves from the torture of the condemned's body to its reform through disciplining practices in prisons. Foucault frames his argument by describing the public punishment perpetrated against Damiens, a man accused of killing his father under the ancien régime.

> [Damiens] was to be "taken and conveyed in a cart, wearing nothing but a shirt, holding a torch of burning wax weighing two pounds"; then, "in the said cart, to the Place de Grève, where, on a scaffold that will be erected there, the flesh will be torn from his breasts, arms, thighs and claves with red-hot pincers, his right hand, holding the knife with which he committed the said parricide, burnt with sulphur . . . and then his body drawn and quartered by four horses and his limbs and body consumed by fire, reduced to ashes and his ashes thrown to the winds."[41]

Since Damiens's crime operates as a violation of the king's body, his public torture seeks to reactivate monarchic power and dissuade onlookers from violating it. However, the modern system of incarceration displaces the body of the sovereign as the site of transgression, thereby producing the culprit as subject of reform. Modern subjectivity, produced through the institutions of the prison and the asylum, become the necessary framework for transitioning from monarchy to nation state, from public punishment to correction, cure, and reform.

Like the cart that parades Damiens before making him disappear, Sayf is made to disappear in front of his family and neighborhood. The public display of Sayf's abduction and *ikhtifā'* aligns the premodern institution of punishment and justice with that of the modern state, represented by the asylum's ambulance. Sayf's madness and homosexuality, like the patricide in Damiens's case, mark the killing of the father at two levels. First, the punishment and ritualized public abduction seek to restore the family honor, soiled by Sayf's expression of homosexuality through antisocial dress and actions. Second, they mark the erasure of Abu Gamal's patriarchal position, because it was his son Gamal who orchestrated Sayf's abduction and not him. In fact, the narrator reveals that the abduction enrages Abu Gamal, who experiences it as an affront to his authority. Sayf's abduction and incarceration thus produce the father as weak, displaced from his patriarchal position by the older son. It also produces Sayf's homosexuality and madness as a site of *ikhtifā'* (disappearance). The act and ritual of *ikhtifā'* as punishment frame the process through which homosexuality is treated and disciplined in *Lusus*.

Abu Golayyel's novel captures the desire of power to see homosexuality disappear. However, the notion of *ikhtifā'* is tied to another important notion from the same root, *takhaffī* (disguise). This disguise operates in the novel's context as a form of drag, expressed in Sayf's clothing and behavior. *Ikhtifā'* and *takhaffī* as forms of drag thus apply to the performativity of Sayf's desire before and after incarceration. Once released from the asylum, Sayf *yatakhaffā* (disguises himself) as a woman in order to seduce and have sex with the narrator.[42] Furthermore, Sayf expresses his desire *bi-l-khifyā* (in secret), first by marrying and second by venturing out of the *ḥāra* at night, cruising the streets of Cairo in search of men. These forms of *takhaffī*, duly noted by Sayf's wife and family, are accepted forms of homosexuality, which has been forced into the space of disguise and veiling. What is imagined as a traditional form of homosexuality, which coexists with marriage, is exposed to its moment of coercive production in Abu Golayyel's novel. Thus we move from Sayf's (and Samir's) subversive and campy drag expressed in flamboyance and dress to form of cross-dressing, which is produced by coercive and violent social and political forces.

The notion of *ikhtifā'* is also associated with possession by the jinn. To make Sayf disappear is to relinquish him to the state of possession by that which is *makhfī* (veiled) and appears only in specific contexts, namely at night.[43] *Ikhfā'* Sayf (making him disappear), by declaring him *majnūn* and incarcerating him through neighborhood gossip and family "contacts" rather than through a psychiatric assessment, is tied to possession's association with homosexuality as a condition of being consumed by one's own desire likened to the spirits. The alignment of *majnūn* with the *makhfī*—whose reason is veiled, according to Ibn Manzur—on the one hand, and of *majnūn* with the homosexual, on the other, characterizes Sayf's condition and its relation to the social. In this context, Foucault's reading of both homosexuality and madness intersects with popular and superstitious beliefs about possession as well as representations of 'Udhri poets such as Majnun and Jamil. These associations complicate the treatment of Sayf's sexuality by preventing its epistemological closure through a clear East/West, modern/premodern framework. Sayf disappears through a power structure that involves the family, the neighborhood, and the state.

The narrator describes Sayf's return from the asylum, brandishing a medical report attesting to his sanity. This report, which Sayf shows to all those who gossiped about his madness and witnessed his abduction, is presented as proof of his cure. Thus, the public abduction is complemented by a public exoneration through an official report that is brandished and paraded, like Sayf when he was abducted. The key point here is not only the report but also its public display, its production in the face of others as a document or attestation to sanity. Showing it to one of the neighbors, a teacher, the latter exclaims that Egyptians should have their national ID cards substituted for government-issued medical reports on their sanity.[44] The condition of sanity as opposed to madness thus arises as the condition of political subjectivity, wherein the family intervenes in and shapes the deployment of state power (the psychiatric institution). In this model, citizens are interpellated through models of psycho-normativity, inextricable from hetero-normativity. However, complicating the picture even further is a doctor's note accompanying Sayf's official attestation. Addressed to the family, the doctor writes that Sayf's true cure is not through institutionalization and psychiatric treatment but rather through a stable household, encouraging his parents to marry him off immediately. The note exposes the failure of the psychiatric institution to cure Sayf, relegating the task to the family's traditional "cure" of homosexuality within the confines of marriage. Upon reading the report, Sayf's mother ululates as the family decides to marry him off to his cousin Nada. The doctor's note bypasses the Foucauldian asylum and its modern episteme, reverting instead to an "old-fashioned" cure that seeks to neutralize homosexuality's visibility by making it disappear in the arranged marriage.

Associating homosexuality with madness, the novel exposes the role of family and state violence in suppressing homosexuality's public expression, neutralizing its madness, and eliminating its affects. When Sayf is taken away in the madmobile, the narrator imagines Sayf interacting with other mad people in the insane asylum. As in a movie scene, Sayf appears in the narrator's fantasy dressed all in white, his hair undone, being questioned (*sīn jīm*, interrogation) like a criminal in a police station by the asylum's staff.[45] Similar to Samir's questioning at the HIV clinic in London, the treatment of homosexuality (*mu'ālajat al-junūn*) in *Lusus* disavows a fictionalization of social and political violence. This violence produces homosexuality through the *sīn jīm* as an illness requiring treatment and elimination. In Abu Golayyel's staging of homosexuality in this working-class context of the new *ḥāra*, one could read the deployment of conservative forces that seek to make homosexuality invisible. However, homosexuality arises as a target but also as a site of embodied resistance to the deployment of power's apparatus.

MAJNUN STRIKES BACK

Suppressing Sayf's homosexuality "cures" his madness and transforms him into a law-abiding, married citizen. At another level, this suppression produces him as the heroic and tragic figure in the novel, overwhelmed by yet resisting various structures of violence. Reflecting on Sayf's *ikhtifā'* through abduction in broad daylight, the narrator claims: "Sayf wasn't insane. He wasn't mad, nor was he narrow or shortsighted. . . . He was simply a rebellious actor and a giddy lover [*'āshiq walhān*]."[46] Entering the madmobile in a highly visual and cinematic scene, Sayf pulls his tongue at his older brother, spits in his father's face, and insults his mother. Resisting the violence perpetrated against him, Sayf performs defiance and rebellion through bodily affects and invectives. In this way, he rejects the role he is forced to play.

Characterizing Sayf as *ʿāshiq walhān* (*ʿishq* is the ideal form of homoerotic love in Arabic poetry),[47] the narrator marks the queer subject's rebellion as a denial of the apparatus of oppression's legitimacy. "Pulling his tongue," "spitting," and "swearing"— the staging of the body—though they fail to rescue Sayf from his public punishment and incarceration, constitute sites of resistance to the violence of a normative interpellation that seeks to make him and his homosexuality disappear.

Sayf's body narrative and its affects not only operate to code homosexuality as a recognizable "species" as Foucault claims but also as a mad striking back that unsettles Arabic literary representations of homosexuality as well. Abu Golayyel frames this narratively through intertextual references to Naguib Mahfouz's novels and Hassan al-Imam's filmic adaptation of Mahfouz's works.[48] In fact, the narrator describes Sayf as a character from al-Imam's films, performing rebellion in the contemporary setting of the *ḥāra*. Combining madness in the Arabic cultural context and in Foucault's model with current articulations of a queer sexuality, the novel presents Sayf as the only character who is forced into submission. Sayf as a rebellious actor serves to anchor the critique of political and social forms of disciplining in queer representations in modern Arabic literature and film. Just as al-Shaykh's character Samir could be compared to Majnun—the ʿUdhri poet accompanied by the animals—and Klinger in *MASH*, Sayf is compared to the Mahfouzian hero in novels and film. The rebellion of the mad and homosexual Sayf is directed against the corruption of social and political authority, and against the homosexual character's depiction as a marginal figure in modern Arabic novels as well. Through the trials of Sayf in this contemporary setting, *Lusus* enacts a break with this mode of representation and unsettles the modern in "modern Arabic literature." The character of the persecuted homosexual could no longer be organically situated in Mahfouz's *ḥāra*. The association of Sayf's sexuality with madness thoroughly complicates the Mahfouzian plot, displacing its aesthetic framework and social and political context. Sayf's madness and affects thus create dissonance in the mode of representation of homosexuality in Arabic literature, thereby undermining its coherence, fixity, and type.

Focusing on Kirsha's character in Mahfouz's *Midaq Alley*, a married café owner who pursues young men, Frédéric Lagrange notes that "the homosexual in the contemporary Egyptian novel or short story is seldom a central figure, rather just another typical character of the popular *ḥāra* of Cairo."[49] Kirsha's "typicality" is seamlessly incorporated into the social structure of the *ḥāra*. Though Kirsha is a marginal figure in Mahfouz's work from the 1950s, Kirsha causes scandal once he publicly expresses his desire. When he entertains a local youth, inviting him to his café and spending nights with him outside the home, Kirsha becomes the object of physical violence. This occurs when his wife, Umm Husayn, attacks her husband's lover in public, before turning against Kirsha and physically assaulting him and shaming him in front of the café customers and passersby. When Kirsha *yujhir bimā yusirruh* (*yujhir*, *ajhar*, speak out, express, i.e., expresses his desire publically), he incurs scorn and violence.[50] Mahfouz characterizes Kirsha as a "homosexual," leaving the word in the Latin script.[51] Even in Mahfouz's novel, the public expression of homosexuality leads to scandal and violence.

The notion of *yujhir* or *jahara* (express, speak out),[52] which is also used to describe "coming out" in contemporary Arabic discourse on homosexuality, is complementary with the notion of *sirr* (hidden, secret). This structure of visibility and invisibility thus reintroduces *ikhtifā*' as an articulation of a homosexuality that could only be veiled or practiced in secret (*bi-l-sirr*). This highlights as well the association of homosexuality with madness as a condition of veiling and unveiling of desire, from Jamil's declaration of love for Buthayna to Kirsha's expression of homosexuality in Mahfouz's work. Here, the association of secrecy with revelation, suppression with expression, frames homosexuality in modern Arabic literature. However, and though both Kirsha and Sayf transgress social norms by expressing their queer desire in their respective environments, Kirsha is complicit with the structure of power in the Mahfouzian *ḥāra*. He is married, deals drugs, and owns a popular café. Whereas Sayf is coerced into marriage through violence, abduction, and institutionalization, in Kirsha's case the reference to madness is restricted to the wife, depicted as a *majnūna* (mad woman)[53] when she publicly attacks her husband. Given this important distinction, madness in Mahfouz characterizes the wife's act of shaming her husband for his public expression of desire rather than Kirsha's homosexuality as such.

Associating homosexuality with madness and departing from the Mahfouzian narrative and the tradition with which it is associated ("the contemporary Egyptian novel" and "modern Arabic literature" more generally), Abu Golayyel introduces a queer model of rebellion in his novel. While *Innaha London* presents Samir as a queer character in quest of sexual fulfillment and meaning in between Beirut and London and beyond the East/West binaries, Sayf emerges in *Lusus* as a tragic figure who rebels against social and political institutions by exposing their complicity, violence, and corruption. Abu Golayyel's novel stages a new articulation of sexual identity and practices by rewriting and reframing the Mahfouzian plot and transposing its urban landscape into a contemporary social and political setting. *Lusus* thus allows us to move the debate about current articulations of Arab sexuality from modernity and tradition, East and West, and gay-lesbian identities and traditional Arab-Islamic structures of desire, to a discussion of social, political, and aesthetic transformations arising from the contemporary novel. This ties in with Roger Allen's remark about the association of modern Arabic literature with Mahfouz's work from the 1950s and 1960s discussed in chapter 1. Not only does this association collapse Sayf with Kirsha by refusing to acknowledge the aesthetic transformations of Arabic texts and the development of their social and political contexts, but it also reduces Arab cultural models to the binaries of modernity/tradition and East/West. The treatment of "the modern" in modern Arabic literature as an unchanging and clearly circumscribed time period, associated with specific political struggles, intellectual debates, and literary works, is out of touch with Arab social, political, and cultural transformations. In order to unsettle this interpretive paradigm, I read Arab modernity as a dynamic process full of possibilities, which unfolds in literary texts through aesthetic transformation, comparative frameworks, and modes of embodiment.

CONCLUSION

The association of homosexuality with madness in the works discussed in this chapter aligns the collapse of the state during Lebanon's civil war and the condition of diaspora that this conflict produced with the erosion of social and political legitimacy in Egypt, which eventually led to the fall of the Mubarak regime in 2011. Both contexts highlight the advent of various forms of violence and displacement as a way of framing the articulation of queer desire. Dissident and antisocial, homosexuality is combated in order to veil the corruption and violence of the state and the family. While the aunt beats Samir and marries him off in *Innaha London*, in *Lusus* Gamal locks up Sayf and marries him off in an attempt to suppress the public expression of his homosexuality. In both cases, the family works in tandem with the state's "modern" institutions in order to assert a form of authority that keeps homosexuality in a state of *ikhtifāʾ* (disappearance) and the homosexual in a state of *takhaffī* (disguise). In this setting, the eroded legitimacy of the Arab state is inextricable from the corruption and moral bankruptcy of the "traditional" family.

Abu Golayyel's and al-Shaykh's narratives debunk the idealization of tradition (the Cairene *ḥāra*, the Arab family) as the repository of authenticity, morality, and resistance to Western hegemony and state power. Simultaneously, these novels unsettle the treatment of modernity as a homogeneous and hegemonic project that seamlessly regulates and produces Arab sexuality. The queer character in these texts resists modes of social and political normativity in Egypt, Lebanon, and England. Focusing on the affects of the queer character in the novels, one could read his madness as a framework for sexual articulation but also as a site of rebellion, transgression, and anger (mad as in "angry"). Investigating the *aḥdāth* or the homosexual events in London, Beirut, and Cairo reveals a new text and set of encounters that refigure literary models, articulations of desire, and political authority beyond the East/West, modern/premodern framework.

In the novels I discussed, Arab-Islamic forms of homosexual practice could no longer be considered authentic or a priori, resisting "Western" cultural and political hegemony from the nineteenth century onward. My reading demonstrates that a traditional form of Arab homosexuality, practiced within the confines of marriage, is in fact produced through forms of coercion arising from the diaspora, Beirut, and the modern-day, working-class Cairene *ḥāra*. Both Sayf and Samir are forced into the position of the "traditional" men-loving man or premodern sodomite—a married man who practices his homosexual desire in secret, at night, or in disguise. In *Lusus* and *Innaha London*, this sexual and social model and the very notion of "tradition" itself are produced and normalized through forms of ideological and physical violence perpetrated by the family and state institutions, both in Europe and in the Arab world. Thus my argument shifts the debate on queer Arab sexuality from the exclusive critique of European modernity and Western discursive practices to an investigation of this sexuality's production through a complex network of forms of authority, literary and cultural contexts, and ideologies. My examination of bodily affects, accidents, miscommunication, and transgressive acts yields the complex understanding necessary to expose this mode of production and critique its epistemological and political violence. The homosexual narrative identified in these texts thus depicts instances of anger, collapse, rebellion, and transgression that systematically rupture the coherent picture, the stereotype, and the fixity of the Arabic text along strict canonical and historical lines.

The queer subjectivity emerging from al-Shaykh's and Abu Golayyel's works and the violence deployed to suppress it need to be read in relation to the social and political transformations that have gripped the Arab world from 2010 onward. Public expressions of desire, both sexual and political, embodied in Tahrir Square and staged in novels, expose the erosion of patriarchal authority, which could only maintain itself through modes of violence and corruption. Specifically, reading *Lusus* after the fall of the Mubarak regime in Egypt, one could argue that the novel stages the corruption of the modern Arab state that is no longer tied to modernity as a clearly identifiable project emerging from the Enlightenment and mediated through colonialism and forms of intellectual and cultural exchange with Europe. *Lusus* emerges from the multiplication of critiques of corruption in Egypt, which gave rise to new configurations of social and political activism from Kifaya to the April 6 movements.[54] The trials of Arab modernity arise from this aesthetic and political context, which is witnessing the emergence of new models of subjectivity and political and literary practices, in between home and the diaspora, the blog and the novel. Instead of examining modernity exclusively at the level of ideology and political conflict—secularism and colonialism—it should be investigated in asymmetrical and unpredictable events (*aḥdāth*), queer, local, and diasporic, emerging from *other* texts, which have been made to disappear (*ikhtifā'*) from literary canons and intellectual and political debates both in the Arab world and in the American academy. Engaging this mode of exclusion in the next chapter as well, I examine Ahmed Alaidy's trials of Arab subjectivity and language, arising from the ruins of a social and political system that failed to "update" and "upgrade." Exploiting this system's weakness and vulnerability, a new generation of angry and uncompromising Arab authors hack and dismantle antiquated state institutions and delegitimize their discursive practices. This radical and violent critique produces new aesthetic models and forms of authority. I argue that Alaidy's literary and political trials disrupt canons and deterritorialize language through bodily affects, narrative discontinuities, and mixing of genres, making it possible to connect al-Shidyaq's work to Abu Golayyel's and Alaidy's and beyond.

CHAPTER SIX

Hacking the Modern

I didn't know that these people existed. I didn't know when
people took to the streets, it would be people like this. I
thought Mubarak had killed this spirit among Egyptians.
—KHALED FAHMY, *Chronicle of Higher Education*, January 30, 2011

They are way ahead of us in this new age, and we
have to play catch-up. (my translation)
—MOHAMED IBRAHIM, *Al-Jazeera Arabic*, February 3, 2011

We are not politicized. (my translation)
—ANONYMOUS DEMONSTRATOR FROM TAHRIR
SQUARE, *BBC Arabic Radio*, February 6, 2011

With the proliferation of Arabic blogging, e-mailing, chatting,
text messaging, and other forms of techno-writing, contemporary
Arabic literature is undergoing a series of structural and linguistic transformations. Specifically, the encounter with the virtual
and the effects of globalization are ushering in a new set of intertextual references that cut across languages, media, and genres.
A new generation of Arab authors is entering the scene of writing
from the world of blogging and scriptwriting, publishing blogs as
novels. In addition, many young novelists are appropriating the
structure of blogs in their literary production, some veiling their
true identity with pen names, others putting it on display by fantasizing narratives of persecution and censorship.[1] A new Arabic
writing is emerging from this interplay between virtuality and
print, affects and contemplative writing, and Arabic and English.
In these texts, we find English words left in the Latin script or at
times transliterated; stream of consciousness; the fragmentation
of the narrator's function; repetition; and various subversions of

narrative structure. In many instances, the difference between the blog and the novel is unclear. In Marie-Thérèse Abdel-Messih's words, "The generation of an electronic environment has led to a break with former narrative modes."[2] Full of affects and discontinuities, this writing presents an interactive textuality that is increasingly calling attention to the way literature is read and translated.

The affects in new texts, expressing anger and frustration, cannot be separated from the bodily affects generated by revolts from Tunisia to Syria from 2010 onward. Scenes of writing and demonstrating work in tandem to stage the production of aesthetic and political change. Though this relation requires further investigation, one could claim that the demand for human rights, equal representation, and economic opportunities on the one hand, and an unprecedented access to forms of communication from print to social media on the other, align new writing with political practices. Recognizing this dynamic interplay elucidates the relation between writing and the political in a rapidly changing technological and social environment. It also anchors these changes in aesthetic transformations and publishing practices, which are disrupting literary canons and displacing intellectual authority. This interplay produces new literary and political possibilities, which systematically interrogate and reframe questions of modernity in between Europe and the Arab world, citizen and state, and author and reader across generations and time periods.

This chapter investigates new Arabic writing's aesthetic shifts and stylistic transformations. I focus on Egyptian author Ahmed Alaidy's novel *An Takun ʿAbbas al-ʿAbd* (*Being Abbas el Abd*) (2003, henceforth: *ʿAbbas al-ʿAbd*) and read it as a manifesto for a new writing characterized by textual disruption, affects, sabotage, and mimicry. I argue that this new author, likened to a hacker, infiltrates the publishing establishment from which he was excluded and disrupts the codes of Arabic literary production. Appropriated from techno-language and used as a verb in Alaidy's text, "hacking" functions as a mode of subversion that empowers a new generation of writers to expose moribund social

and political systems through a new language and media. From
the forms of embodiment that disrupt and refigure genres (*madḥ*,
riḥla, novel) in *Nahda*, postcolonial, and diasporic texts analyzed
in previous chapters, I focus in this chapter on the incorporation of a multiplicity of "literary" and "nonliterary" genres (text
message, blog, advertisement, religious supplication) that unsettle
the novel's economy (writing, reading, publishing). I argue that
in Alaidy's work, affects are no longer inscribed on the body of
the disoriented Arab traveler in Europe, but rather condition the
text's production, language, and mechanics. These affects take
shape through forms of repetition of sentences and words, and
whimsical use of punctuation, bolding, spacing, and italicizing.
Alaidy moves us from the literary staging of the experience of
modernity to interactive writing, which calls on the reader to
experience and react to the text itself. The trials of Arab modernity unfold in Alaidy's work through a series of staged *aḥdāth*
(events, accidents) embodied in various episodes and encounters
in Cairo's streets, cafés, and public restrooms, and in the production and circulation of the Arabic text as well. Engaging critical works by David Damrosch, Alain Badiou, Sabry Hafez, and
Muhsin al-Musawi, my investigation challenges readings of syncretism and hybridity that either celebrate this new writing or rel-
egate it to globalization's neocolonial dynamics.

THE LITERARY SCENE

Both established writers like Elias Khoury (b. 1948), Hoda Barakat (b. 1952), and Gamal al-Ghitani (b. 1945) as well as new
ones from across the Arab world are contributing to a flourishing literary scene that is making writing "cool" again. Inter-
net-savvy and conversant with the products and transformations brought about by globalization, a new generation of Arab
writers relates to English not as a foreign language but rather
as the language that is constitutive of their cultural landscape
and their subjectivities. From blogs and websites to satellite TV,
films, and literature, global culture is pervasive in contemporary

texts. In this landscape, a new generation is arising from a cultural experience that can no longer be understood in terms of neatly organized binaries of resistance/imperialism, East/West, and tradition/modernity. Social media, tweeting, and texting are mediating the articulations of new identities and experiences. This generation is experimenting with linguistic registers, mixing genres, addressing the reader, and blurring the distinction between virtuality and print.

These literary voices are benefiting from technological development and the Internet as well as from the decentralization and privatization of the publishing industry in the Arab world. Dar al-Shorouk in Egypt is publishing such works as Khalid Khamisi's *Taxi* (2007), a Cairene taxi rider's diary, and Ghada Abdel Aal's *'Awza Atgawwiz* (*I Want to Get Married*) (2008), a satirical blog about marriage turned novel and TV show.[3] Dar Merit, the Cairo-based publisher of Hamdi Abu Golayyel's *Lusus Mutaqa'idun* (*Thieves in Retirement*), is likewise giving voice to many young literary talents who are coming to writing from the world of blogs, film scripts, and journalism. From Yasser 'Abd al-Latif's *Qanun al-Wiratha* (The law of inheritance) (2002), a novel about migration, return, and the character's relation to the city, to Muhammad 'Ala' al-Din's highly modernist *Injil Adam* (The gospel according to Adam) (2006), about an obsessive character, a stalker who fantasizes about seduction, rape, and murder, young authors are producing noteworthy works. Merit's editor, Muhammad Hashim, who was awarded the Jeri Laber International Freedom to Publish Award in 2006 and the Hermann Kesten Prize of the German PEN Club in 2011, has succeeded in creating both a vibrant publishing house and a salon that meets daily at Merit's offices in central Cairo, steps from Tahrir Square. In this new forum, authors gather and debate cultural and political issues, organize political action and review manuscripts, thereby anchoring the relation between literature and the political, and the aesthetic and its social context. This new generation, which has been overlooked or dismissed by critics and pundits as being apolitical, vulgar, and consumerist, has succeeded in mobilizing for a political revolution and a revolution in writing.

Despite some resistance to this kind of literary production, critical attention has been gradually emerging both in the Arab world and beyond. In 2010, the *New Yorker* published an article on new Arabic fiction, shedding light on innovative and noteworthy works including Rajaa Alsanea's *Banat al-Riyad* (*Girls of Riyadh*) (2005) and Sinan Anton's *I'jam* (*I'jam: An Iraqi Rhapsody*) (2004).[4] As part of the Hay Festival, a group of thirty-nine authors under the age of thirty-nine was showcased at a conference in Beirut in 2009.[5] This event presented new literary talents from across the Arab world, consecrating their work as an integral part of a flourishing literary scene. In addition to *Akhbar al-Adab*, which systematically engages new writing, major Arabic newspapers including *Al-Hayat* and *Al-Akhbar* are also running reviews of new works, making critics and readers increasingly aware of and interested in this literary production.[6] The Cairo-based periodical *Wasla* is devoted exclusively to the Arab blogosphere, publishing social, political, and literary articles and reviews.[7] Academic studies by Moneera al-Ghadeer, Sabry Hafez, Muhsin al-Musawi, Marilyn Booth, and others focus on the aesthetic transformations in recent Arabic literature, examining them in the context of social, technological, and political change.[8]

The critical reception of a new generation of Arab authors needs to be explored in relation to the reception of Arab modernist innovators from the 1960s onward.[9] Fabio Caiani's investigation of new Arabic poetics, focusing on literature from the 1980s and 1990s and engaging works by such authors as Edward Kharrat (b. 1926) and Elias Khoury, offers a formalist context for analyzing contemporary fiction.[10] Stefan Meyer's discussion of modernist trends in Arabic literature and their relation to existentialism, the absurd, and other European literary and philosophical influences provides an important framework for engaging new writing. Elaborating on arguments by Pierre Cachia and Roger Allen, among others, Meyer reads modernist Arabic literature in the encounter with European and American literary fiction, focusing on questions of political *engagement* and narrative structure in Arabic texts. Comparing Sonallah Ibrahim's (b. 1937) *Tilk al-Ra'iha* (*The Smell of It*) (1966) to Camus's *L'Etranger* (1942),[11] Meyer argues that Ibrahim's short and fragmented sentences recreate the interiority in Camus's work. Though it is necessary to engage the European intertext in analyzing Ibrahim's work and modern Arabic literature more generally, it is important to avoid foreclosing it by emphasizing questions of borrowing through a causal and linear trajectory originating in the West. As I have demonstrated in the previous chapters, the comparative engagement with Arabic works requires dynamic negotiation and interpretation across cultural, historical, and literary contexts.

Marking Sonallah Ibrahim's experience of imprisonment, *Tilk al-Ra'iha* presents a first-person narrative about a man released from jail. The main character's daily activities mimic that of his prison experience, blurring the line between freedom and captivity, inside and outside, and animal behavior—driven by crude senses—and that of humans. Written in a mechanical and choppy style, and structured by the routine visits of the parole officer, the story puts in question the construction of space and time. These visits confer upon the main character an identity framed through the regularity of the practices of power. At one point, Ibrahim presents the main character in his bedroom, reading a literary essay about the French realist author Guy de Maupassant's (1850–1893) understanding of literature as a vehicle for aesthetic transcendence and beautification of the world. Then, turning to his own writing without success, he drops his pen, lies on his bed, and masturbates.

Ibrahim's novella shocked the literary establishment at the time, which suppressed its publication in its integral form. In the preface of a later edition, Ibrahim mentions how Yahya Haqqi (1905–1992), doyen of Arab literati, railed against the work.[12] According to Haqqi, Ibrahim's text generates disgust and aversion and therefore could not be considered "literature" (*adab*). However, Yusuf Idris (1927–1991), the quintessential short-story author who eventually writes *Tilk al-Ra'iha*'s introduction, compares the critic to a metallurgist. He assesses Ibrahim's work as the latter mixes metals and folds them in order to produce something different, untranslatable, and new. In a reference to alchemy, Idris deconstructs Ibrahim's first name, "Son'-Allah" (*sana'a*, make, produce an artifact), elaborating on his manipulation of metals both in material and spiritual terms. Lacking the language to describe Ibrahim's text, Idris suggests that the story causes him to feel "danger, hope, and claustrophobia" (*al-khatar, al-amal, al-dīq*).[13] Acknowledging his inability to frame *Tilk al-Ra'iha* given the tradition or canon to which his work and that of Haqqi belong, Idris suspends judgment about the story's literary value, considering it part of a yet unidentifiable mode of writing, full of possibilities.[14]

The danger and doubt arising from Sonallah Ibrahim's text characterize the experience and reception of new writing today. Idris's sentiment is echoed in this characterization of blogging as a new writing practice: "What is great about blogging is that you're completely free for no one will ask you to qualify your writing. You can read, understand, and react to blogs and feel moved by them without having to decide whether you're reading a short story, a prose poem, or a journalistic article. . . . . Blogging is primarily a space for crying out. . . . Our generation feels that there is no time for complications. . . . Its language is often rebellious, not subject to the rules set by the conservative Egyptian social establishment and its antiquated tradition" (my translation).[15] Blogging's promise of freedom threatens the literary establishment and defies its sanctioned genres. Emerging from a space at the intersection of "literature" and "pulp," the novel and the blog, new texts question the legitimacy of literary canons and challenge their ideological and political production. The rebellion against established genres thus coincides with a critique of the social and political institutions with which these genres are associated. Finding a voice in a new cultural setting to express both political views and poetic imagination characterizes the project of an alienated youth that is actively engaged in staging and subverting the material conditions of its alienation and exclusion.

NEW WRITING MANIFESTO

'Abbas al-'Abd, an experimental novel that appeared from Dar Merit in 2003, exemplifies some of the new directions Arabic fiction has gone in the virtual age. Alaidy (b. 1974) entered the literary scene from the world of writing scripts for television and film, comic strips, political poems, and satire for a variety of Egyptian newspapers. His novel stages the rants of an angry narrator, a Cairene youth who goes about dating girls, riding public transportation, and discussing politics, culture, and history. 'Abbas al-'Abd presents a split character who performs various narrative functions. As Abdel-Messih notes, "the first/third-person narrative voice shifts inadvertently between past/present temporalities, showing forced relationships and failed relationality in disconnected situations."[16] 'Abdallah, a depressed young man who spends most of his time hallucinating in his room, serves a primary narrative function. 'Abbas is 'Abdallah's friend; he comes to 'Abdallah as a voice or as an image, pushing him to engage the world around him through acts of violence and sabotage, street fights, and graffiti. 'Awni is 'Abdallah's uncle, a psychiatrist who tortured his nephew when he was a child. There are two girls, both named Hind, whom the narrator tries to date. The last character is Shahinda, who works as a nurse at the mental asylum to which the narrator was sent as a child.

In his review of the novel, Hazem Abyad argues that Alaidy's text conjures up a disembodied space, a city stripped of its materiality, and that it relies on postmodern pastiche and parody, breaking in this way with questions of causality and originality.[17] This characterization provides the necessary perspective for interpreting Alaidy's text, which stages a series of unpredictable encounters, followed by ruminations and diatribes on Egyptian culture and history. A vulgar and violent narrative expresses anger over current social conditions. While discussing the relation between

Egypt and the West, 'Abbas tells the narrator: "'You want us to progress?? So burn the history books and forget your precious dead civilization. Stop trying to squeeze the juice from the past. Destroy your pharaonic history. . . . We will only succeed when we turn our museums into public lavatories (marāḥīḍ 'āmma).'"[18] In this way 'Abbas lashes out against Egypt's national identity. He "explodes like a sewer pipe that can't hold the shit anymore" (infajar ka-majrūr lam ya'ud yuṭīq al-ihāna),[19] breaking the link between modern-day Egypt and its glorious past. Progress, in 'Abbas's view, requires a break with the past and a destruction of the history books through which the past is imagined as constitutive of national identity. Burning history books and turning museums into public toilets delegitimize the way the past is mediated through educational and cultural institutions and maintained through political ideology. 'Abbas, the angry voice in Alaidy's novel, exposes the discrepancy between Egypt's imagined past and contemporary social and political decay. The "sewer pipe" that is redirected at the source of decay and waste in governmental institutions and discourse anchors the new literary text as a site of expulsion. The novel no longer represents a social reality or offers a critique of its ills and shortcomings through dialectical engagement or allegorical representation. Instead, Alaidy's text stages the sewers both as product and excrement of a decaying social and ideological model. The "sewer pipe's" explosion in the text thus constitutes a dynamic site of resistance through the displacement of affects. This complicates the relation between the text as product of its social and political environment and the text as "waste" or "pulp," which cannot be considered "literature."

According to 'Abbas, breaking with Egypt's romanticized past involves breaking with the "generation of the Defeat." In a reference to the 1967 war with Israel, or Naksa, a turning point in Arab political and cultural history, 'Abbas tells 'Abdallah: "Egypt had its generation of the Defeat. We're the generation that came after it. The 'I've-got-nothing-to-lose generation.' We're the autistic generation, living under the same roof with strangers who have names similar to ours. . . . Pull-shit. You need to

UPGRADE your wisdom and UPDATE your experience."[20] Here
'Abbas identifies the means by which a model of Egyptian identity
that breaks along generational lines can be overcome. *Tawaḥḥud*
(autism) is fictionalized as the condition of Arab youth, chatting
and texting and relating to their parents, who happen to live with
them in the same house, as complete strangers.[21] Connected to
one another and the Internet through nonverbal communication,
this generation is disconnected from the family and the state.
These modes of communication inscribe Alaidy's text as a site of
"explosion" and interactive writing, sewer-like. In this context,
identity formation becomes metonymic, constituted through
affects and physical proximity, thereby supplanting the historical
and civilizational master narrative through which Egyptian identity is imagined and maintained.

Appropriating computer language, 'Abbas asks the narrator
to update and upgrade his system and install a new server that
would supersede the cultural model that holds Egyptians hostage.
With the expletive "pull-shit," a combination of "bullshit" and
"don't pull this crap on me," which is given in English in the Arabic text, 'Abbas violently shakes not only 'Abdallah but the reader
of the text as well, forcing him/her to take notice of this need to
update, upgrade, that is, install new software, and move on. The
discourse of technology thus transforms the barbaric burning of
history books and the destruction of museums into acts of computer uploads and upgrades, signaling the advent of a generation
that is radically rethinking its social and political identity. In this
context, the question of experience becomes the strategic site for
dismantling and reconstituting communal bonds. "Updating" no
longer applies to the social and political institutions of the Egyptian state, which are stuck in the past and are thus out of touch
with this new generation, but rather to the experience of the 'abd
as in 'Abd-allah, 'Abbas's interlocutor, which conjures up the
Egyptian colloquialism, the "common man" ('abd). Arising from
texting and blogging, Alaidy's work recuperates a new mode of
experience that appropriates nonverbal communication in order
to shake up and awaken the common person from his/her torpor,

urging him/her to take action and reexperience his/her environment in new ways.

Updating and upgrading one's server are forms of *prise de conscience* that replace political *engagement* (*iltizām*) understood in
the French literary and political context. *Engagement* characterizes a previous Arab generation that demanded and believed
in a particular and perhaps utopic model of social and political
change yet ended up being crushed by authoritarian rule and military defeats. Arab modernity—with which the Egyptian nation-
state is associated—is staged in Alaidy's text as a dystopic and
antiquated project. This project operates as a computer application developed by an older and dysfunctional program, which
is—and perhaps always was—incompatible and unsupported.
Breaking with the "generation of Defeat," Alaidy interrogates its
project of modernity, the failure of which was merely exposed
in the 1967 war or *Naksa*. While the text calls for updating and
refiguring new modes of experience, it also opens the possibility
for a political subjectivity that breaks with modernity as imagined by some *Nahda* thinkers and embodied in such state institutions as libraries and museums. Alaidy's text sets the stage for an
upgraded and updated modern that unsettles Arab intellectual
and political modernity associated with Pan-Arab ideologies, for
instance. This dismantling and reframing of the new subject of
experience—"the common man"—and of the author and reader
of blogs, Twitter feeds, and Alaidy's text, constitute the new trials
of Arab modernity. In this context, "trials" designate the youths'
"putting on trial" of an ideological model and political structure that is collapsing or has already collapsed. This leads us to
introduce a new meaning for *aḥdāth* as the "youths," thereby
highlighting a generational framework that subverts political and
epistemological hierarchies. Moving from cultural and historical development to computer development of programs and inter-
faces, the new text becomes a stage for coding, trying, and refiguring social, political, and aesthetic models simultaneously.

Alaidy's text gradually stages a sabotage of the cultural products associated with the "generation of Defeat." The generation

that matured in the 1950s and 1960s is best known for its novels, the quintessential genre of Arab literary modernity. Engaging works by Ghassan Kanafani (1936–1972) and Halim Barakat (b. 1936), Edward Said argues that the act of writing after
1967 meant creating the *scene* for the reenactment of disaster
and the dramatization of "*periodicity*, that is, the active historical process by which Arab reality, if it is to have existential status,
must form itself."[22] The new generation of Arab authors imagined in Alaidy's text is no longer concerned with being suspended
between past and future, but rather engages the present as something that just *is*, a flickering, regenerating moment that appears,
disappears and reappears. The break with the "generation of
Defeat" entails in this new-writing manifesto a dismantling of
the novel's literary form. *'Abbas al-'Abd* launches an unwaver-
ing attack against the novel and the literary establishment that
sustains it for ideological and commercial reasons by excluding,
traditionally, young upstart authors and ignoring their current
reality. As the narrator says:

> IF THIS WERE A NOVEL, IT WOULD NOW BE TIME FOR YOU
> TO STOP and have a sandwich. Unfortunately, however, it isn't.
> This is not a novel. No one likes to read about the torments of the
> demigods when it is revealed to them what semidemihumans they
> are. These are the works that go along with the critics to the lavatory
> to assist them in floating free of the burden of fat buttocks.[23]

Here the narrator redefines the genre of the text he is narrating by blurring distinctions between virtual and material, literary
and nonliterary. This liminal work resists—in fact, unequivocally
renounces—the genre of the novel itself. Through this postmodern gesture, the narrator disabuses the reader of the idea that
the text he is narrating is a novel. In this call to action, this text
raises doubts regarding the nature, social function, and ideological framework of the genre as such. The text interpellates the
reader and calls on him/her to intervene through blank spaces
interspersed throughout *'Abbas al-'Abd*, yielding an interactive
writing full of affects, akin to that of blogs, text messages, and

social media. This new text calls on the reader to become aware
of his/her social and political reality by updating his/her experience and participating in the act of writing. The reader's experience of and reaction to this new text, full of affects and disruptions, shape the text's production. Unlike the reader of the
"literature of Defeat" who is conjured up as a participant in a
historical struggle, seeking to mend the break between the Arab
past and future after 1967,[24] Alaidy's reader is interpellated as
the subject of an immediate experience inscribed in the body and
expressed in the affects of frustration, anger, and sabotage. In
this light, 'Abbas al-'Abd performs an aesthetic subversion, which
is staged as a call for an embodied participation in new cultural
production and political acts, gestures, and performances. The
demise of the novel does not announce the end of writing. On the
contrary, the end of the novel, which is relegated in Alaidy's text
to the sewers of modernity in its Egyptian context, witnesses the
rise of new writing and new subjectivities that are not yet fully
defined or recognizable. Modern Arabic literature's association
with the project of modernity in the 1950s and 1960s, as Roger
Allen observes, is exposed and dismantled in Alaidy's text. The
new writer, alleged avatar of a consumerist and apolitical age and
whose work is relegated to vulgar pulp fiction, writes back like
an exploding sewer pipe. Alaidy stages and recodes the imagery
of excrement with which his generation of writers is associated,
redirecting it at the literary and political establishment that is
blind to its own waste. This new writing arises in between "pull-
shit"—in the hyphen—through an act of violent rebellion against
the canon, the government, and the condition of Egypt's youths
(as in *aḥdāth*) and society.

The traditional novel, according to Alaidy, is incompatible
with new social and political reality, language, and media. This
notion of incompatibility needs to be understood in the computer language context of "updating" and "upgrading" through
which Alaidy inscribes his attack on literary canons and social
and political institutions. Thus Alaidy exploits the literary genre
to which his work arguably belongs by acts of upgrades and

updates, mixing Arabic and English, using parentheses and question marks to excess, and systematically repeating words and sentences. In order to expose the demise of the novel (the one Haqqi laments when reading Ibrahim's *Tilk al-Ra'iha*), Alaidy uploads to his own work genres like advertisement, religious supplication (*du'ā'*), and user manual. In one instance, he sings the praises of a fictitious drug, Partacozine:

> You want to be unchained, to be free? You want to live your life to the full? This is your chance. . . . Partacozine will make your life more eventful and less painful. "Let's go everyone. In the Name of God the Healer." Raise your hands to Heaven in supplication and let's all say together: O God, save Partacozine from all evil and bless us in it! Aaaaaamen. "Did you know that Partacozine was much attacked at first?" O God, curse the Zionists, the evildoers, and Your enemies, Aaaaaamen. . . . O God, grant success to all who wish well to us and to Partacozine, O lord of the Worlds! Aaaaaaaaaamen. "Partacozine starts working after five minutes." Aaaaaaaaaamen.[25]

In this passage, Alaidy mixes the genre of advertisement with that of *du'ā'*, often uttered during Friday prayer in countries across the Arab world. Partacozine is thus presented as a miracle drug for the Muslim *umma* (nation). Alaidy's postmodern parody of *du'ā'* incorporates into its religious and ideological context an advertisement for antidepressants. The use of parody, according to Linda Hutcheon, calls attention to the constructedness of literary genres and aesthetic traditions, exposing in this way the ideological framework of canon formation. "Parody seems to offer a perspective on the present and the past which allows an artist to speak *to* a discourse from *within* it, but without being totally recuperated by it. Parody appears to have become, for this reason, the mode of the marginalized, or of those who are fighting marginalization by a dominant ideology."[26] In *'Abbas al-'Abd*, parody and the mixing of literary with nonliterary genres shape cultural production. Critiquing the appropriation of the project of Arab modernity in political discourse, Alaidy parodies the achievement of "Arab victory" and the mending of the historical ruptures of 1948 and 1967 through the defeat of Zionists and imperialists. This liberationist master narrative of Arab literary and political modernity is itself an advertisement, disseminated and marketed by Arab autocratic regimes and Islamists alike. This propaganda distracts from the necessary engagement with the state of psychological collapse of the Arab subject, now in need of drugs to withstand his/her own reality. In this way Alaidy parodies *duʿāʾ* and its political context but also consumerism and aspects of globalization that are reflected in the proliferation of drugs in the Arab world. This double parody operates both as a social and political critique of the Arab nationalist mantra—defeating Zionism and liberating Arab land—on the one hand, and as a literary intervention in the genre of the novel on the other.

Moreover, the alliteration of Partacozine and the intonation of *duʿāʾ* activate the linguistic affects in acts of deterritorializing language and genre. The opening of the mouth in "aaaaaam" and the pushing down with "eeeeen" create openings and fissures in the text itself, disrupting its writing yet connecting it to other media and recitation forms. This desacralization of the language, exaggerating the "a" sound through repetition and marking the "een" or "in" sound (as in *Āmīn*) by linking it to Partacoz(ine) takes Alaidy's text beyond the figurative and the representational, the discursive and the metaphorical. These sounds, openings of the mouth and the pressing of certain letters on the keyboard, the holding down of the finger for the "aaaa" to appear and proliferate in the text, introduce the guttural and the technological, the repetitive and the obsessive in the language itself, tampering with it, mixing it up. The attention to sounds and textual disruptions thus complicates the theories of parody or modernist experimentation with which new writing is often associated. In Alaidy's text, questions of sound, materiality, and phonetics are staged to unsettle language structure but also moribund social and political systems.

In its attempt to further infiltrate genre and deterritorialize language, exposing fundamental weaknesses and contradictions, the text rails against the materiality of the book itself, deploying the user-manual genre in order to provide instructions for destroying books, and especially long novels. The narrator enumerates the steps in the act of sabotage:

> Glue together the books in the public libraries, according to the following recipe:
>
>   1. Be sure to choose an appropriate time. . . .
>   2. Choose a provocatively large book, i.e., one of more than five hundred pages. . . .
>   3. You are at liberty to choose either an author or a topic you hate. . . .
>   4. Remove the lid on the liquid gum.
>   5. Pour the gum into the center of the book while flipping the pages, bearing in mind that "Knowledge is Light."
>   6. Stick the front and back covers of the book to the first and last pages, then cross out the author's name, using an X. . . .
>   7. Put the book back on a shelf other than its usual shelf. . . . The day is coming when the last barrier separating paper-backs from bags of potato chips will disappear. . . . The day is coming when they'll put a picture on the front of every book of a man tossing it into a trash can, and write underneath it:
>
> ### Help Make the World
> ### A Cleaner Place![27]

Alaidy here incorporates the genres of street signs (ḥāfiẓ ʿalā al-naẓāfa, no littering) and instruction manuals into the novel, transforming postmodern parody into sabotage. The recipe in this case is reminiscent of the anarchist cookbook, wherein food preparation becomes a violent affair. Deconstructing the relation between food and knowledge, reading and nourishment, Alaidy transforms the book into an object to be discarded like an empty bag of chips. Assuming the position of a saboteur who goes into the library to destroy the book, Alaidy's character unleashes a critique of the power structure that the book represents. The attack on library books calls attention to the educational system that is constitutive and symptomatic of the social and political decay exposed in the text. This allows the reader to entertain the erasure of both the book's materiality and its political and epistemological significance. Alaidy's narrator calls on the reader to acknowledge a new political reality and take part in changing it through micro-acts of rebellion and destruction. A new model of *engagement* (*iltizām*) arises from Alaidy's text, which transforms the reader into an accomplice and a saboteur, and the text into an interactive stage for comments, feedback, and performances of cathartic violence.

The destruction of the novel's materiality exposes its vulnerability not only as a genre now infiltrated by other nonliterary genres and pulp fiction but also as a product, an object placed on a library shelf, in the hands of the reader. This destruction of the book simultaneously undermines the act of reading, which mediates the production of the imagined national community in Benedict Anderson's sense.[28] Alaidy's reference to "autism" is thus a reference to the erasure of the symbolic bonds through which the community is constituted. The autistic generation no longer produces or imagines the national community by reading long novels, but generates it instead through sounds ("aaaaaam" and "eeeeen") and affects inscribed in Alaidy's text, blogs, and in the chants, vibrations, and signs held by demonstrators across the Arab world from 2010 onward. The new generation in Alaidy's writing is a barbaric horde of autistic saboteurs, unable to engage the social given the ideological framework of a moribund political system and its association with a project of modernity that has gone—has always already been—"down the drain."

Alaidy's violent reaction against a form of centralized social and ideological control exposes the crisis and bankruptcy of existing models of education and literary genres. The destruction of the book is the beginning of the uneducation and the reeducation of the public, updating their experience and upgrading their relation to knowledge. The destruction of the long novel in Alaidy's text could also be contextualized in relation to al-Shidyaq's lament about contemplative writing's demise and the advent of the modern text, which arises from the smoke and darkness of the polluted city discussed in chapter 3. The new text, full of affects and fragments, narrative disruptions and linguistic play, is the product of this virtual interplay wherein readers are interpellated no longer as participants in an imagined community, but as active participants in a new process of writing and interpretation, and political and social change. A far cry from Mafhouz's portrayal of the Cairene *ḥāra* in the 1950s, Alaidy's urban space is both physical and virtual, strategically positioned in between the *'ashwā'iyyāt* (slums) of modern-day Cairo and its upscale neighborhoods. With access to the Internet, cell phones, and satellite TV, this community of authors, readers, and activists undermine the ideological production of the novel as a site of idealization of tradition and the production of community. The dichotomy of modernity and tradition, the old-fashioned *ḥāra* and the modern neighborhoods of Cairo collapse both as sociological and political constructs framing and framed by literary works. Contemporary writing breaks with these binary oppositions by refiguring and devising new forms of subjectivity and writing practices produced in between the Internet and print, Cairo's slums and *wisṭ al-balad* (city center). The plot of the Mahfouzian novel, which depicts the rise and fall of such protagonists as Hamida in *Midaq Alley* and Gabalawi in *Children of the Alley*, for instance, is subverted in new writing. Contemporary literary and political events (*aḥdāth*) produce new texts and forms of subjectivity, from the queer character in Abu Golayyel's work discussed in the previous chapter to the techno-saboteur in Alaidy's manifesto. The staging of the experience of modernity set in Cairo or in London, whether it's associated with European technology or Arab regimes, exposes and dismantles models of aesthetic and political authority.

HACKING THE POLITICAL

In an interview published in *Critical Inquiry* in 2008, the French philosopher Alain Badiou sets out to imagine the possibility of the political in the age of globalization.[29] Badiou notes that "contrary to Hegel, for whom the negation of the negation produces a new affirmation, I think we must assert that today negativity, properly speaking, does not create anything new. It destroys the old, of course, but does not give rise to a new creation."[30] In this context, Badiou suggests that the riots of November 2005 in France failed to produce social and political change because the Arab youth continue to feel excluded and marginalized. As opposed to 1968, when students and workers, sharing *engagement*, came together to effect change, Badiou argues that today that convergence "is missing" because "the youths of the *banlieues*" are "shut up in a collective isolation. Things will probably change, but for the moment this is the reason why nothing came of these revolts. And, for the moment, all they can do is revolt."[31] Badiou's assessment is based on a very specific model of political action that emerges from Hegelian dialectics and spreads through socialist and nationalist ideological models. Given this development, Badiou identifies the absence of a dialectical synthesis and thus of a meaningful social and political change tied to specific revolutionary action. According to Badiou, the French *banlieue* is shut out from historical change.

However, Badiou's reading of the revolutionary model is unable to explain or account for *other* movements and events (*aḥdāth*) as sites of transformation and redefinition of the political taking place online, in public squares, and in literature. In this context, the project of Arab modernity, exposed and attacked in Alaidy's text, could not be separated from the Hegelian model and its production of Arab nationalist social and political systems. This model is bankrupt in Alaidy's staging of the political; it is trapped in a hermeneutical circle that draws on models of class struggle in the Marxist context, and on the history of revolutions from 1789 onward. This Eurocentric interpretive model fails to account for the kinds of transformation staged in the text, and for those shaping Arab social and political reality today. Furthermore, the attention to the *banlieue*, likened to Cairo's slums, as the exclusive site and origin of political action was proven erroneous. As the events of the Arab Spring have demonstrated, and, as Alaidy's text projects, this change arises in between center and periphery, the 'ashwā'iyyāt (slums) and Tahrir Square (city center), and the upper and working classes. The space of experimentation and trials, in between Cairo's slums and upper-class neighborhoods, the material and the virtual, interrogates these binary oppositions and unsettles political authority, interpretive models, and literary canons.

Sabry Hafez's reading of new writing in Egypt echoes Badiou's observation. Hafez investigates the poetics of the 1990s generation of authors, examining their works through the lens of political, class, and urban transformations.

> If the writing "I" is no longer able to secure its position as the controlling consciousness of the text, and the author no longer has confidence in his or her narrator, it is because both have become variations of the subaltern self, inhabiting a subaltern country that has lost its independence, its dignity and its regional role. This creates a crisis in which the "I" is unable to identify with itself, let alone with an "other" or a cause. Yet it also offers a narrative capable of relating external reality "from the inside," as if an integral part of it, while at the same time seeing it from the outside, the viewpoint of the marginalized, appropriate to its own insignificance. The new Arabic novel is immersed in the most minute details of its surrounding social reality, yet it is unable to accept it. The "novel of the closed horizon" is the genre of an intolerable condition.[32]

Hafez's understanding of the conditions of alienation relegates new writing by young Egyptian authors to a "closed horizon," reinforcing the metaphor of autism articulated in Alaidy's text. Hafez uses his analysis of the changing map of Cairo, which is based on urban development studies done by André Raymond and Abu-Zaid Rajih, to understand the new novel, arguing that literary narratives reflect this material reality.[33] In this context, the shrinking of physical spaces in Cairo leads new authors into impossible, claustrophobic literary spaces. One might elaborate on Hafez's reading of the material conditions of alienation by taking into account the effects of technological development and the Internet on this new literary and political landscape, which would spare us the engagement with the question of the end of history in a post-*Naksa*, postdialectical age. Micro-acts of bricolage, staged in new writing, unsettle this closed horizon and create the possibility of change and resistance. Ahmed Alaidy and many other writers of his generation write comic strips in newspapers and scripts for films as well as blog. This vibrancy allows us to read new texts as contributing to a clockwork of change, incrementally and locally intervening in discourse and ushering in new ideas and aesthetic and political practices. In her reading of the 1990s generation and of Ahmed Alaidy's work by focusing on the "family," Samia Mehrez argues that "it is precisely this generation of urban, savvy and streetwise 'I've-got-nothing-to-lose' youth that has carried contemporary Egyptian avant-garde beyond family and nation, opening up new literary imaginings and linguistic possibilities that promise uncharted referential, technical and aesthetic territories."[34] The attention to the aesthetic, grounded in social and political reality, brings to light these transformations and frames them as constitutive of novelty and change.

Analyzing hacking in Ahmed Alaidy's text allows us to engage new writing in ways that go beyond the logic of negativity and destruction that Badiou and Hafez identify, breaking with its binaries of modernity/tradition, East/West, center/periphery. "Hack" (*ḥāk*) is transliterated from English in Alaidy's text and then translated as *ikhtirāq al-niẓām* (infiltrating the system, though *niẓām* means both system and regime, as in Mubarak's old *niẓām* in Egypt).[35] Alaidy invokes hacking to expose the task of the new Arab author in this liminal space of writing. "Hack" is introduced in a conversation about a seventeen-year-old Russian youth who succeeded in hacking the Pentagon's website and uploading MP3 music files. Adding that hackers are now everywhere, targeting even the government (*ḥattā l-ḥukūma bi-tithāk*), 'Abbas defines the function of the interactive writer and reader.[36] Uploading MP3 files to the Pentagon site is an act of infiltration and penetration, and of mixing of genres, just like Alaidy's mixing of supplication with advertisement in Partacozine's praise. Just as the seventeen-year-old Russian exposes the system's vulnerability and penetrates the "impenetrable," Alaidy's text exposes Egypt's antiquated and incompatible social and political system.

"Hack" means "to cut or sever with repeated irregular or unskillful blows," "to make chopping strokes or blows," "to write computer programs for enjoyment," and "to gain access to a computer illegally."[37] Alaidy draws on these different meanings, rendering hacking both an act of sabotage, as in gluing and destroying the library book, and of play, experimentation, trial, and computer programing. In Alaidy's manifesto, the author is a techno-saboteur, ushering in a different relation to writing and tradition, and departing from the project of modernity associated with Mahfouz, Haqqi, and others. After taking the axe to the long novel by hacking and cutting it down, what remains are fragments, reproduced in Alaidy's work through "ahhhhh" and "ohhhhh." These fragments—also waste or excrement as in the sewer explosion metaphor introduced earlier—are akin to text messages and comments written on blogs and Facebook pages, further blurring the distinction between techno-writing and literature. In this context, Alaidy's dedication at the beginning of the work, addressing his "partners in crime,"[38] resembles a confession to a criminal act, which consecrates the act of writing—new writing—as a crime. This act turns the reader into an accomplice and the critic into a detective who tries to decode the crime. Hacking thus characterizes the intervention of a new generation in cultural production through acts of violence, penetration, dissimulation, programing, and writing. Conceptualizations of the self that emerge through a new language and aesthetic sensibility reflected in distorted narrative structures with blank spaces and affective inscriptions entail an articulation of a course of action and a critique from the bottom up, challenging an ideological project that could no longer dissimulate or veil its illegitimacy. The hacking metaphor describes an incessant infiltration and mapping out of new literary and artistic spaces. Thus, new writings can no longer be dismissed as a vulgar phenomenon but rather must be acknowledged as an important

cultural production with wide-ranging social and political repercussions. The aesthetic strategies adopted in new works could also
be identified in the other texts discussed throughout this book,
from al-Tahtawi's "hacking" of *madḥ* and *riḥla* genres to al-Shidyaq's *kashf* (unveiling, stripping naked) the discourse on civilization.
These processes of infiltration and sabotage, embodied in *Nahda*,
postcolonial, and new writings, are constitutive of the "modern"
in modern Arabic literature.

CONCLUSION

Elaborating on arguments by Ella Shohat and Homi Bhabha,
among others, Muhsin al-Musawi argues that critical production
of hybridity and syncretism continues to veil material conditions of
production and other social frameworks necessary to literature's
circulation and reception.[39] Examining Sonallah Ibrahim's 1991
novel *Al-Lajna* (*The Committee*), al-Musawi argues that although
the novel critiques global capital, exposing the nation-state's complicity in the neocolonial onslaught on the Arab and developing
world, "this global order would soon have the same status as the
nation-state as long as there are selfish interests, corruption, and
repression."[40] However, al-Musawi claims that in many new writings, "the ideological application to the nation is rarely touched on;
the politics of globalization is put aside, and neither American capital nor European contexts are debated or criticized."[41] Al-Musawi
goes on to analyze the role of the technological in framing the role
of the nation-state and its reach in a new age:

> The preoccupations of literary modernity are no longer the only
> ones in the minds of writers, nor are postmodern discursive anxi-
> eties. What is at stake now relates to identity, territorial fact and
> meaning, as well as to one's cherished tradition and culture. This
> needs to be examined from a focused and insightful historical
> perspective that takes into account the movement from colonial-
> ism and the nation-state to a global reality of mixed agenda and far
> reaching consequences.[42]

Al-Musawi identifies the stakes in the investigation of a new Arab aesthetics. The contemporary text could not be discarded as a form of posturing from a position of social and economic privilege but rather acknowledged as a vital negotiation of one's place in relation to the political and the historical. The quest for a new language in these writings and the critic's ability to recognize and explain this quest are of great consequence given the extent to which the Arab world is assailed by social violence, poverty, and political oppression. The danger lies not just in dismissing the violent political and economic symptoms of globalization but also in dismissing the young generation's attempt to speak with a new voice. This voice would spare it the stifling effects of those very symptoms that might lead this generation further into frustration, resentment, and despair. The transformations that the Arab world has undergone since the end of 2010 highlight the political and social potential of this generation of tech-savvy writers and activists. Their writing thus needs to be read with greater urgency in relation to social and political transformations. This is not meant to reduce the text to a mere reflection of the Arab social and political scene, but rather to situate aesthetic transformations within their appropriate sociopolitical contexts and acknowledge the increasingly blurred distinction between writing and blogging, fiction and political action. In Egypt specifically, new writers, multitasking as bloggers and cartoonists, activists and journalists, systematically refigure the relation between the literary and the political, "national literature" and "global fiction."

David Damrosch engages in his work new spaces of literary production in the encounter between the local and the global. Moving beyond antiquated frameworks that have thus far informed and at times governed literary critical reception of minor literatures, Damrosch argues that literary production needs to be examined in the interplay between cultural and ideological forces, between the sites of literary production and the sites of circulation of literature.[43] While Damrosch reads "world literature not as a canon of texts but as a mode of circulation and of reading" beyond these texts' cultural and national boundaries, it is necessary to simultaneously understand these works in light of both their social and political contexts, and the system of language and writing through which their authors articulate imagination, fantasy, and identity.[44] The importance of the frameworks advanced by Damrosch and others lies in the fact that this writing is no longer associated with authors deprived of agency. As Alaidy and his fellow authors take control and hack the system of publishing, their work could not be read as a "victim literature," which is produced by the oppressed, the colonized, or the *banlieue* dwellers in Badiou's formulation. This does not mean that social and political realities are elided but rather that writing is a scene that offers the possibility of negotiation, dynamic movement, resistance, and change.

A reading that acknowledges the ability of a new generation to create ripples, make sounds, and get its voice across is very political. Alaidy's hacking, in this context, contributes to an aesthetic project that calls on new writers to take up a difficult "breaking loose" from their predecessors. From the critique of the *Naksa* generation and the mistrust of Arab ideological movements since the 1950s arise new political possibilities. Infiltrating the system of writing through forms of hacking could be debated as an ethical issue or as a symptom of the vulgarization of culture. This, however, would be to fall prey to the elitist models against which this generation is rebelling in the first place. Manipulating the publishing industry through new narrative structures and blogs ends up, in one way or another, empowering young writers who contribute to social and political change.

The emphasis on reading new genres that connect films with Arabic literature, the novel and the blog, and Arabic and English, unsettles the prevailing political and historical approaches to Arabic literature discussed in chapter 1. A critical investigation of new writing gives urgency to the reconceptualization of the Arab experience of modernity, which I undertake in this book, and serves to interrogate the appropriation of Arabic literature in cultural debates about colonialism, tradition, and secularism, to name a few. Reading literary sites of embodiment as *aḥdāth* (events, accidents) by aligning *Nahda* with contemporary fiction challenges the instrumentalization of "modern Arabic literature" as a discrete historical and sociological category through which one may gauge the truth about Islam and Arabs. Engaging these debates highlights this study's critical repercussions on the way we understand and disseminate Arabic writing in the virtual age.

Alaidy reworks al-Shidyaq's critique of civilization in a contemporary setting, staging its decay and devising modes of hacking and subversion that expose its eroded legitimacy. Through the proliferation of sounds and affects, repetitions and disruptions, Alaidy's text identifies the ideological collapse of the state and of its master narrative of historical and cultural continuity. The *Nahda* critical practices I identified in chapters 2 and 3 continue to unfold with this generation of new writers. These practices unveil the social and political system's failure and corruption, and expose the violence deployed to mask it. Like al-Shidyaq, Alaidy's *ḥāk* is staged through linguistic play and modes of embodiment. The subversion of social and political structures and models of legitimacy takes shape through a deterritorialization of language and, specifically, the language of the intellectual in the service of the political establishment. Alaidy empties language through repetition, mixing genres, and affects. This deterritorialization, as I argued in the chapter on al-Shidyaq as well, opens up new possibility for imagining the social and the political, and generates in the process new forms of literary practices arising at the intersection of the virtual and the material, the Internet and Tahrir Square, the novel and the blog. The Arab Spring, which was orchestrated and staged by Alaidy's generation, is now associated with a new *Nahda*. This association needs to be examined and theorized not merely as a repetition of or continuity with a particular cultural project from the nineteenth century, but rather as the adoption of new literary and political practices and techniques from which meaning and subjectivity arise. The trials of Arab modernity unfold in Alaidy's text through ruptures, discontinuity, play, and negotiation, which systematically interrogate questions of linearity, borrowing, and causality. Understanding the political at this historical stage requires an investigation of this trajectory of breakdowns and contradictions that is constitutive of social and cultural models.

CHAPTER SEVEN

Conclusion

Writing the New Political

In this book I presented different articulations of modernity in Arabic travel narratives, novels, and experimental writing from the nineteenth century to the present. Starting with the staging of the Arab encounter with Europe, I challenged the reading of modernity (*ḥadātha*) as innovation (*iḥdāth*) in relation to tradition, and anchored it instead in the notion of event (*ḥadath*) or events (*aḥdāth*), which also means incidents, trials, and episodes. Introducing these notions by drawing on literary theory and philosphy served to identify in the Arabic text a dynamic unfolding that unsettles European modernity's imagined homogeneity. Decentering modernity as a fixed set of practices and ideas moves the debate away from the mechanics of Arab borrowing from the West. Rather than establishing or defining a canon, I exposed and critiqued the way canon limits and circumscribes notions of modernity and literature. The comparative approach adopted in this book allowed me to identify a series of practices, rhythms, techniques, and encounters through which modernity becomes problematized, interrogated, tried out, and imagined.

My strategy consisted in unsettling the question of representation by engaging modernity in gestures, movements, and affects, which I examined in a dynamic interplay across historical and cultural contexts. I argued that modernity takes shape in a series of trials, never realized or complete, arising from experiences of anxiety and disorientation, fascination and confusion. These spaces of fantasy and literary embodiment reposition the political by systematically undermining its ideological production and exposing its modes of physical and discursive violence. The new political, which arises from al-Tahtawi's fantasy about Muhammad ʿAli and Samir's fits of madness at an HIV clinic in London, is open and unfolding, and thus could only be identified, gauged, and approximated in the *aḥdāth* I examine. Rather than engage al-Tahtawi's views on government and on the role of the *ʿulamāʾ* (religious scholars) in a new age, or scrutinize al-Shaykh's views on Arab homosexuality for that matter, I explored poetic associations and drag in al-Tahtawi's and al-Shaykh's texts, which arise from experiences of fragmentation and fits of madness. My exploration involved a close comparative reading of aesthetics, poetic fragments, and "pulp fiction," which are often dismissed or overlooked. This reintroduction of and engagement with *other* texts elucidated the interplay between writing practices and political authority.

Starting with al-Tahtawi and focusing on his poetic associations as sites of fantasy and embodiment of a modern experience discussed by Benjamin, I demonstrated that this *Nahda* text not only lends itself to Euro-American theoretical frameworks but that it is, in some respect, constitutive of them as well. The comparative approach to al-Tahtawi's work involved an investigation across cultural registers and philosophical traditions, going back and forth between Arabic and European texts, and modern and classical ones, in order to highlight a dynamic interplay that spares us, once and for all, questions of borrowing, originality, and the use of theory in Arabic literary studies.

Moreover, my reading of al-Tahtawi's work at the intersection of *madḥ* and *riḥla* highlighted a new articulation of *Nahda* appropriation of tradition in the nineteenth century, a problematic that informs and shapes intellectual debates about Arab modernity and authenticity. The question of innovation vis-à-vis tradition or the return to tradition as a resistance to Western practices and thought proved to be simplistic at best. Appropriating Alaidy's "hacking" in this context, one could argue that al-Tahtawi "hacks" the Arab-Islamic tradition in order to express a different relation to religious and political authority, both in Egypt and in Europe. This chapter demonstrated that tradition is dynamic, shifting, and constantly repositioned in the modern Arabic text. Al-Tahtawi's infiltration of Arab-Islamic history through the incorporation and transformation of genres (madḥ and riḥla), religious tradition (Islam, al-Azhar), and history (Sayf al-Dawla) identifies a comparative pattern already at work within Nahda writing.

The Nahda, until very recently, had been the domain of historical and political studies of Euro-Ottoman relations. Such scholars as Albert Hourani and Hisham Sharabi have focused on the Arabic text as representative of social and political forces that could be incorporated into specific intellectual debates about East/West relations. Analyzing al-Tahtawi's poetic fragments produced a different account of the Nahda narrative, thereby highlighting multiple sites of confrontation, which could not be reduced to political conflict and the tradition/modernity binaries. Specifically, chapter 2 highlighted the transformation of the Muslim scholar into a state bureaucrat and reformer; analyzing al-Tahtawi's poetic association provided a crucial insight into the resistance, anxiety, and fantasy involved in this transformation.

Moving from al-Tahtawi to al-Shidyaq and focusing on the question of civilization, chapter 3 examined the way it has been "stripped naked" in Kashf. Processes of embodiment of the intellectual struggle involved in identifying and explaining civilization as a coherent cultural and historical project expose civilization's violent, ideological production. In describing his reactions to English food across class and regional contexts, al-Shidyaq unveils the play of contradictions at work in the very notion of civilization itself. Deploying registers of anger, shame, mockery, capriciousness, shock, and disbelief, al-Shidyaq forces his reader to witness, attest, and feel revolted by what is frustrating and oppressing him. This interactive and postmodern writing serves to position *Kashf* in relation to *other* texts in the Arabic literary tradition and to those produced in the virtual age.

From al-Shidyaq's confusion and frustration in Europe arise a radical dismantling of civilization as the British understand and practice it. In this context, the Arabic text is involved in a systematic confrontation with and deconstruction of orientalist and colonial models from the nineteenth century onward. Just like al-Tahtawi reframes and repositions the relation between power and knowledge, al-Azhar and Muhammad 'Ali, the modernity tried out in al-Shidyaq's *Kashf* in no way engages European modernity dialectically or accepts at face value its association with civilization as progress and liberation that could be imported to the East. Al-Shidyaq's *other* modernity brings to light a trajectory of ruptures and traces, thereby calling attention to micro-texts, anecdotes, and parody through which Arab modernity is imagined and practiced in the nineteenth century. These modern practices, which coincide with textual innovation and play from al-Shidyaq to Alaidy, deterritorialize and reframe the master narrative of Arab modernity by unsettling its association with European and later Arab models of progress and development.

Radwa Ashour's treatment of al-Shidyaq's contribution as emblematic of an alternative *ḥadātha* (modernity)—*mumkina*, full of possibilities—dovetails with recent reassessments of the *Nahda* in the works of Kamran Rastegar, Yoav Di-Capua, Shaden Tageldin, Stephen Sheehi, Elizabeth Holt, Samah Selim, Nabil Matar and other scholars taking to task the *Nahda* master narrative.[1] These readings aim to dismantle the *Nahda* as a coherent body of texts produced by intellectuals in their ivory towers, or, as al-Shidyaq himself puts it, in "Damascus's elegant gardens." The *Nahda* I examine is produced on the street. The emphasis of this scholarly trend is on local activism, advertising, fashion, and other local sites of cultural production. Moving away from its grand narrative and focusing instead on practices, events, and trials undertaken by travelers, journalists, and common people throughout the Arab-Ottoman world, this deconstruction of the *Nahda* reveals the body of the Arab traveler as a site of unraveling and production of the East/West relation. The body signifies, performs, and breaks down by collapsing as well as dismantling the master narratives of European civilization and of Arab modernity alike.

Incorporating the African-Arab experience into the *mashriqi* (Levantine) narrative of the encounter with Europe and the project of Arab modernity more generally, the chapter on Tayeb Salih investigated the literary staging of colonialism in modern Arabic literature. Edward Said discusses the way the 1967 defeat against Israel or *Naksa* created a rupture in the Arab historical narrative of progress and development from the nineteenth century onward. However, what undermines this project of Arab modernity is not only colonial onslaught in its various manifestations but the exclusion of other experiences, texts, sounds, and voices from within the Arab world. It is impossible to fully engage 1967 and read the new generation of Arab authors who set themselves apart from the "generation of Defeat" without confronting those excluded from the *Nahda* narrative. Anchoring Arab modernity in the Sudan by examining the encounter with European colonialism displaces the *Mashriq-Maghrib* or *Mashriq*-Europe axis of Arab modernity. An engagement with Tayeb Salih's work in this context multiplies the sites of modernity's trials and events in Arab debates and cultural production.

Moreover, chapter 4 sought to collapse scenes of disaster by tracing trajectories of loss and exposing colonial trauma. This reading reintroduced models of ambivalence and instability not only in the relation between colonizer and colonized, but in the way the West is produced, imagined, and endowed with specific agency as well. My comparative approach served to interrogate the postcolonial genealogy and the psychoanalytic frameworks deployed to read Salih's text specifically. Treating *Mawsim* as just another manifestation of colonial angst, structured through a dysfunctional Oedipus that arises both from the Sudanese family and social context and from the violence of colonial structures, fails to account for the work's complexity.

The stench of corpses lying on battlefields in Europe and in the Sudan, and the shrieks and murmurs of grieving women are embodied in Salih's novel, calling attention to themselves through murmurs, outbursts, and various affects. The author tries out different modes of mourning, unleashing the ghosts in an attempt to exorcise them by offering them proper burial or by dismissing and casting them away. *Mawsim*'s *aḥdāth* arise in between different experiences of loss, structures of mourning, and sites of disaster in the Sudan and in Europe. Arab modernity is tried in these literary embodiments, which unsettle historical narratives, literary canons, and scholarly traditions. This chapter demonstrated that the theoretical model able to engage the postcolonial novel must be identified in the interstices of Salih's text, and in between the narrator's fantasy, projection, and various attempts to interpret Mustafa's experience in England by recognizing voices, accents, and faces.

From the Sudanese *other* within colonial discourse and the Arab master narrative of modernity I moved in chapter 5 to the queer *other* in order to investigate the trials of Arab modernity in London and in the Cairene *ḥāra*. In this context, my examination of Abu Golayyel's and al-Shaykh's works focused on the association of homosexuality with madness in *Innaha London* and *Lusus*. Through a comparative reading of the figure of Majnun, an impassioned lover and a mad rebel protesting, doing drag, and acting out, I argued that literary expressions of queer desire operate as sites of resistance to social and political normativity, both in the Arab world and in the diaspora. Discussing the aesthetic transformations of the contemporary novel and drawing on Arab-Islamic literary and philosophical works, I critically engaged Michel Foucault's understanding of sexual and epistemological developments and tied in current debates about Arab homosexuality. I showed how discursive models of sexuality are situated in modernity's intertwinement with structures of power and systems of belief ranging from the *ḥāra* and the European metropolis, the Arab family and the nation state. Specifically, the affects of *junūn* in al-Shaykh's and Abu Gollayel's texts chart other sites of the modern that are simultaneously queer and working-class, Arab and European, and literary and political. Queering modernity's *aḥdāth* served in this context to further challenge its treatement as a static and homogeneous Western import.

Moreover, recent political and aesthetic events could not be read independently of the articulations of sex and gender explored in chapter 5. Thus, if we were to read Abu Gollayel's work retrospectively, we could associate the characters of Gamal with Gamal Mubarak and Abu Gamal with Husni Mubarak, Egypt's deposed president. In this light, the novel ties in the collapse of despotic regimes to the erosion of patriarchal authority, which could be maintained only through modes of violence and oppression. This erosion is simultaneous with the rise of multiple configurations of political subjectivity and literary genre. As this chapter demonstrated, only a dynamic reading across languages, cultures, and literary traditions could expose the intertwinement of these forms of subjectivity as they arise from a specific political and cultural context.

Postcolonial readings of Arabic literature often dismiss expressions of queer Arab sexuality as upper-class phenomena, complicit with Western hegemonic practices. They also dismiss a new generation of men and women with access to technology and conversant with Western popular culture as consumerist and apolitical. These epistemological and political binaries thus exclude the possibility of mobilizing people from across the social and political spectrum as we have witnessed from 2010 onward. A tech-savvy generation succeeded in mobilizing workers, disenfranchised ethnic and religious groups, women and men, young and old. *Other* possible (*mumkina*, full of possibilities) readings, undertaken in this book, are not simply attempts to expose these theoretical shortcomings, but to contest as well their insufficient engagement with the complexity of current cultural production arising from increasingly hard-to-categorize spaces and media.

Current literary practices generate new meaning but also identify hitherto unexplored intertextual trajectories that reflect and mediate our return to the past. In this context, al-Shidyaq's *kashf* needs to be juxtaposed to and put in dialogue with Alaidy's "hacking," the subject of chapter 6. Just as al-Shidyaq embodied the experience of modernity through modes of ingestion and expulsion, disgust and collapse, Ahmed Alaidy stages in his work the collapse of social and political models by infiltrating and deterritorializing Arabic language and the political. Alaidy's "hacking" and al-Shidyaq's *kashf* are forms of unveiling of decay and exposing civilization's barbarism. Hacking and *kashf* reveal processes of *ikhtifā'*, i.e., of the "disappearing" and the veiling of the decay—the system's corruption and illegitimacy.

Reading Alaidy's text alongside al-Shidyaq's and others' serves to contextualize this study in the present, situating it in relation to current transformations and multiplications of writing modes. The West and its association with modernity are no longer recognizable for Alaidy and his generation. Writing in English and Arabic, blogging and producing novels and incorporating filmic references, this generation is rendering antiquated scholarly and political paradigms that continue to draw on the nation in its 1950s articulation as the prism through which literature is produced and read and political change occurs. Taking on the very meaning of literature by infiltrating its modes of production, circulation, and reading public, new writing calls on the critic to engage with narrative fragments, texting, and blogging as the new language of this "I've-got-nothing-to-lose-generation." In the process, this *very* political and *very* literary generation, effecting political change and contributing to a flourishing literary scene, is dismantling traditional paradigms of literature and the political.

Just when we thought that the Arab project of modernity was defunct and buried, calls for equal rights and representation are resonating throughout the Arab world, with people confronting autocratic governments with their bodies, anger, and frustration. The trials of Arab modernity, now more than ever, are in need of exploration at the level of affects and embodiment in Arab public squares and online. Talk of a new *Nahda* creates the urgency for a comparative reading that aligns al-Tahtawi and al-Shidyaq with Alaidy and his contemporaries. The examination of the interplay of the literary and the political offers the possibility of theorizing *engagement* (*iltizām*) in between the literary text and social media, writing and demonstrating. The trials of Arab modernity are taking shape in these liminal spaces, in new forms of writing and political activism, refiguring literary genres and models of subjectivity.

This so-called "apolitical" generation, which was instrumental in effecting political change, not only unsettles the traditional literary and political paradigms in the present, but also interrogates these paradigms' applicability to the 1950s and 1960s, and to al-Shidyaq and al-Tahtawi as well. The inability to recognize and the failure to interpret the sociopolitical context that gave rise to the Arab Spring in late 2010 is intimately tied to the master narratives that have thus far disseminated *Nahda*, postcolonial, and diasporic works. The focus on Arab intellectual debates, political ideology, and canonical texts and authors, which have been treated as "representative" of Arab culture from the nineteenth century onward, rendered *other* texts and social and political practices invisible. The failure to investigate these practices and events as a literary staging of Arab modernity produces a scholarly ivory tower, disconnected from its social and cultural context. The interpretive shift I propose in this book by exploring modes of *kashf* and "hack" is not meant to dismiss Arab intellectual debates and "high literature," but rather to deconstruct the binary oppositions through which they are produced. This deconstruction juxtaposes the canon with what is imagined as being outside of it—minor literature, vulgar texts, and poetic fragments—by reintroducing questions of experience, affect, and the encounter. This literary comparative project examined these sites as generative of new meaning with wide-ranging repercussions on literary, political, and anthropological studies. In this context, gauging these sites as staging alternative and multiple trajectories of Arab modernity— *aḥdāth mumkina*—from the *Nahda* onward puts in question the theoretical frameworks that focus exclusively on questions of representation and misrepresentation in modern Arabic literature. Arabic texts do not merely "represent" the West, tradition, and modernity, but rather decenter, produce, and dismantle them. The trials of Arab modernity arise from the literary staging of these processes and their corresponding events.

As I have shown in chapter 3, Aesop's staging of his body as a site of an alternative textuality according to Marin is an event that changes the course of the master narrative and creates new possibility of meaning and movement. Body narratives, performances, ingestions and expulsions of food and ideas, tight clothes and expressions of queerness hack models of normativity and expose in the process literary canons and systems of truth. These systems are literary and political, tied to Roger Allen's critique of the anchoring of modern Arabic literature in Mahfouz's trilogy but also in the reduction of its corpus to anticolonial struggle and the binaries of tradition and modernity within the confines of the nation state. The interplay of the literary and the political, the dynamic comparative movement across cultural registers and historical periods is excluded, sidelined, and dismissed in the majority of scholarly discussions both in the Arab world and the American academy.

The social and political developments that gripped the Arab world in late 2010 create an urgency to investigate multiple sites of literary production in *Nahda* and contemporary texts. Both in Arab public squares and in Alaidy's and his contemporaries' texts, we move from the novel as a fixed and clearly circumscribed genre and from the revolution as a clearly identifiable and consorted political action to literary and political practices emerging at the intersection of social and political contexts, technological development, and new media. These literary and political *scenes* are spaces of experimentation and trials, which produce new textualities and set in motion social and political change. Stunning pundits and intellectuals, these scenes and events characterize a systematic refashioning of questions of modernity, the state, freedom, sexuality, and literature. They also produce models of subjectivity that need to be further explored in acts of hacking and sabotage, thereby taking Arabic literary scholarship in new and unpredictable directions.

1. INTRODUCTION: DEBATING MODERNITY

Epigraph: Michel Foucault, *The Foucault Reader*, ed. Paul Rabinow (New York: Pantheon, 1984), 39.

1. Adonis makes this argument in his 1974 book *Al-Thabit wa-l-Mutahawwil: Bahth fi al-Ibda' wa-l-Itba' 'ind al-'Arab*, 4 vols. (Beirut: Dar al-Saqi, 2006). See also *An Introduction to Arab Poetics* (London: Saqi, 2003).

2. See Muhammad ibn Mukarram ibn Manzur, *Lisan al-'Arab*, ed. 'Ali Shiri, 18 vols. (Beirut: Dar Ihya' al-Turath al-'Arabi, 1988), 3–4:52–54.

3. Claire Colebrook, *Gilles Deleuze* (New York: Routledge, 2010), 57.

4. For clarity and simplification, I will be using *ahdāth* throughout the book to mean the plural of *hāditha*, *hadath*, and *hādith*.

5. Qasim Amin, *Tahrir al-Mar'a; Al-Mar'a al-Jadida* (Cairo: Al-Markaz al-'Arabi li-l-Bahth wa-l-Nashr, 1984). See also Leila Ahmad's critique of Amin's position in *Women and Gender in Islam* (New Haven: Yale University Press, 1992), 144–68.

6. Taha Hussein, *Mustaqbal al-Thaqafa fi Misr* (Cairo: Al-Hay'a al-Misriyya al-'Amma li-l-Kitab, 1993).

7. For an account of modern Arab intellectual thought and debates, see Elizabeth Suzanne Kassab, *Contemporary Arab Thought: Cultural Critique in Comparative Perspective* (New York: Columbia University Press, 2010).

8. Georges Tarabishi, *Al-Muthaqqafun al-'Arab wa-l-Turath* (London: Riad el-Rayyes, 1991).

9. Sadiq Jalal al-Azm, *Al-Naqd al-Dhati ba'd al-Hazima* (Beirut: Dar al-Tali'a, 1968). Al-Azm is not alone in undertaking such self-critique;

the 1967 defeat caused a crisis in Arab intellectual thought, bringing about a radical examination of the project of Arab modernity.

10. Talal Asad, *Formations of the Secular: Christianity, Islam, Modernity* (Stanford, Calif.: Stanford University Press, 2003).

11. Using the example of Hizbullah in Lebanon, Lara Deeb claims that articulations of modernity could be identified in a set of contemporary social practices and forms of authority (see Lara Deeb, *An Enchanted Modern: Gender and Public Piety in Shi'i Lebanon* [Princeton, N.J.: Princeton University Press, 2006]).

12. Richard Shusterman, *Body Consciousness: A Philosophy of Mindfulness and Somaesthetics* (New York: Cambridge University Press, 2008), xii.

13. Ibid.

14. Ibid., 3.

15. William Connolly, *Neuropolitics: Thinking, Culture, Speed* (Minneapolis: University of Minnesota Press, 2002), 61.

16. Ibid., 44.

17. See also the work of Martha Nussbaum, who reintroduces emotions into legal and political analyses. Emotions, according to her, are constitutive of the legal apparatus and thus play a crucial role in cementing communal bonds (Martha Craven Nussbaum, *Hiding from Humanity: Disgust, Shame, and the Law* [Princeton, N.J.: Princeton University Press, 2004]).

18. Charles Hirschkind, *The Ethical Soundscape: Cassette Sermons and Islamic Counterpublics* (New York: Columbia University Press, 2009), 22.

19. Ibid., 20.

20. Leigh Eric Schmidt, *Hearing Things: Religion, Illusion, and the American Enlightenment* (Cambridge, Mass.: Harvard University Press, 2002).

21. Hirschkind, *Ethical Soundscape*, 18.

22. For an engagement with questions of experience, encounter, and the Derridean metaphysics of presence, see John Borneman and Abdellah Hammoudi, eds., *Being There: The Fieldwork Encounter and the Making of Truth* (Berkeley: University of California Press, 2009), esp. 237–58.

23. Brian Massumi, *Parables for the Virtual: Movement, Affect, Sensation* (Durham, N.C.: Duke University Press, 2002), 27.

24. Melissa Gregg and Gregory J. Seigworth, "An Inventory of Shimmers," in *Affect Theory Reader*, ed. Gregg and Seigworth (Durham, N.C.: Duke University Press, 2010), 1–25, 1.

25. Rei Terada, *Feeling in Theory: Emotion after the "Death of the Subject"* (Cambridge, Mass.: Harvard University Press, 2003).

26. Kaja Silverman, *Flesh of My Flesh* (Stanford, CA: Stanford University Press, 2009), 26.

27. Eve Kosofsky Sedgwick, *Touching Feeling: Affect, Pedagogy, Performativity* (Durham, N.C.: Duke University Press, 2003), 6–7.

28. Ibid., 6.

29. Ibid., 7. For a discussion of the "performative," see Jonathan Culler, *The Literary in Theory* (Stanford, Calif.: Stanford University Press, 2007), 137–65.

30. For a critique of the logic of Arabic literary "genesis," see Samah Selim, "The Narrative Craft: Realism and Fiction in the Arabic Canon," *Edebiyat* 14.1–2 (2003): 109–28, 114.

31. Gayatri Chakravorty Spivak, *Death of a Discipline* (New York: Columbia University Press, 2003), 55.

32. Natalie Melas, *All the Difference in the World: Postcoloniality and the Ends of Comparison* (Stanford, Calif.: Stanford University Press, 2006), 39.

33. Ibid., 38.

34. Roger Allen, "Literary History and the Arabic Novel," *World Literature Today* 75.2 (2001): 205–13. Mahfouz's trilogy consists in *Bayn al-Qasrayn*, *Qasr al-Shawq*, and *Al-Sukkariyya* [*Palace Walk, Palace of Desire*, and *Sugar Street*] (1956–57).

35. Marilyn Booth made this statement at University of Texas at Austin, January 26, 2010.

36. Edward Said, introduction to Halim Barakat's 1969 novel *'Awdat al-Ta'ir ila al-Bahr* [*Days of Dust*] (Washington, D.C.: Three Continents Press, 1983), ix–xxxiv, xxi.

37. Muhsin al-Musawi, *The Postcolonial Arabic Novel: Debating Ambivalence* (Leiden: Brill, 2003), 68–69.

38. Muhsin al-Musawi, *Islam on the Street: Religion in Modern Arabic Literature* (Plymouth, U.K.: Rowman and Littlefield, 2009), 109–25.

39. Sedgwick, *Touching*, 8.

40. Edward Said, *Humanism and Democratic Criticism* (New York: Columbia University Press, 2004), 13.

41. Ibid., 6.

42. Ibid.

43. Ibid., 59. Addressing literary reception and exchange between Persia, the Arab world, and Europe by situating modernity in innovations and the social transformation of the role of literature in the nineteenth century, Kamran Rastegar addresses Said's reclaiming of philology in the conclusion to his book *Literary Modernity between the Middle East and Europe: Textual Transactions in*

Nineteenth-Century Arabic, English, and Persian Literatures (New York: Routledge, 2007), 145–48.

44. For a recent comparative example of such analysis, see Sahar Amer, *Crossing Borders: Love between Women in Medieval French and Arabic Literatures* (Philadelphia: University of Pennsylvania Press, 2008).

45. See Rasheed el-Enany, *Arab Representations of the Occident: East West Encounters in Arabic Fiction* (New York: Routledge, 2006).

46. See Dipesh Chakrabarty, *Provincializing Europe: Postcolonial Thought and Historical Difference* (Princeton, N.J.: Princeton University Press, 2000).

47. For an example of this, see Stefan G. Meyer, *The Experimental Arabic Novel* (Albany: State University of New York Press, 2000).

48. Albert Hourani, *Arabic Thought in the Liberal Age (1798–1939)* (New York: Cambridge University Press, 1983).

2. FANTASY OF THE IMAM

Epigraph: Montesquieu, *Persian Letters*, translated by Margaret Mauldon (Oxford: Oxford University Press, 2008), 30.

1. Samer Ali, *Arabic Literary Salons in the Islamic Middle Ages: Poetry, Public Performance, and the Presentation of the Past* (Notre Dame, Ind.: University of Notre Dame Press, 2010), 93. Ali argues that Ibn al-Jahm was in fact a Baghdadi but that the Sufi reception of the poet presented him as a country bumpkin undergoing aesthetic maturity and personal growth in Baghdad.

2. Ibid., 92.

3. Ibid., 88.

4. Ibrahim Abu-Lughod, *Arab Rediscovery of Europe* (Princeton, N.J.: Princeton University Press, 1963).

5. Rifaʿa Rafiʿ al-Tahtawi, *Takhlis al-Ibriz fi Talkhis Bariz aw al-Diwan al-Nafis bi-Iwan Baris* (Beirut: Al-Muʾassassa al-ʿArabiyya li-l-Dirasat wa-l-Nashr, 2002). The title literally means "Extraction of pure gold in the abridgement of Paris." Unless indicated otherwise, for the English translation I use Daniel Newman, *An Imam in Paris: Al-Tahtawi's Visit to France (1826–1831)* (London: Saqi, 2004).

6. Khaled Bayomi, "*Nahdah* Visions and Political Realities in the Arab East," in the Third Nordic Conference on Middle Eastern Studies: Ethnic Encounter and Culture Change, Joensuu, Finland, 19–22 June, 1995, www.smi.uib.no/paj/Bayomi.html. See also Ezzat Orany, "'Nation,' 'patrie,' 'citoyen' chez Rifaʿa al-Tahtawi et Khayr-al-Din

al-Tunisi," *Mélanges de l'institut Dominicain d'études orientales du Caire* 16 (1983): 169–90.

7. See Hourani, *Arabic Thought in the Liberal Age.*

8. Al-Musawi, *Islam on the Street,* xxiii.

9. Gilbert Delanoue describes these poems "dont Rifaʿa aime à far-cir son texte, selon les exigences du bon style de l'époque" [with which Rifaʿa likes to stuff his text, in accordance with the stylistic conven-tions of the time] (my translation) (Gilbert Delanoue, *Moralistes et politiques Musulmans dans l'Egypte du XIXème siècle [1798–1882]* [Lille, France: Service de Reproduction des Thèses, Université de Lille III, 1980], 395). Daniel Newman points out that "the relation between the poems and the text to which they are supposed to refer is usu-ally tenuous and always contrived" (Newman, introduction to *Imam,* 15–92, 91).

10. Ibid., 96, 100.

11. Ibid., 86.

12. This scholarship includes the works of Adonis, Hisham Shar-abi, Hazem Nuseibeh, and Ibrahim Abu-Lughod.

13. Muhammad ʿAli's "destruction of the systems of tax-farms and interference with *awqāf* [religious endowments] struck at the root of their (*ulamāʾ*) social position and of the system of Islamic schools. In their place and that of the Mamluks, he formed a ruling group which included Turkish, Kurdish, Albanian, Circassian soldiers, and also Europeans, Armenians, and others conversant with the politics and finances of Europe" (Hourani, *Arabic Thought,* 52). This was aimed at forming a "mercenary" aristocratic class, loyal only to Muham-mad ʿAli and through which he would govern Egypt (Anouar Louca, *ʿAwdat Rifʿat al-Tahtawi* [Susa, Tunisia: Dar al-Maʿarif li-l-Tibaʿa wa-l-Nashr, 1997], 68).

14. While he initiated the process of "westernization," Muham-mad ʿAli, writes Hourani, had no interest in the "political ideas of Europe" (Hourani, *Arabic Thought,* 52).

15. Ibid.

16. Anouar Louca suggests that the idea to send an Egyptian mis-sion to France was formulated in 1812 by Edmé-François Jomard (see Anouar Louca, *Voyageurs et écrivains Egyptiens en France au XIX siècle* [Paris: Éditions Didier, 1970], 33). It is all the more important that Jomard, who later becomes the supervisor of the first mission, takes special interest in al-Tahtawi's education. From 1831 to 1849, there were up to 360 Egyptian students studying various disciplines in European cities (Newman, introduction, 79).

17. Delanoue, *Moralistes,* 365.

18. Anouar Louca, *L'Or de Paris* (Paris: Éditions Sindbad, 1988), 11–35.

19. As a result of his encounters with the French at L'Institut d'Egypte during the occupation, al-'Attar, rector of al-Azhar from 1831 to 1834, advocates the critical borrowing from Europe (Delanoue, *Moralistes*, 329–39). For a recent investigation of al-'Attar's relation to the French in Egypt, see Shaden Tageldin, *Disarming Words: Empire and the Seductions of Translation in Egypt* (Berkeley: University of California Press, 2011), 66–107.

20. At Bulaq (Cairo's port), Napoleon established Egypt's first printing press in 1798. Closed after the French evacuation in 1801, Bulaq reopened in 1821 under Muhammad 'Ali for the publication of mostly scientific and military books in translation (Mundhir Ma'aliqi, *Ma'alim al-Fikr al-'Arabi fi 'Asr al-Nahda al-'Arabiyya* [Beirut: Dar Iqra', 1986], 90). For a complete list of Bulaq's publications from 1822 to 1843, see "Catalogue Général," *Journal Asiatique* 4.2 (1843): 24–61.

21. C. E. Dawn, "Ottomanism to Arabism: The Origin of an Ideology," in *The Modern Middle East*, ed. Albert Hourani, Phillip Khoury, and Mary Wilson (Berkeley: University of California Press, 1993), 375–393, 378.

22. Newman, introduction, 44.

23. Ibid., 90.

24. Al-Tahtawi, *Imam*, 99/*Takhlis*, 23.

25. Abu-Lughod writes that before the nineteenth century, Arab travelers to Europe were scarce, and consisted of such people as Fakhr al-Din, Emir of Mount-Lebanon, who traveled to Tuscany. Other travelers were Lebanese students who went to Italy to study theology but did not write travel narratives or anything of the kind. The impetus to travel to and to write about Europe starts again at the beginning of the nineteenth century with Muhammad 'Ali's missions to France (Abu-Lughod, *Arab Rediscovery*, 67). In "Travel Books in Modern Arabic Literature" (*Muslim World* 52 [1962]: 207–15), Anwar G. Chejne, in addition to listing the various Arab travelers to Europe in the nineteenth century, mentions the trips of Ilyas ibn Hanna of Mosul from 1668 to 1683 to Europe and America, and of Makariyus, Patriarch of Aleppo, to the Balkans and Russia in the middle of the seventeenth century (ibid., 210). For a detailed account of Arab travelers to Europe in the seventeenth century, see Nabil Matar, ed., *In the Lands of the Christians: Arab Travel Writing in the Seventeenth Century* (New York: Routledge, 2002). See also Louca, *Voyageurs*, 13–24.

26. Niqula ibn Yusuf al-Turk, *Histoire de l'expédition des Français en Egypte* (1839) (Cairo: L'imprimerie de l'institut Français d'archéologie orientale, 1950).

27. See *Rihlat al-Saffar ila Faransa (1845–1846)* (Beirut: Al-Mu'assassa al-'Arabiyya li-l-Dirasat wa-l-Nashr, 2007).

28. Mohammed Sawaie, "Rifa'a Rafi' al-Tahtawi and his Contribution to the Lexical Development of Modern Literary Arabic," *International Journal of Middle Eastern Studies* 32 (2000): 395–410, 401.

29. Ibid., 405.

30. Myriam Salama-Carr, "Negotiating Conflict: Rifa'a Rafi' al-Tahtawi and the Translation of the 'Other' in Nineteenth-Century Egypt," *Social Semiotics* 17.2 (2007): 213–27, 217.

31. Ibid., 219.

32. Ibid., 223.

33. Tageldin, *Disarming Words*, 132.

34. Khaled Fahmy argues that nationalist readings of Muhammad 'Ali's rise to power and modernization of Egypt's infrastructure through "westernization" rely on the imaginary continuity of an Egyptian national model traceable to Egypt's pharaonic past. Fahmy argues that Muhammad 'Ali, as governor of Egypt, expressed his military and political power within the framework of his Ottoman authority rather than as the nationalist ruler of the Egyptian state in the nineteenth century (Khaled Fahmy, *All the Pasha's Men* [New York: Cambridge University Press, 1997], 26).

35. Newman, introduction, 71.

36. Walter Benjamin, *Illuminations*, ed. Hannah Arendt and trans. Harry Zohn (New York: Schocken, 1968), 162.

37. Ibid., 157.

38. Quoted in Walter Benjamin, *The Writer of Modern Life: Essays on Charles Baudelaire*, ed. Michael Jennings and trans. Howard Eiland et al. (Cambridge, Mass.: Belknap Press of Harvard University Press, 2006), 13.

39. Ibid., 20.

40. Ibid., 21–22.

41. For a detailed description of the trip and the mission in general, see Louca, *Voyageurs*, "L'Ecole Egyptienne de Paris," 33–54.

42. Al-Tahtawi, *Imam*, 137–38/*Takhlis*, 56–57.

43. To anchor the pre-Islamic anxiety of departure, we can consider the ambivalence of al-Shanfara's idiomatic construction in the pre-Islamic ode, *Lamiyyat al-'Arab*, in which the ṣu'lūk's abandonment of the campsite is presented as the tribe's own departure: *aqīmū banī ummī ṣudūra maṭiyyikum, fa-innī li-qawmin siwākum la-amyalu* (Get up the chest of your camels and leave, sons of my mother. I lean to a tribe other than you) (Michael Sells, trans., *Desert Tracings* [Middletown, Conn.: Wesleyan University Press, 1989], 24).

44. ʿAbd al-Rahman al-Jabarti, *History of Egypt*, trans. and ed. Thomas Philipp and Moshe Perlmann, 4 vols. (Stuttgart: Franz Steiner Verlag, 1994), 3:15.

45. Al-Jabarti describes the soldiers' desecration of al-Azhar mosque and school during a revolt a few months into the occupation.

46. It was common that Muslim travelers to Europe in the nineteenth century justified their trips in the name of the pursuit of scientific knowledge (see H. Pérès, "Voyageurs musulmans en Europe aux XIXe et XXe siècles," *Mémoires de l'institut Francais d'archéologie orientale* 68 [1935]: 185–95).

47. *Riḥla* in medieval Arabic texts refers to the trip for the acquisition of knowledge. Al-Tahtawi's use of *imtaṭaynā* (ride) to describe his embarkment anchors the trip in the *riḥla* genre. The well-known representatives of this genre are Ibn Jubayr's (1145–1217) trip from Granada to Mecca and Ibn Battuta's (1304–1369) travels all the way to China. In Ibn Battuta's case, the *riḥla* intersects with the genre of *ʿajāʾib* (marvels) because his trip involves encounters and destinations that could not be confirmed or explained historically (see I. R Netton, "Riḥla," *Encyclopaedia of Islam*, 2nd ed., ed. P. Bearman et al. [Brill Online], www.brillonline.nl/subscriber/entry?entry=islam_SIM-6298).

48. Louca, *ʿAwdat*, 82–83.

49. Al-Tahtawi, *Takhlis*, 69.

50. Al-Tahtawi, *Imam*, 153.

51. Al-Tahtawi, *Takhlis*, 68.

52. Al-Tahtawi, *Imam*, 153.

53. Louca, *ʿAwdat*, 116.

54. Jacques Lacan, *Ecrits* (Paris: Éditions du Seuil, 1966), 94.

55. Louca, *ʿAwdat*, 117.

56. In his reading of the "world as exhibition" and critique of orientalist and colonial ordering mechanism in the nineteenth century, Timothy Mitchell refers to al-Tahtawi's stay in France and his encounter with the mirrors in Marseille more specifically. Mitchell argues that Arab travelers in Europe were "Objects on exhibit." Al-Tahtawi and his colleagues were parodied in a vaudeville play. They experienced the advent of visual mimicry, simulacra, and a new "dialectics of seeing" brought about by the Arcades project in Paris in the 1820s, and, later on, the exhibitions. Al-Tahtawi's experience in the café could thus be read in light of an unsettling collapse of reality and appearance (see Timothy Mitchell, *Colonising Egypt* [Berkeley: University of California Press, 1991], 4–5, 12).

57. Louca clearly observes that al-Tahtawi's quoting of Arabic poetry

in this encounter constitutes a return to his Arab-Islamic roots, and more specifically, to the pre-Islamic or *jāhilī* poetic genre, in which the author conjures up the beloved at the site of ruins. However, he claims that this is indicative of *ta'alluq* (maturity, brilliance) (Louca, *'Awdat*, 119), ignoring the Lacanian context upon which he seeks to draw.

58. Benjamin, *Writer*, 16.

59. Susan Buck-Morss, *Dialectics of Seeing: Walter Benjamin and the Arcades Project* (Cambridge: MIT Press, 1991), 186.

60. Al-Tahtawi, *Takhlis*, 79.

61. Al-Tahtawi, *Imam*, 164.

62. Al-Tahtawi, *Takhlis*, 80.

63. Al-Tahtawi, *Imam*, 164.

64. Al-Tahtawi, *Takhlis*, 80.

65. Al-Tahtawi, *Imam*, 165.

66. Al-Tahtawi, *Takhlis*, 80.

67. Al-Tahtawi writes the poem in order to celebrate Muhammad 'Ali's and his son Ibrahim's victory over the Ottomans at Acre in 1831 (Delanoue, *Moralistes*, 434).

68. Baudelaire's encounter with the weather echoes al-Tahtawi's both emphasizing the experience of impotence. Benjamin references Baudelaire's representation of his experience of the weather in *Spleen et Idéal*, LXXVII, Spleen III:

Je suis comme le roi d'un pays pluvieux,
Riche, mais impuissant [impotent], jeune et pourtant très vieux

[I'm like the king of a rainy country,
Rich but helpless, decrepit though still a young man] (Benjamin, *Writer*, 3)

The same imagery is repeated in the poem "Spleen" from *Les Fleurs du mal*:

Quand le ciel bas et lourd pèse comme un couvercle
Sur l'esprit gémissant en proie aux longs ennuis,
Et que de l'horizon embrassant tout le cercle,
Nous verse un jour noir plus triste que les nuits (Charles Baudelaire, *Les Fleurs du mal* [Paris: Éditions Gallimard, 1964], 88)

[When the low, heavy sky weighs like a lid
On the groaning spirit, victim of long ennui,
And from the all-encircling horizon
Spreads over us a day gloomier than the night] (Geoffrey Wagner, *Selected Poems of Charles Baudelaire* [New York: Grove, 1974], http://fleursdumal .org/poem/161)

These moments, linked to the weather particularly, further tie in al-Tahtawi's experience in Paris to Baudelaire's in Benjamin's reading.

The play of light and the experience of gloom are urban settings that trigger poetic association. These encounters emphasize the subject's experience of pain and fragmentation. The modern encounter is thus one involving a violent confrontation with modernity in terms of technological development, urban landscape, and weather.

69. Al-Tahtawi, *Takhlis*, 200–201.

70. Ibid., 193.

71. Ibid.

72. Al-Tahtawi, *Imam*, 273.

73. Moreover, given the strong sexual connotation of the word *watar* (aim; the phrase *qaḍāʾ al-watar* could mean sexual gratification), this term thus characterizes his task as a fulfillment of a sexual desire, which al-Tahtawi emphasizes by using the expression *qaḍāʾ al-awtār* in describing sex and prostitution in Paris elsewhere in *Takhlis* (al-Tahtawi, *Takhlis*, 97).

74. Ibid., 193–94.

75. Al-Tahtawi, *Imam*, 273.

76. Ibid., 194.

77. The verses are from a poem al-Mutanabbi composed in praise of Dallir bin Lashakruz, a commander who rushed to the rescue of al-Mutanabbi's hometown, Kufa, when the Banu Kalb tribe invaded in 961 (Abi al-ʿAlaʾ al-Maʿarri, *Sharh Diwan al-Mutanabbi*, ed. ʿAbd al-Majid Diab, 4 vols. [Cairo: Dar al-Maʿarif, 1992], 4:260).

78. Al-Tahtawi substitutes the word *luqyān* (attaining, receiving) in al-Mutanabbi's verse for the word *idrāk* (catching up, becoming aware, realizing). This substitution, though it doesn't fundamentally change the meaning of the verse, calls attention to the introduction of an epistemological category characterized by movement and speed. *Adrak* means "to catch up with something by taking it off guard," but also "to become aware of it and realize it in the process."

79. Ali, *Salons*, 98.

80. Ibid., 112.

81. This rearticulation will take a different turn during al-Tahtawi's exile in the Sudan following Muhammad ʿAli's death. While serving his *sentence* from 1850 to 1854, al-Tahtawi translates *Les Aventures de Télémaque* (1699), a mirror-for-princes work by François Fénélon (1651–1715). The book serves as a critique of autocratic rule (Newman, introduction, 53).

82. This section was added to *Takhlis*'s second edition. While it figures in the recent Arabic editions of *Takhlis*, it is not included in Newman's translation, just alluded to in a footnote (al-Tahtawi, *Imam*, 188), so I use my translation to render the encounter.

83. Al-Tahtawi, *Takhlis*, 108.

84. Ibid.

85. Ibid. It is important to keep in mind that al-Farabi was a close reader of Plato.

86. Ibid.

87. This reading casts in a new (comparative) light the debates on the relation between the intellectual and power (*al-muthaqqaf wa-l-sulṭa*) theorized by such thinkers as Edward Said (*Representations of the Intellectual* [New York: Vintage, 1996]); Abdallah Laroui (*Al-ʿArab wa-l-Fikr al-Tarikhi* [Casablanca: Al-Markaz al-Thaqafi al-ʿArabi, 1992]); Saad Eddin Ibrahim (*Azmat al-Muthaqqafin wa-l-Thaqafa al-ʿArabiyya* [Cairo: Markaz ibn Khaldun li-l-Dirasat al-Inmaʾiyya, 2006]); Samah Idris (*Al-Muthaqqaf al-ʿArabi wa-l-Sulta* [Beirut: Dar al-Adab, 1992]); and Muhammad ʿAbed al-Jabiri (*Al-Muthaqqafun fi al-Hadara al-ʿArabiyya: Mihnat ibn Hanbal wa-Nakbat ibn Khaldun* [Beirut: Markaz Dirasat al-Wihda al-ʿArabiyya, 1995]).

88. This is from Baudelaire's poem "Invitation au voyage" (*Les Fleurs du mal*), referenced earlier in my discussion of Benjamin (Benjamin, *Writer*, 21–22).

89. Al-Musawi, *Islam*, 17.

3. AVERSION TO CIVILIZATION

First epigraph: Jonathan Swift. *The Works of Jonathan Swift*, 19 vols. (Edinburgh: A. Constable, 1814), 7:457.

Second epigraph: Quoted in Immanuel Kant, *Anthropology, History, and Education*, ed. Günter Zöller and Robert B. Louden (New York: Cambridge University Press, 2007), 269.

1. For a definition of *ʿaṣabiyya* (group solidarity) and a discussion of its association with the rise and fall of empires, see Ibn Khaldun, *Al-Muqaddima* (Beirut: Dar Ihyaʾ al-Turath al-ʿArabi, 1960), 128–42. Just as the Bedouins benefited from *ʿaṣabiyya* in order to create the Islamic Empire, the Osman clan benefited from it in order to create the Ottoman Empire (Delanoue, *Moralistes*, 64).

2. Rifaʿa Rafiʿ al-Tahtawi, *Kitab al-Murshid al-Amin li-l-Banat wa-l-Banin* (1872), *Aʿmal* (Beirut: Al-Muʾassassa al-ʿArabiyya li-l-Dirasat wa-l-Nashr, 1973), 2:469–70.

3. Ahmad Faris al-Shidyaq, *Al-Wasita fi Maʿrifat Ahwal Malta wa-Kashf al-Mukhabbaʾ ʿan Funun Urubba* (Beirut: Al-Muʾassassa al-ʿArabiyya li-l-Dirasat wa-l-Nashr, 2004). *Tamaddun* (civilization) and *funūn ūrūbbā* (arts of Europe) are used interchangeably in this edition's title, which is composed of two separate books. The Malta

travelogue, first published in 1836, is republished along with *Kashf* in 1863. These two books are often published together but are in fact two separate works (Aziz al-Azmeh and Fawwaz Trabulsi, eds., introduction to *Ahmad Faris al-Shidyaq: Silsilat al-A'mal al-Majhula* [henceforth: *A'mal*] [London: Riad el-Rayyes, 1995], 7–47, 11).

4. For an excellent study of food consumption and aversion as sites of negotiating social and political identities in the Indian subcontinent's colonial context, see Parama Roy, *Alimentary Tracts: Appetites, Aversions, and the Postcolonial* (Durham, N.C.: Duke University Press, 2010). Her work reintroduces "often-overlooked social and bodily grammars of colonial encounter and postcolonial development—grammars that can substantially recast existing accounts of events, communities, and persons" (ibid., 24).

5. See al-Azmeh and Trabulsi, introduction, 12–25.

6. Al-Shidyaq's biographer, 'Imad al-Solh, puts this date at 1826. Al-Solh also contests a number of assumptions about al-Shidyaq's life and cultural production (see 'Imad al-Solh, *Ahmad Faris al-Shidyaq: Atharuh wa-'Asruh* [Beirut: Sharikat al-Matbu'at li-l-Tawzi' wa-l-Nashr, 1987], 31).

7. For an excellent article on al-Shidyaq's translation of the Bible, see Nadia al-Bagdadi, "The Cultural Function of Fiction: From the Bible to Libertine Literature. Historical Criticism and Social Critique in Ahmad Faris al-Shidyaq," *Arabica* 46.3–4 (1999): 375–401.

8. Al-Azmeh and Trabulsi, introduction, 30.

9. For a detailed discussion of *Al-Jawa'ib*'s history and publications, see al-Solh, *Al-Shidyaq*, 85–133.

10. *Leg over Leg: Volume 1*, trans. Humphrey Davies (New York: New York University Press, 2013) (forthcoming). The title is also translated as "Thigh upon Thigh on the Question of Who Am I" (see Dwight Reynolds, ed., *Interpreting the Self: Autobiography in the Arabic Tradition* [Berkeley: University of California Press, 2001], 58).

11. Sabry Hafez, who argues that *Saq* is the first autobiographical text of modern Arabic literature, understands its title, *Saq 'ala al-Saq*, as a posture of affront deployed to herald its acceptability in the new paradigm of civilization and savoir-faire, Europe-like (Sabry Hafez, "The Language of the Self: Autobiographies and Testimonies," *Alif: Journal of Comparative Poetics* 22 [2002]: 7–33, 20). Radwa Ashour argues that *Saq* is a modern *maqāma* (Radwa Ashour, *Al-Hadatha al-Mumkina: Al-Shidyaq wa-l-Saq 'ala al-Saq, al-Riwaya al-Ula fi al-Adab al-'Arabi al-Hadith* [Cairo: Dar al-Shorouk, 2009], 36). Originating in the tenth century with the work of Badi' al-Zaman al-Hamadhani (967–1007), the *maqāma* is a rhymed narrative about

a vagrant character engaging in various adventures and tricks in the marketplace. The picaresque is thought to have its roots in the *maqāma* (see "Maqāma," in *Encyclopedia of Arabic literature*, ed. Julie Scott Meisami and Paul Starkey, 2 vols. (London: Routledge, 1998), 2:507–8; see also Roger Allen, *The Arabic Literary Heritage: The Development of its Genres and Criticism* [New York: Cambridge University Press, 1998], 270).

12. Ahmad Faris al-Shidyaq, *Al-Saq 'ala al-Saq fi ma huwa al-Faryaq, aw Ayyam wa-Shuhur wa A'wam fi 'Ajam al-'Arab wa-l-A'jam* (Beirut: Dar Maktabat al-Hayat, 1966), 83. For the critical reference, see Al-Azmeh and Trabulsi, introduction, 32–33.

13. Rastegar, *Literary Modernity*, 107.

14. Sabry Hafez, Nadia al-Bagdadi, Radwa Ashour, Dwight Reynolds, and a few others make this argument.

15. Al-Bagdadi, "Cultural Function," 397.

16. Ashour, *Al-Hadatha*, 133.

17. I refer here to the works of Kamran Rastegar, Nadia al-Bagdadi, Radwa Ashour, and others, all referenced in this chapter.

18. Ahmad ibn Fadlan, *Rihlat ibn Fadlan: Ila Bilad al-Turk wa-l-Rus wa-l-Saqaliba* (Beirut: Al-Mu'assassa al-'Arabiyya li-l-Dirasat wa-l-Nashr, 2003), 67.

19. Ibid., 109.

20. Ibid., 103.

21. Ibid., 106.

22. In addition to Voltaire and Montesquieu, al-Shidyaq is compared in the European tradition to Swift and Rabelais, among others.

23. Edward Said, *Orientalism* (New York: Vintage, 1979), 176.

24. Al-Shidyaq, *Kashf*, 190. All translations of al-Shidyaq's texts and secondary Arabic sources quoted in this chapter are mine.

25. Homi Bhabha, *The Location of Culture* (New York: Routledge, 1994), 66.

26. Al-Shidyaq, *Kashf*, 368.

27. Selection from *Al-Jawa'ib* in al-Shidyaq, *A'mal*, 209.

28. Ibid., 267.

29. Norbert Elias, *The Civilizing Process: Sociogenetic and Psychogenetic Investigations*, trans. Edmund Jephcott and ed. Eric Dunning, Johan Goudsblom, and Stephen Mennell (Oxford: Blackwell, 2000), 5.

30. For *kashf*'s various meanings, see Ibn Manzur, *Lisan*, 13–14:72–73.

31. Al-Shidyaq, *Kashf*, 501–3.

32. While *mawrid* means "source, resource, site, and place," *wakhīm*

means "unhealthy, pernicious, and indigestible" (Ibn Manzur, *Lisan*, 15–16:175, 190–92).

33. For a detailed study of phonology and linguistics in al-Shidyaq's work, see Muhammad Zarkan, *Al-Jawanib al-Lughawiyya 'ind Ahmad Faris al-Shidyaq* (Damascus: Dar al-Fikr, 1988), 70–105.

34. T. S. Eliot's *The Wasteland* (1922) had a very important impact on Arabic literary modernism (see Terri DeYoung, "T. S. Eliot and Modern Arabic Literature," *Year Book of Comparative and General Literature* 48 [2002]: 3–22).

35. Al-Azmeh and Trabulsi call the village Purley (introduction, 18–19), but it's more likely called Barley, as Geoffrey Roper remarks in "Ahmad Faris al-Shidyaq and the Libraries of Europe and the Ottoman Empire," *Libraries and Culture* 33.3 (1998): 233–48, 236.

36. Al-Shidyaq, *Kashf*, 129–30.

37. Ibid., 126.

38. *Tābūt*, which usually means "coffin," is used here to mean "dirt box" or "manure cart."

39. It's important to note that Samuel Lee was also the priest at the parish of the nearby town of Royston (Roper, "Shidyaq," 236). Furthermore, in *Saq*, al-Shidyaq relates how a priest in Mount Lebanon offers him a piece of bread that was so hard and stale it almost broke his tooth. This humorous episode should be read as a satirical and embodied critique of the church (al-Shidyaq, *Saq*, 135–36).

40. See Usama Makdisi, *Artillery of Heaven: American Missionaries and the Failed Conversion of the Middle East* (Ithaca, N.Y.: Cornell University Press, 2008), 103–37.

41. Al-Bagdadi notes that upon learning of his brother's death, al-Shidyaq heads to Malta and starts working with the Protestant missionaries there (al-Bagdadi, "Cultural Practices," 398). Although this immediate departure is due to concern for his personal safety, it should also be read as a form of displacement of a traumatic experience. Furthermore, al-Shidyaq's son dies while residing in the village. The death of the son and of the brother should be aligned here as well.

42. Louis Marin, *Food for Thought*, trans. Mette Hjort (Baltimore: Johns Hopkins University Press, 1997), 45.

43. Ibid., 48.

44. Ibid.

45. Ibid., 51.

46. Ibid.

47. Ibid., 53.

48. In *Saq*, al-Shidyaq satirizes Faryaq's reception in the streets of

London when he describes how people would gather around him and his wife, unable to distinguish their gender due to their foreign garments (al-Shidyaq, *Saq*, 435).

49. Compounding this view with his description of the eating manners of the upper class, al-Shidyaq describes their lack of hygiene as they eat without adequately cleaning their hands and in fact touching their hair and other parts afterward (al-Shidyaq, *Kashf*, 169). From scarcity of food and lack of culinary sophistication to poor hygiene, his reading of food and reactions to British eating habits undermine the unity of the concept of civilization, blurring its imagined binary opposition at a variety of levels.

50. For a detailed discussion of the semiotics of meat preparation, see Claude Lévi-Strauss, "Culinary Triangles," in *Food and Culture: A Reader*, ed. Carole Counihan and Penny Van Esterik (East Sussex, U.K.: Psychology Press, 1997), 28–35.

51. Al-Shidyaq, *Kashf*, 267.

52. Ibid., 268.

53. *Kashf*'s editor explains in a footnote that *jakhr* means "rotten meat smell" (ibid.). However, *jakhr* also means the liquid oozing from the rabbit's orifice in a reference to menstruation (Ibn Manzur, *Lisan*, 3–4:86). This blurs the distinction between inside and outside and captures the *mukhabba'* as that which is both hidden and flagrant at the same time. In *Kitab al-Hayawan* (Cairo: Maktabat Mustafa al-Halabi, 1965), al-Jahiz mentions that the rabbit's menstruation makes its meat disgusting to those who are sensitive to such things (232).

54. Al-Shidyaq, *Kashf*, 268–69.

55. Sigmund Freud, *Civilization and Its Discontents*, trans. James Strachey (New York: Norton, 1989), 54. Freud's text, in which he introduces the concept of *thanatos* (death drive), emerges from the horrors of World War I and coincides with the rise of fascism in Europe. His work belongs to a body of works that present European modernity or civilization following the two world wars as containing the germ of its own destruction. See also Theodor Adorno and Max Horkheimer, *Dialectic of Enlightenment*, trans. John Cumming (New York: Seabury, 1976).

56. Kristeva mentions "cette chose qui ne démarque plus . . . l'effondrement d'un monde qui a effacé ses limites" (that thing that no longer demarcates . . . the collapse of a world that erased its limits) (my translation) (Julia Kristeva, *Pouvoirs de l'horreur* [Paris: Éditions du Seuil, 1980], 11).

57. Charles Baudelaire, *The Flowers of Evil*, trans. Keith Waldrop (Middletown, Conn.: Wesleyan University Press, 2006), 42.

Les jambes en l'air, comme une femme lubrique,
Brûlante et suant les poisons,
Ouvrait d'une façon nonchalante et cynique
Son ventre plein d'exhalaisons.

Le soleil rayonnait sur cette pourriture,
Comme afin de la cuire à point,
Et de rendre au centuple à la grande Nature
Tout ce qu'ensemble elle avait joint;

Et le ciel regardait la carcasse superbe
Comme une fleur s'épanouir.
La puanteur était si forte, que sur l'herbe
Vous crûtes vous évanouir. (Baudelaire, *Les Fleurs du mal*, 42)

58. Winfried Menninghaus, *Disgust: The Theory and History of a Strong Sensation*, trans. Howard Eiland and Joel Golb (Albany: State University of New York Press, 2003), 134.

59. This is the cornerstone of the racialist, orientalist European discourse from Holbach and Montesquieu to Volney and beyond.

60. Elias, *Civilizing Process*, 103.

61. Gilles Deleuze and Félix Guattari, *Kafka: Towards a Minor Literature*, trans. Dana Polan (Minneapolis: University of Minnesota Press, 1986), 13.

62. Ibid., 20.

63. Al-Azmeh and Trabulsi, introduction, 32.

64. Al-Shidyaq, *Kashf*, 488. This is al-Shidyaq's deconstruction of the process of civilization in Elias's sense, i.e., the veiling of food preparation, which occurs "behind the scene."

65. Ibid., 488.

66. Ibid., 490.

67. Edouard Glissant, *Poétique de la relation* (Paris: Éditions Gallimard, 1990), 62.

68. Muhsin al-Musawi, *The Postcolonial Arabic Novel*, 163.

69. Edward Said, *Reflections on Exile and Other Essays* (Cambridge, Mass.: Harvard University Press, 2000), 173.

70. Al-Azmeh and Trabulsi, introduction, 24.

71. See *Dialectic of Enlightenment*.

72. Deleuze and Guattari, *Kafka*, 18.

73. Ibid.

74. In this chapter, I explore al-Shidyaq's *kashf* as a form of "hacking," unveiling, and exposing the "stink" in the system that requires to be updated and upgraded.

4. STAGING THE COLONIAL ENCOUNTER

First epigraph: Suhayl Idris, *Al-Hayy al-Latini* (Beirut: Dar al-Adab, 2006), 162.

Second epigraph: Alaa Al Aswany, *Chicago* (Cairo: Dar al-Shorouk, 2007), 171.

1. This categorization is from Rasheed el-Enany, *Arab Representations of the Occident*).

2. Waïl S. Hassan, *Tayeb Salih: Ideology and the Craft of Fiction* (Syracuse, N.Y.: Syracuse University Press, 2003), 17.

3. These narratives inspired many Arab leaders and elite who came to power in the 1950s and 1960s especially. Muhsin al-Musawi argues that Gamal 'Abd al-Nasser fashioned his persona based on Tawfiq al-Hakim's main character, Muhsin, in *'Usfur min al-Sharq*.

4. The Berber commander who conquered Spain for the Muslims in 711.

5. Edward Said argues that this staging or *scene* is the reenactment of historical and cultural forces (Said, introduction to *Days of Dust*, xx).

6. This is also staged in Arab intellectual thought, specifically in the performance of the *muthaqqaf* (intellectual), the bearer of the lost project. This is what George Tarabishi seeks to achieve through his psychoanalytic reading of the return to *turāth* (heritage) after 1967 (see Georges Tarabishi, *Al-Muthaqqafun al-'Arab wa-l-Turath*).

7. Roger Allen, *The Arabic Novel: An Historical and Critical Introduction* (Syracuse, N.Y.: Syracuse University Press, 1995), 159–60.

8. The encounter with colonial modernity is addressed and complicated in the postcolonial text through engagement with questions of mourning and hybridity. See also Abdelkebir Khatibi, *Love in Two Languages*, trans. Richard Howard (Minneapolis: University of Minnesota Press, 1990); and Homi Bhabha, *The Location of Culture*.

9. Assia Djebar, *Fantasia: An Algerian Cavalcade*, trans. Dorothy S. Blair (Portsmouth, N.H.: Heinemann, 1993), 157.

10. Tayeb Salih, *Season of Migration to the North*, trans. Denys Johnson-Davies (Oxford: Heinemann, 1970), 9.

11. Ibid., 1.

12. Ibid., 3.

13. Hassan provides August 16, 1898, as the exact date of Mustafa's birth (Hassan, *Tayeb*, 91).

14. R. S. Krishnan, "Reinscribing Conrad: Tayeb Salih's *Season of Migration to the North*," *International Fiction Review* 23.1–2 (1996): 7–15, 1–2.

15. Frantz Fanon, *Peau noire, masques blancs* (Paris: Éditions du Seuil, 1965).

16. Salih, *Season*, 30–31.

17. Al-Musawi, *The Postcolonial Arabic Novel*, 196.

18. Mustafa describes his awareness of sexuality as a *shahwa jinsiyya mubhama* (vague sexual desire) when this maternal figure wrapped her arms around him for the first time. This scene, which visually unfolds at a train station in Cairo, frames Mustafa's awareness of his sexuality (Salih, *Season*, 29/*Mawsim al-Hijra ila al-Shamal* [Beirut: Dar al-Jil, 1999], 34).

19. Joseph John and Yosif Tarawneh, "Tayeb Salih and Freud: The Impact of Freudian Ideas on 'Season of Migration to the North,'" *Arabica* 35 (1988): 328–49, 334.

20. Muhammad Siddiq, "The Process of Individuation in Al-Tayyeb Salih's Novel *Season of Migration to the North*," *Journal of Arabic Literature* 9 (1978): 67–104.

21. Saree Makdisi, "The Empire Renarrated: *Season of Migration to the North* and the Reinvention of the Present," *Critical Inquiry* 18 (1992): 804–20, 808.

22. Salih, *Season*, 34.

23. When Mustafa dies at the end, Hosna is forced to marry a man many years her senior. When he forces himself on her, Hosna kills him and then commits suicide.

24. Salih, *Mawsim*, 45/*Season*, 14–15.

25. Al-Musawi, *The Postcolonial Arabic Novel*, 197.

26. Mieke Bal, *Narratology: Introduction to the Theory of Narrative* (Toronto: University of Toronto Press, 1997), 142.

27. Ibid., 19.

28. Sigmund Freud, "Mourning and Melancholia," in *The Standard Edition of the Complete Psychological Works of Sigmund Freud*, ed. and trans. James Strachey, 24 vols. (London: Hogarth, 1953–74), 14:237–60.

29. Moneera al-Ghadeer, *Desert Voices: Bedouin Women's Poetry in Saudi Arabia* (London: Tauris, 2009), 47.

30. Cathy Caruth, ed., *Trauma: Explorations in Memory* (Baltimore: Johns Hopkins University Press, 1995), 4–5.

31. Ibid., 10.

32. Salih, *Season*, 19.

33. Sudanese-British author Jamal Mahjoub describes the battlefield of the colonial war in the Sudan as a site of disaster similar to the one depicted by Djebar. Describing Kitchener's extermination of the Sudanese at the battle of Omdurman on September 2, 1898, Mahjoub

writes: "The battle had taken only four hours or so. Four hours—and eleven thousand enemy dead at the cost of forty-eight Englishmen. A strange mixture of awe and revulsion went through [him] like a shudder: a man could not feel honour at having wreaked such havoc. The age of war was a quaint memory; this was the age of meticulous slaughter" (Jamal Mahjoub, *In the Hour of Signs* [Oxford: Heinemann, 1996], 24). This triumph of the colonial mission and modern technology, according to Mahjoub, haunts both its perpetrators and the author revisiting the scene of carnage.

34. Maurice Halbwachs argues that collective and individual memories are two interconnected and socially constructed phenomena that change as a result of historical and ideological forces (see Maurice Halbwachs, *On Collective Memory*, ed. and trans. Lewis A. Coser [Chicago: University of Chicago Press, 1992]).

35. Salih, *Season*, 45.

36. In *Specters of Marx* (1994), Jacques Derrida, the literary critic turned medium in séance, conjures up the spirits that pervade the literary text, framed through a structure of haunting. In *Hamlet*'s case, argues Derrida, the specter of the dead king exposes betrayal and murder and sets the stage for the plot's development. Manifested in the voice that comes to Hamlet, the dead king in Shakespeare's play announces the narrative and determines its trajectory. The king operates as a function of haunting. Derrida argues that "this spectral someone other looks at us, we feel ourselves being looked at by it, outside of any synchrony, even before and beyond any look on our part, according to an absolute anteriority (which may be on the order of generation, of more than one generation) and asymmetry." For Derrida, the specter is a "present absence" that sees without being seen. Haunting is coextensive with this moment of origin, the beginning of consciousness—plot, narrative, and subjectivity (Jacques Derrida, *Specters of Marx: The State of the Debt, the Work of Mourning, and the New International*, trans. Peggy Kamuf [New York: Routledge, 1994], 7).

37. Salih, *Season*, 34.

38. For an exploration of the question of masculinity and masquerade, see Waïl S. Hassan, "Gender (and) Imperialism: Structures of Masculinity in Tayeb Salih's *Season of Migration to the North*," *Men and Masculinities* 5.3 (2003): 309–24. For an article exploring the question of hybridity in the relation between the narrator and Mustafa, see Patricia Geesey, "Cultural Hybridity and Contamination in Tayeb Salih's *Mawsim al-Hijra ila al-Shamal (Season of Migration to the North)*," *Research in African Literatures* 28 (1997): 128–39.

39. I agree with Ali Abdallah Abbas, who considers it a mistake to read Mustafa's sexual exploits as anticolonial resistance (see Ali Abdallah Abbas, "The Father of Lies: The Role of Mustafa as Second Self in *Season of Migration to the North*," in *Tayeb Salih's Season of Migration to the North: A Casebook*, ed. Mona Takieddine Amyuni [Beirut: American University of Beirut, 1985], 27).

40. Salih, *Season*, 29.

41. Ibid., 33–34.

42. Ibid., 156–57.

43. It's important to note that the French lover in Idris's *Al-Hayy al-Latini* [The Latin Quarter] is called Jeanine.

44. For a comparative reading of the figure of *Othello* in *Mawsim*, see Barbara Harlow, "Othello's *Season of Migration*," *Edebiyat* 4.2 (1979): 157–75.

45. The Battle of Lepanto between Catholic city-states (including Venice) and the Ottoman Empire in 1571, which is fictionalized in *Othello*, could be aligned with Omdurman and World War I in Salih's narrative.

46. Salih, *Season*, 31.

47. Benita Parry, "Reflections on the Excess of Empire in Tayeb Salih's *Season of Migration to the North*," *Paragraph: A Journal of Modern Critical Theory* 28.2 (2005): 72–90, 78.

48. Ibid., 155. For a discussion of this term, see Ibn Manzur, *Lisan*, 10:146–49.

49. Hassan, *Tayeb*, 17.

50. Ibn Manzur, *Lisan*, 9:430–34.

51. Ibid., 10:31–39.

52. Salih, *Season*, 164.

53. The last scene portrays the narrator swimming and almost drowning in the Nile. The novel ends with his survival, "choosing life" as a form of disentanglement from Mustafa's tale and an avoidance of the latter's fate (ibid.,169).

54. Musa al-Halool, "The Nature of the Uncanny in *Season of Migration to the North*," *Arab Studies Quarterly* 30 (2008): 31–38.

55. Parry, "Reflections," 76.

56. Ibid., 79.

57. For a comparative critique of modernity/tradition and colonial/anticolonial binaries in Salih's text, see Gayatri Chakravorty Spivak's *Death of a Discipline*, 56–66, 76–79.

58. Salih, *Season*, 95.

59. Ibid., 49–50.

60. Hassan, *Tayeb*, 87.

5. MAJNUN STRIKES BACK

First epigraph: Naguib Mahfouz, *Hams al-Junun*, in *Al-Mu'allafat al-Kamila* (henceforth: *Mu'allafat*), 4 vols. (Beirut: Maktabat Lubnan, 1990), 1:5.

Second epigraph: Gayatri Gopinath, *Impossible Desires: Queer Diasporas and South Asian Public Cultures* (Durham, N.C.: Duke University Press, 2005), 11.

Third epigraph: *Bareed Mista3jil: True Stories* (Beirut: Meem, 2009), 34. The transliteration corresponds to the actual book title, which appropriates Arabic techno-speak by substituting the letters 'ayn for "3," *hamza* for "2," and so on.

1. For an article on lesbianism in modern Arabic literature, see Hanadi al-Samman, "Out of the Closet: Representations of Homosexuals and Lesbians in Modern Arabic Literature," *Journal of Arabic Literature* 39.2 (2008): 270–310.

2. Valerie Traub, "The Past Is a Foreign Country? The Times and Spaces of Islamicate Sexuality Studies," in *Islamicate Sexualities: Translations across Temporal Geographies of Desire*, ed. Kathryn Babayan and Afsaneh Najmabadi (Cambridge, Mass.: Center for Middle Eastern Studies of Harvard University, 2008), 1–40, 2.

3. Joseph Massad, *Desiring Arabs* (Chicago: Chicago University Press, 2007), 174.

4. Michel Foucault, *History of Sexuality, Volume 1: An Introduction*, trans. Robert Hurley (New York: Vintage, 1990), 43.

5. Ibid., 57.

6. Dina al-Kassim, "Epilogue: Sexual Epistemologies, East in West," in *Islamicate Sexualities*, 297–340, 300.

7. Emily Apter, *The Translation Zone: A New Comparative Literature* (Princeton, N.J.: Princeton University Press, 2006), 6.

8. Gopinath, *Impossible Desires*, 13.

9. Hanan al-Shaykh, *Only in London*, trans. Catherine Cobham (New York: Pantheon, 2001), 1.

10. For a reading of cultural hybridity and acculturation in the novel, see Susan Alice Fischer, "Women Writers, Global Migration, and the City: Joan Riley's *Waiting in the Twilight* and Hanan al-Shaykh's *Only in London*," *Tulsa Studies in Women's Literature* 23.1 (2004): 107–20. See also Syrine Hout, "Going the Extra Mile: Redefining Identity, Home, and Family in Hanan al-Shaykh's *Only in London*," *Studies in the Humanities* 30.1–2 (2003): 29–45.

11. Al-Shaykh, *Only in London*, 2, 5.

12. Ibid., 3. Samir is an unknowing trafficker: the pet monkey he

was paid to deliver to its owner in London was in fact made to swallow diamonds.

13. Hanan al-Shaykh, *Innaha London ya 'Azizi* (Beirut: Dar al-Adab, 2001), 7.

14. Al-Shaykh, *Only in London*, 3.

15. Muhammad Hayyan al-Samman, *Khitab al-Junun fi al-Thaqafa al-'Arabiyya* (London: Riad el-Rayyes, 1993), 58. In the context of the Ottoman Empire, the shadow-play character, Karagoz, could also be mentioned as a site of performative resistance to social and political order and morality (see Dror Ze'evi, *Producing Desire: Changing Sexual Discourse in the Ottoman Middle East, 1500–1900* [Berkeley: University of California Press, 2006], 125–48).

16. Ibn Manzur, *Lisan*, 3–4:217–21.

17. See Leyla Rouhi, *Mediation and Love: A Study of the Medieval Go-Between in Key Romance and Near-Eastern Texts* (Leiden: Brill, 1999), 148–49.

18. Roger Allen, *An Introduction to Arabic Literature* (New York: Cambridge University Press, 2000), 105.

19. Al-Shaykh's use of the monkey in the novel is reminiscent of George Michael's 1987 song "Monkey." The chorus goes as follows: "Why can't you do it? Why can't you set your monkey free? Always giving in to it, do you love the monkey or do you love me? Why can't you do it? Why do I have to share my baby with a monkey?" (www.lyricsmania.com/lyrics/george_michael_lyrics_138/faith _lyrics_701/monkey _lyrics_7949.html). Furthermore, the expression "having a monkey on one's back" characterizes a drug addiction. In this context, Samir's sexuality, which he tries to tame through sedatives on the plane, thus coincides with addiction. While London operates as the junkie's paradise, the addiction characterizes an all-consuming passion that must be expressed, Majnun-like.

20. Al-Shaykh, *Only in London*, 3.

21. There are many references in the text to the monkey as *majnūn* (al-Shaykh, *Innaha London*, 44).

22. Al-Shaykh, *Only in London*, 88.

23. Ibid., 91.

24. Ibid., 91–92.

25. Foucault, *History*, 78.

26. Al-Shaykh, *Only in London*, 92–93.

27. Ibid., 150.

28. Ibid., 89–90.

29. Ibid., 149.

30. See Keith Harvey, "Describing Camp Talk: Language/Pragmatics/Politics," *Language and Literature* 9.3 (2000): 240–60.

31. Judith Butler, *Gender Trouble* (New York: Routledge, 1990), 185.

32. Realizing the precarious nature of her situation, Zahra decides to commit an act of *junūn* at a dinner party by dressing up in a flamboyant manner and dancing for the guests. This performance alienates her husband and leads him to divorce her. From *junūn*'s association with depression to *junūn* as an act of resistance to social norms, Zahra appropriates in this one instance a form of drag to protest social normativity and propriety (Hanan al-Shaykh, *The Story of Zahra*, trans. Peter Ford [New York: Anchor, 1996], 91). For a reading of Zahra's *junūn* as a form of protest, see Miriam Cooke, *Other Voices: Women's Writers on the Lebanese Civil War* (Syracuse, N.Y.: Syracuse University Press, 1996), 50–55.

33. Hamdi Abu Golayyel, *Thieves in Retirement*, trans. Marilyn Booth (Syracuse, N.Y.: Syracuse University Press, 2006), xiv.

34. Once, Sayf bought women's clothes, including a *blūza bidūn akmām* (sleeveless top) ("body" is left in the Latin script in the text), but was prevented from wearing them by his brothers, and by Gamal especially (Hamdi Abu Golayyel, *Lusus Mutaqa'idun* [Cairo: Dar Merit, 2002], 19).

35. Abu Golayyel, *Thieves*, 12.

36. Abu Golayyel, *Lusus*, 28–30.

37. Ibid., 14.

38. Ibid., 16.

39. Ibid., 28. For the etymology of *ikhtifā'* see Ibn Manzur, *Lisan*, 5–6:116–18.

40. Abu Golayyel, *Lusus*, 27.

41. Michel Foucault, *Discipline and Punish: The Birth of the Prison*, trans. Alan Sheridan (New York: Vintage, 1995), 3.

42. For a similar episode, see Youssef Idris's short story *Hiya* ["She"], in *Bayt min Lahm wa-Qisas Ukhra* [House of flesh and other stories] (Cairo: 'Alam al-Kutub, 1971).

43. See P. N. Boratav et al., "DJinn," in *Encyclopedia of Islam*, ed. P. Bearman et al., Brill Online, www.brillonline.nl/subscriber /entry?entry=islam_COM-0191.

44. Abu Golayyel, *Lusus*, 85.

45. Ibid., 28.

46. Abu Golayyel, *Thieves*, 12.

47. Khaled el-Rouayheb, *Before Homosexuality in the Arab-Islamic World, 1500–1800* (Chicago: University of Chicago Press, 2005), 85.

48. Hassan al-Imam (1919–1988) was a prolific Egyptian film-maker who adapted to the screen such Mahfouzian novels as *Midaq Alley* (1963), *Bayna al-Qasrayn* (1964), and *Qasr al-Shawq* (1967).

49. Frédéric Lagrange, "Male Homosexuality in Modern Arabic Literature," in *Imagined Masculinities: Male Identity and Culture in the Modern Middle East*, ed. Mai Ghoussoub and Emma Sinclair-Webb (London: Saqi, 2000), 169–98, 178.

50. Naguib Mahfouz, *Zuqaq al-Midaq*, in *Mu'allafat*, 1:660.

51. Ibid., 1:686.

52. Ibn Manzur, *Lisan*, 3–4:225–26.

53. Mahfouz, *Zuqaq*, 684.

54. Kifaya (*kifāya*, enough) is the Egyptian Movement for Change founded in 2004 by a number of writers, politicians, and activists critical of the Egyptian government's corruption and policies, and vehemently opposed to the *tawrīth*, the rumored handing over of power by Husni Mubarak to his son Gamal. Founded in 2008, the April 6 Youth Movement, loosely affiliated with Kifaya, was instrumental in driving the protests that led to the collapse of the Mubarak regime in January 2011.

6. HACKING THE MODERN

First epigraph: Quoted in Ursula Lindsey and Aisha Labi, "Hundreds of American Students Lie Low in Egypt, as Protests Continue," *Chronicle of Higher Education*, January 30, 2011, http://chronicle.com /article/Hundreds-of-American-Students/126159/.

Second epigraph: Interview by *Al-Jazeera Arabic TV*, February 3, 2011.

Third epigraph: Interview by *BBC Arabic Radio*, February 6, 2011.

1. In *Al-Akharun* [*The Others*] (2006), for instance, Seba Al-Herz (the author's pen name) appropriates the structure of anonymity from the *Arabian Nights* and stages the body as a site of writing, a hyper-text full of danger and unpredictability. As for Rajaa Alsanea, she claimed in some interviews that she had received death threats. In *Banat al-Riyad* [*Girls of Riyadh*] (2005), Alsanea displaces the novel to the virtual, fantasizing its origin in technology through a series of transcribed e-mails sent once a week. At some point in the novel, the narrator, who is also called Rajaa, claims that the Saudi government is threatening to shut down her Internet service due to her e-mails' scandalous nature.

2. Marie-Thérèse Abdel-Messih, "Hyper Texts: Avant-Gardism in Contemporary Egyptian Narratives," *Neohelicon* 36.2 (2009): 515–23, 515.

3. *I Want to Get Married*, trans. Nora Eltahawy (Austin: Center for Middle Eastern Studies at University of Texas, 2010).

4. Claudia Roth Pierpont, "Found in Translation: The Contemporary Arabic Novel," *New Yorker*, January 18, 2010, 74–80.

5. Samuel Shimon, ed., *Beirut 39: New Writing from the Arab World* (New York: Bloomsbury, 2010).

6. *Al-Hayat*'s literary reviewer is Hazem Abyad; *Al-Akhbar*'s is Muhammad Khayr.

7. Founded in 2010 by the Arabic Network for Human Rights Information, *Wasla* is produced entirely by bloggers (see http://wasla .anhri.net).

8. See Marilyn Booth, "Translator v. author (2007): Girls of Riyadh Go to New York," *Translation Studies* 1.2 (2008): 197–211; and Moneera Al-Ghadeer, "Girls of Riyadh: A New Technology Writing or Chick Lit Defiance," *Journal of Arabic Literature* 37.2 (2006): 296–302; and for an issue dedicated to new writing in Egypt, see *Banipal* 25 (2006).

9. For an important theoretical framework to read these texts beyond the postmodern, see Stephan Guth, "Individuality Lost, Fun Gained: Some Recurrent Motifs in Late Twentieth-Century Arabic and Turkish Novels," *Journal of Arabic and Islamic Studies* 7 (2007): 25–49. See also, for a historical and sociological investigation of cultural and literary dynamics in Egypt from the 1960s to the present, Richard Jacquemond, *Conscience of the Nation: Writers, State, and Society in Modern Egypt*, trans. David Tresilian (Cairo: American University of Cairo Press, 2008).

10. Fabio Caiani, *Contemporary Arab Fiction: Innovation from Rama to Yalu* (New York: Routledge, 2007). See also *Arabic Literature: Postmodern Perspectives*, ed. Angelika Neuwrith, Andreas Pflitsch, and Barbara Winckler (London: Saqi, 2010).

11. Stefan Meyer, *The Experimental Arabic Novel*, 17.

12. Sonallah Ibrahim, *Tilk al-Ra'iha wa-Qisas Ukhra* (Minya, Egypt: Dar al-Huda, 2003), 11.

13. Ibid., 25.

14. The reception of Ibrahim's work could be understood in the context of the fall of the *udabā'* (literati) in the 1960s. Yoav Di-Capua discussed this process in "The Arab Experience of Existentialism," a talk presented at the Middle Eastern Studies Luncheon Seminar, University of Texas at Austin, October 13, 2009.

15. Quoted in Ibrahim Farghali, http://arabblogandpoliticalcom munication.blogspot.com/2005/11/blog-post_25.html.

16. Abdel-Messih, "Hyper Texts," 521.

17. Hazem Abyad, review of *An Takun ʿAbbas al-ʿAbd*, *Al-Hayat*, December 25, 2003, www.arabworldbooks.com/ArabicLiterature /review20.htm.

18. *Being Abbas el Abd*, trans. Humphrey Davies (Cairo: American University of Cairo Press, 2006), 34; Alaidy, *ʿAbbas al-ʿAbd*, 39.

19. Ibid.

20. Ibid. 36,

21. For a discussion of the collapse of the family as a national icon in new Arabic fiction, see Samia Mehrez, *Egypt's Culture Wars: Politics and Practice* (New York: Routledge, 2008), 123–43.

22. Said, introduction, xxv.

23. Alaidy, *Being Abbas*, 51.

24. Said, introduction, xxviii–xxxix.

25. Alaidy, *Being Abbas*, 63–64.

26. Linda Hutcheon, "The Politics of Postmodernism: Parody and History," *Cultural Critique* 5 (1986–87): 179–207, 206.

27. Alaidy, *Being Abbas*, 92–93. Capitalization, spacing, and bolding are all present in the original text and translation.

28. Benedict Anderson, *Imagined Community: Reflections on the Origin and Spread of Nationalism* (London: Verso, 1983).

29. Alain Badiou, "'We Need a Popular Discipline': Contemporary Politics and the Crisis of the Negative," interview by Filippo Del Lucchese and Jason Smith, *Critical Inquiry* 34.4 (2008): 645–59.

30. Ibid., 652.

31. Ibid., 659.

32. Sabry Hafez, "The New Egyptian Novel: Urban Transformation and Narrative Form," *New Left Review* 64 (2010): 47–62, 62.

33. André Raymond, *Cairo*, trans. Willard Wood (Cambridge, Mass.: Harvard University Press, 2000); Abu-Zaid Rajih, "Al-Insan wa-l-Makan: Al-Qahira Namudhaja," *Misr: Nazra nahwa al-Mustaqbal*, ed. Shukri Muhammad ʿAyyad (Cairo: Dar Asdiqaʾ al-Kitab, 1999), 11–33.

34. Mehrez, *Egypt's Culture*, 143.

35. "Hack," which I also translate as *tansif* (*nasafa*, to blow up; *tansif*, slow and systematic process of delivering blows; undermining and intervening; manipulating the consistency of the thing). This translation emerged from a conversation with Professor Michael Cooperson (UCLA).

36. Alaidy, *Being Abbas*, 96/*ʿAbbas al-ʿAbd*, 98. There is a play on the meaning of the words *hāk* (infiltrate) and *nāk* (fuck) in this phrase.

37. See www.merriam-webster.com/netdict/hack.

38. These partners include Chuck Palahniuk, Sonallah Ibrahim, and other writers from Alaidy's milieu.

39. Muhsin al-Musawi, "Engaging Globalization in Modern Arabic Literature: Appropriation and Resistance," *Modern Language Quarterly* 68.2 (2007): 305–29. For a detailed discussion of modern Arabic literature and the postcolonial novel more specifically, see al-Musawi's *The Postcolonial Arabic Novel*.

40. Al-Musawi, "Engaging Globalization," 322.

41. Ibid., 319.

42. Ibid., 329.

43. David Damrosch, "Comparative Literature?" *PMLA* 118.2 (2003): 326–30.

44. David Damrosch, *What Is World Literature?* (Princeton, N.J.: Princeton University Press, 2003), 5.

7. CONCLUSION: WRITING THE NEW POLITICAL

1. See Samah Selim, "Fiction and Colonial Identities: Arsène Lupin in Arabic," *Middle Eastern Literatures* 13.2 (2010): 191–210; and "The People's Entertainments: Translation, Popular Fiction and the *Nahdah* in Egypt," in *Other Renaissances: A New Approach to World Literature*, ed. Brenda Dean Schilgen, Gang Zhou, and Sandra L. Gilman (New York: Palgrave Macmillan, 2007), 35–58; Elizabeth Holt, "Narrative and the Reading Public in 1870s Beirut," *Journal of Arabic Literature* 40.1 (2009): 37–70; Nabil Matar, ed., *In the Lands of the Christians*; Stephen Sheehi, *Foundations of Modern Arab Identity* (Gainesville: University of Florida Press, 2004); Kamran Rastegar, *Literary Modernity between the Middle East and Europe*; and Shaden Tageldin, *Disarming Words*.

GLOSSARY

'alim (plural, *'ulamā'*) Religious scholar.

'amāra Apartment complex, building.

'anqā' Phoenix.

Azhar (adjective, *azharite*) Islamic University and Center in Cairo.

ḥadātha Modernity.

ḥādith, ḥāditha, hadath (plural, *aḥdāth, ḥawādith*) Event, incident, episode, accident.

ḥāra Neighborhood.

iḥdāth Innovation.

ikhtifā' Disappearance.

ikhtirāq Infiltration.

iltizām *Engagement*, political commitment.

junūn Madness.

kashf Unveiling, revealing, diagnosis, report.

madḥ Praise poetry.

majnūn Mad.

mawrid Source, resource, site.

mawsim Season.

mukhabba' Hidden, concealed.

Nahda Enlightenment, revival, or Arab Renaissance beginning in the nineteenth century.

riḥla Travel narrative.

ṭālib Student.

ta'riya Stripping naked.

wakhīm Unhealthy, indigestible.

BIBLIOGRAPHY

Abbas, Ali Abdallah. "The Father of Lies: The Role of Mustafa Saʿeed as Second Self in *Season of Migration to the North*." In *Tayeb Salih's Season of Migration to the North: A Casebook*, edited by Mona Takieddine Amyuni. Beirut: American University of Beirut, 1985.

ʿAbd al-Latif, Yasser. *Qanun al-Wiratha*. Cairo: Dar Merit, 2002.

Abdel Aal, Ghada. *ʿAwza Atgawwiz*. Cairo: Dar al-Shorouk, 2008.

———. *I Want to Get Married*. Translated by Nora Eltahawy. Austin: Center for Middle Eastern Studies at University of Texas, 2010.

Abdel-Messih, Marie-Thérèse. "Hyper Texts: Avant-Gardism in Contemporary Egyptian Narratives." *Neohelicon* 36.2 (2009): 515–23.

Abu Golayyel, Hamdi. *Lusus Mutaqaʿidun*. Cairo: Dar Merit, 2002.

———. *Thieves in Retirement*. Translated by Marilyn Booth. Syracuse, N.Y.: Syracuse University Press, 2006.

Abu-Lughod, Ibrahim. *Arab Rediscovery of Europe*. Princeton, N.J.: Princeton University Press, 1963.

Abyad, Hazem. Review of *An Takun ʿAbbas al-ʿAbd*. *Al-Hayat*, December 25, 2003. www.arabworldbooks.com/ArabicLiterature/review20.htm.

Adonis. *Al-Thabit wa-l-Mutahawwil: Bahth fi al-Ibdaʿ wa-l-Itbaʿ ʿind al-ʿArab*. 4 vols. Beirut: Dar al-Saqi, 2006.

———. *An Introduction to Arab Poetics*. London: Saqi, 2003.

Adorno, Theodor, and Max Horkheimer, *Dialectic of Enlightenment*. Translated by John Cumming. New York: Seabury, 1976.

Ahmad, Leila. *Women and Gender in Islam*. New Haven: Yale University Press, 1992.

ʿAlaʾ al-Din, Muhammad. *Injil Adam*. Cairo: Dar Merit, 2006.

Alaidy, Ahmed. *An Takun 'Abbas al-'Abd*. Cairo: Dar Merit, 2003.

———. *Being Abbas el Abd*. Translated by Humphrey Davies. Cairo: American University of Cairo Press, 2006.

Ali, Samer. *Arabic Literary Salons in the Islamic Middle Ages: Poetry, Public Performance, and the Presentation of the Past*. Notre Dame, Ind.: University of Notre Dame Press, 2010.

Allen, Roger. *The Arabic Literary Heritage: The Development of its Genres and Criticism*. New York: Cambridge University Press, 1998.

———. *The Arabic Novel: An Historical and Critical Introduction*. Syracuse, N.Y.: Syracuse University Press, 1995.

———. *An Introduction to Arabic Literature*. New York: Cambridge University Press, 2000.

———. "Literary History and the Arabic Novel." *World Literature Today* 75.2 (2001): 205–13.

Alsanea, Rajaa. *Banat al-Riyad*. Beirut: Dar al-Saqi, 2006.

Amer, Sahar. *Crossing Borders: Love between Women in Medieval French and Arabic Literatures*. Philadelphia: University of Pennsylvania Press, 2008.

Amin, Qasim. *Tahrir al-Mar'a; Al-Mar'a al-Jadida*. Cairo: Al-Markaz al-'Arabi li-l-Bahth wa-l-Nashr, 1984.

Anderson, Benedict. *Imagined Community: Reflections on the Origin and Spread of Nationalism*. London: Verso, 1983.

Anton, Sinan. *I'jam*. Beirut: Dar al-Adab, 2004.

Apter, Emily. *The Translation Zone: A New Comparative Literature*. Princeton, N.J.: Princeton University Press, 2006.

Asad, Talal. *Formations of the Secular: Christianity, Islam, Modernity*. Stanford, Calif.: Stanford University Press, 2003.

Ashour, Radwa. *Al-Hadatha al-Mumkina: Al-Shidyaq wa-l-Saq 'ala al-Saq, al-Riwaya al-Ula fi al-Adab al-'Arabi al-Hadith*. Cairo: Dar al-Shorouk, 2009.

al Aswany, Alaa. *'Amarit Ya'qubyan*. Cairo: Dar Merit, 2002.

———. *Chicago*. Cairo: Dar al-Shorouk, 2007.

al-Azm, Sadiq Jalal. *Al-Naqd al-Dhati ba'd al-Hazima*. Beirut: Dar al-Tali'a, 1968.

Babayan, Kathryn, and Afsaneh Najmabadi, eds. *Islamicate Sexualities: Translations across Temporal Geographies of Desire*. Cambridge, Mass.: Center for Middle Eastern Studies at Harvard University, 2008.

Badiou, Alain. "'We Need a Popular Discipline': Contemporary Politics and the Crisis of the Negative." Interview by Filippo Del Lucchese and Jason Smith. *Critical Inquiry* 34.4 (2008): 645–59.

al-Bagdadi, Nadia. "The Cultural Function of Fiction: From the Bible to Libertine Literature. Historical Criticism and Social Critique in Ahmad Faris al-Shidyaq." *Arabica* 46.3–4 (1999): 375–401.

Bal, Mieke. *Narratology: Introduction to the theory of Narrative.* Toronto: University of Toronto Press, 1997.

Banipal 25 (2006).

Barakat, Hoda. *Hajar al-Dahk.* Beirut: Dar al-Nahar, 1990.

Bareed Mista3jil: True Stories. Beirut: Meem, 2009.

Baudelaire, Charles. *Les Fleurs du mal.* Paris: Éditions Gallimard, 1964.

———. *The Flowers of Evil.* Translated by Keith Waldrop. Middletown, Conn.: Wesleyan University Press, 2006.

———. *Selected Poems of Charles Baudelaire.* Translated by Geoffrey Wagner. New York: Grove, 1974. http://fleursdumal.org /poem/161.

Bayomi, Khaled. "*Nahdah* Visions and Political Realities in the Arab East." Paper presented at the Third Nordic Conference on Middle Eastern Studies: Ethnic Encounter and Culture Change, Joensuu, Finland, 19–22 June 1995. www.smi.uib.no/paj/Bayomi .html.

Benjamin, Walter. *Illuminations.* Edited by Hannah Arendt and translated by Harry Zohn. New York: Schocken, 1968.

———. *The Writer of Modern Life: Essays on Charles Baudelaire.* Edited by Michael Jennings and translated by Howard Eiland et al. Cambridge, Mass.: Belknap Press of Harvard University, 2006.

Bhabha, Homi. *The Location of Culture.* New York: Routledge, 1994.

Booth, Marilyn. "Translator v. Author (2007): Girls of Riyadh Go to New York." *Translation Studies* 1.2 (2008): 197–211.

Borneman, John, and Abdellah Hammoudi, eds. *Being There: The Fieldwork Encounter and the Making of Truth.* Berkeley: University of California Press, 2009.

Boratav, P. N., et al. "DJinn." In *Encyclopaedia of Islam,* edited by P. Bearman et al. Brill Online, www.brillonline.nl/subscriber/ entry?entry=islam_COM-0191.

Buck-Morss, Susan. *Dialectics of Seeing: Walter Benjamin and the Arcades Project.* Cambridge, Mass.: MIT Press, 1991.

Butler, Judith. *Gender Trouble*. New York: Routledge, 1990.

Caiani, Fabio. *Contemporary Arab Fiction: Innovation from Rama to Yalu*. New York: Routledge, 2007.

Caruth, Cathy, ed. *Trauma: Explorations in Memory*. Baltimore: Johns Hopkins University Press, 1995.

"Catalogue Général." *Journal Asiatique* 4.2 (1843): 24–61.

Chakrabarty, Dipesh. *Provincializing Europe: Postcolonial Thought and Historical Difference*. Princeton, N.J.: Princeton University Press, 2000.

Chejne, Anwar G. "Travel Books in Modern Arabic Literature." *Muslim World* 52 (1962): 207–15.

Colebrook, Claire. *Gilles Deleuze*. New York: Routledge, 2010.

Connolly, William E. *Neuropolitics: Thinking, Culture, Speed*. Minneapolis: University of Minnesota Press, 2002.

Conrad, Joseph. *Heart of Darkness*. New York: Norton, 2005.

Cooke, Miriam. *Other Voices: Women's Writers on the Lebanese Civil War*. Syracuse, N.Y.: Syracuse University Press, 1996.

Culler, Jonathan. *The Literary in Theory*. Stanford, Calif.: Stanford University Press, 2007.

al-Daif, Rashid. *Tablit al-Bahr*. Beirut: Riad el-Rayyes, 2011.

Damrosch, David. "Comparative Literature?" *PMLA* 118.2 (2003): 326–30.

———. *What Is World Literature?* Princeton, N.J.: Princeton University Press, 2003.

Dawn, C. E. "Ottomanism to Arabism: The Origin of an Ideology." In *The Modern Middle East*, edited by Albert Hourani, Phillip Khoury, and Mary Wilson, 375–93. Berkeley: University of California Press, 1993.

Deeb, Lara. *An Enchanted Modern: Gender and Public Piety in Shi'i Lebanon*. Princeton, N.J.: Princeton University Press, 2006.

Delanoue, Gilbert. *Moralistes et politiques Musulmans dans l'Egypte du XIXème siècle (1798–1882)*. Lille, France: Service de Reproduction des Thèses, Université de Lille III, 1980.

Deleuze, Gilles, and Félix Guattari. *Kafka: Towards a Minor Literature*. Translated by Dana Polan. Minneapolis: University of Minnesota Press, 1986.

Derrida, Jacques. *Specters of Marx: The State of the Debt, the Work of Mourning, and the New International*. Translated by Peggy Kamuf. New York: Routledge, 1994.

DeYoung, Terri. "T. S. Eliot and Modern Arabic Literature." *Year Book of Comparative and General Literature* 48 (2002): 3–22.

Djebar, Assia. *Fantasia: An Algerian Cavalcade.* Translated by Dorothy S. Blair. Portsmouth, N.H.: Heinemann, 1993.

Di-Capua, Yoav. "The Arab Experience of Existentialism." Talk presented at the "Middle Eastern Studies Luncheon Seminar," October 13, 2009, University of Texas at Austin.

———. "Transnational Arab Thought and the Global Culture of the 1960s." Talk presented at a conference entitled "Teaching Arab Intellectual Thought and the Changing Role of the Literati," May 7–9, 2011, Columbia University, New York.

Elias, Norbert. *The Civilizing Process: Sociogenetic and Psychogenetic Investigations.* Translated by Edmund Jephcott and edited by Eric Dunning, Johan Goudsblom, and Stephen Mennell. Oxford: Blackwell, 2000.

el-Enany, Rasheed. *Arab Representations of the Occident: East-West Encounters in Arabic Fiction.* New York: Routledge, 2006.

Fahmy, Khaled. *All the Pasha's Men.* New York: Cambridge University Press, 1997.

Fanon, Frantz. *Peau noire, masques blancs.* Paris: Éditions du Seuil, 1965.

Farghali, Ibrahim. http://arabblogandpoliticalcommunication.blogspot .com/2005/11/blog-post_25.html.

Fischer, Susan Alice. "Women Writers, Global Migration, and the City: Joan Riley's *Waiting in the Twilight* and Hanan al-Shaykh's *Only in London.*" *Tulsa Studies in Women's Literature* 23.1 (2004): 107–20.

Foucault, Michel. *Discipline and Punish: The Birth of the Prison.* Translated by Alan Sheridan. New York: Vintage, 1995.

———. *The Foucault Reader.* Edited by Paul Rabinow. New York: Pantheon, 1984.

———. *History of Sexuality, Volume 1: An Introduction.* Translated by Robert Hurley. New York: Vintage, 1990.

———. *Madness and Civilization: A History of Insanity in the Age of Reason.* Translated by Richard Howard. New York: Vintage, 1988.

Freud, Sigmund. *Civilization and Its Discontents.* Translated by James Strachey. New York: Norton, 1989.

———. "Mourning and Melancholia." In *The Standard Edition of the*

Complete Psychological Works of Sigmund Freud, 24 vols., edited and translated by James Strachey, 14:237–60. London: Hogarth, 1953–74.

Geesey, Patricia. "Cultural Hybridity and Contamination in Tayeb Salih's *Mawsim al-Hijra ila al-Shamal (Season of Migration to the North)*." *Research in African Literatures* 28 (1997): 128–39.

al-Ghadeer, Moneera. *Desert Voices: Bedouin Women's Poetry in Saudi Arabia*. London: Tauris, 2009.

———. "Girls of Riyadh: A New Technology Writing or Chick Lit Defiance." *Journal of Arabic Literature* 37.2 (2006): 296–302.

Glissant, Edouard. *Poétique de la relation*. Paris: Éditions Gallimard, 1990.

Gopinath, Gayatri. *Impossible Desires: Queer Diasporas and South Asian Public Cultures*. Durham, N.C.: Duke University Press, 2005.

Gregg, Melissa, and Gregory J. Seigworth, eds. *Affect Theory Reader*. Durham, N.C.: Duke University Press, 2010.

Guth, Stephan. "Individuality Lost, Fun Gained: Some Recurrent Motifs in Late Twentieth-Century Arabic and Turkish Novels." *Journal of Arabic and Islamic Studies* 7 (2007): 25–49.

Hafez, Sabry. *The Genesis of Arabic Narrative Discourse: A Study in the Sociology of Modern Arabic Literature*. London: Saqi, 1993.

———. "The Language of the Self: Autobiographies and Testimonies." *Alif: Journal of Comparative Poetics* 22 (2002): 7–33.

———. "The New Egyptian Novel: Urban Transformation and Narrative Form." *New Left Review* 64 (2010): 47–62.

al-Hakim, Tawfiq. *'Usfur min al-Sharq*. Cairo: Dar al-Ma'arif, 1974.

"Hack." www.merriam-webster.com/netdict/hack.

Halbwachs, Maurice. *On Collective Memory*. Edited and translated by Lewis A. Coser. Chicago: University of Chicago Press, 1992.

al-Halool, Musa. "The Nature of the Uncanny *in Season of Migration to the North*." *Arab Studies Quarterly* 30 (2008): 31–38.

Haqqi, Yahya. *Qindil Umm Hashim*. Casablanca: Dar Tubqal li-l-Nashr: 1995.

Harlow, Barbara. "Othello's *Season of Migration*." *Edebiyat* 4.2 (1979): 157–75.

Harvey, Keith. "Describing Camp Talk: Language/Pragmatics/Politics." *Language and Literature* 9.3 (2000): 240–60.

Hassan, Waïl S. "Gender (and) Imperialism: Structures of Masculinity in Tayeb Salih's *Season of Migration to the North*." *Men and Masculinities* 5.3 (2003): 309–24.

———. *Tayeb Salih: Ideology and the Craft of Fiction*. Syracuse, N.Y.: Syracuse University Press, 2003.

Haykal, Husayn. *Zaynab*. Cairo: Maktabat Nahdat Misr, 1963.

al-Herz, Seba. *Al-Akharun*. Beirut: Dar al-Saqi, 2006.

Hirschkind, Charles. *The Ethical Soundscape: Cassette Sermons and Islamic Counterpublics*. New York: Columbia University Press, 2009.

Holt, Elizabeth. "Narrative and the Reading Public in 1870s Beirut." *Journal of Arabic Literature* 40.1 (2009): 37–70.

Hourani, Albert. *Arabic Thought in the Liberal Age (1798–1939)*. New York: Cambridge University Press, 1983.

Hout, Syrine. "Going the Extra Mile: Redefining Identity, Home, and Family in Hanan al-Shaykh's *Only in London*." *Studies in the Humanities* 30.1–2 (2003): 29–45.

Hussein, Taha. *Mustaqbal al-Thaqafa fi Misr*. Cairo: Al-Hay'a al-Misriyya al-'Amma li-l-Kitab, 1993.

Hutcheon, Linda. "The Politics of Postmodernism: Parody and History." *Cultural Critique* 5 (1986–87): 179–207.

Ibn Fadlan, Ahmad ibn 'Abbas. *Rihlat ibn Fadlan: Ila Bilad al-Turk wa-l-Rus wa-l-Saqaliba (921)*. Beirut: Al-Mu'assassa al-'Arabiyya li-l-Dirasat wa-l-Nashr, 2003.

Ibn Khaldun, Abu Zayd ibn Muhammad. *Al-Muqaddima*. Beirut: Dar Ihya' al-Turath al-'Arabi, 1960.

Ibn Manzur, Muhammad ibn Mukarram. *Lisan al-'Arab*. 18 vols. Edited by 'Ali Shiri. Beirut: Dar Ihya' al-Turath al-'Arabi, 1988.

Ibn Sina, Abu 'Ali al-Husayn. *Qanun fi al-Tibb*. 3 vols. Beirut: Dar Sadir, 1970.

Ibrahim, Saad Eddin. *Azmat al-Muthaqqafin wa-l-Thaqafa al-'Arabiyya*. Cairo: Markaz ibn Khaldun li-l-Dirasat al-Inma'iyya, 2006.

Ibrahim, Sonallah. *Tilk al-Ra'iha wa Qisas Ukhra*. Minya, Egypt: Dar al-Huda, 2003.

Idris, Samah. *Al-Muthaqqaf al-'Arabi wa-l-Sulta*. Beirut: Dar al-Adab, 1992.

Idris, Suhayl. *Al-Hayy al-Latini*. Beirut: Dar al-Adab, 2006.

Idris, Yusuf. *Bayt min Lahm wa-Qisas Ukhra*. Cairo: 'Alam al-Kutub, 1971.

al-Isbahani, Abu Faraj. *Kitab al-Aghani.* 25 vols. Beirut: Dar al-Thaqafa, 1955–64.

al-Jabarti, 'Abd al-Rahman. *History of Egypt.* 4 vols. Edited and translated by Thomas Philipp and Moshe Perlmann. Stuttgart: Franz Steiner Verlag, 1994.

al-Jabiri, Muhammad 'Abed. *Al-Muthaqqafun fi al-Hadara al-'Arabiyya: Mihnat ibn Hanbal wa-Nakbat ibn Khaldun.* Beirut: Markaz Dirasat al-Wihda al-'Arabiyya, 1995.

Jacquemond, Richard. *Conscience of the Nation: Writers, State, and Society in Modern Egypt.* Translated by David Tresilian. Cairo: American University of Cairo Press, 2008.

al-Jahiz. *Kitab al Hayawan.* Cairo: Maktabat Mustafa al-Halabi, 1965.

John, Joseph, and Yosif Tarawneh. "Tayeb Salih and Freud: The Impact of Freudian Ideas on 'Season of Migration to the North.'" *Arabica* 35 (1988): 328–49.

Kant, Immanuel. *Anthropology, History, and Education.* Edited by Günter Zöller and Robert B. Louden. New York: Cambridge University Press, 2007.

Kassab, Suzanne. *Contemporary Arab Thought: Cultural Critique in Comparative Perspective.* New York: Columbia University Press, 2010.

Khamisi, Khalid. *Taxi.* Cairo: Dar al-Shorouk, 2007.

Khatibi, Abdelkebir. *Love in Two Languages.* Translated by Richard Howard. Minneapolis: University of Minnesota Press, 1990.

Krishnan, R. S. "Reinscribing Conrad: Tayeb Salih's *Season of Migration to the North.*" *International Fiction Review* 23.1–2 (1996): 7–15.

Kristeva, Julia. *Pouvoirs de l'horreur.* Paris: Éditions du Seuil, 1980.

Labi, Aisha, and Ursula Lindsey. "Hundreds of American Students Lie Low in Egypt, as Protests Continue." *Chronicle of Higher Education,* January 30, 2011, http://chronicle.com/article/Hundreds-of-American-Students/126159/.

Lacan, Jacques. *Ecrits.* Paris: Éditions du Seuil, 1966.

Lagrange, Frédéric. "Male Homosexuality in Modern Arabic Literature." In *Imagined Masculinities: Male Identity and Culture in the Modern Middle East,* edited by Mai Ghoussoub and Emma Sinclair-Webb, 169–98. London: Saqi, 2000.

Laroui, Abdallah. *Al-'Arab wa-l-Fikr al-Tarikhi.* Casablanca: Al-Markaz al-Thaqafi al-'Arabi, 1992.

Lévi-Strauss, Claude. "Culinary Triangles." In *Food and Culture: A Reader*, edited by Carole Counihan and Penny Van Esterik, 28–35. East Sussex, U.K.: Psychology Press, 1997.

Louca, Anouar. *'Awdat Rif'at al-Tahtawi*. Susa, Tunisia: Dar al-Ma'arif li-l-Tiba'a wa-l-Nashr, 1997.

———. *Voyageurs et écrivains Egyptiens en France au XIX siècle*. Paris: Éditions Didier, 1970.

Ma'aliqi, Mundhir. *Ma'alim al-Fikr al-'Arabi fi 'Asr al-Nahda al-'Arabiyya*. Beirut: Dar Iqra', 1986.

al-Ma'arri, Abi al-'Ala'. *Sharh Diwan al-Mutanabbi*. 4 vols. Edited by 'Abd al-Majid Diab. Cairo: Dar al-Ma'arif, 1992.

Mahfouz, Naguib. *Al-Mu'allafat al-Kamila*. 4 vols. Beirut: Maktabat Lubnan, 1990.

Mahjoub, Jamal. *In the Hour of Signs*. Oxford: Heinemann, 1996.

Makdisi, Saree. "The Empire Renarrated: *Season of Migration to the North* and the Reinvention of the Present." *Critical Inquiry* 18 (1992): 804–20.

Makdisi, Usama. *Artillery of Heaven: American Missionaries and the Failed Conversion of the Middle East*. Ithaca, N.Y.: Cornell University Press, 2008.

Marin, Louis. *Food for Thought*. Translated by Mette Hjort. Baltimore: Johns Hopkins University Press, 1997.

al-Marrash, Fransis Fath-Allah. *Rihlat Baris*. Beirut: Al-Mu'assassa al-'Arabiyya li-l-Dirasat wa-l-Nashr, 2004.

Massad, Joseph. *Desiring Arabs*. Chicago: Chicago University Press, 2007.

Massumi, Brian. *Parables for the Virtual: Movement, Affect, Sensation*. Durham, N.C.: Duke University Press, 2002.

Matar, Nabil, ed. *In the Lands of the Christians: Arab Travel Writing in the Seventeenth Century*. New York: Routledge, 2002.

Mehrez, Samia. *Egypt's Culture Wars: Politics and Practice*. New York: Routledge, 2008.

Meisami, Julie Scott, and Paul Starkey, eds. *Encyclopedia of Arabic Literature*. 2 vols. London: Routledge, 1998.

Melas, Natalie. *All the Difference in the World: Postcoloniality and the Ends of Comparison*. Stanford, Calif.: Stanford University Press, 2006.

Menninghaus, Winfried. *Disgust: The Theory and History of a Strong*

Sensation. Translated by Howard Eiland and Joel Golb. Albany: State University of New York Press, 2003.

Meyer, Stefan. *The Experimental Arabic Novel: Postcolonial Literary Modernism in the Levant.* Albany: State University of New York Press, 2000.

Mitchell, Timothy. *Colonising Egypt.* Berkeley: University of California Press, 1991.

Montesquieu, *Persian Letters.* Translated by Margaret Mauldon. Oxford: Oxford University Press, 2008.

Mubarak, ʿAli. *ʿAlam al-Din.* Cairo: Maktabat al-Adab, 1993.

al-Musawi, Muhsin. "Engaging Globalization in Modern Arabic Literature: Appropriation and Resistance." *Modern Language Quarterly* 68.2 (2007): 305–29.

———. *Islam on the Street: Religion in Modern Arabic Literature.* Plymouth, U.K.: Rowman and Littlefield, 2009.

———. *The Postcolonial Arabic Novel: Debating Ambivalence.* Leiden: Brill, 2003.

Najmabadi, Afsaneh. *Women with Mustaches and Men without Beards: Gender and Sexual Anxieties of Iranian Modernity.* Berkeley: University of California Press, 2005.

Netton, I. R. "Riḥla." In *Encyclopaedia of Islam,* 2nd ed., edited by P. Bearman et al. Brill Online, www.brillonline.nl/subscriber /entry?entry= islam_SIM-6298.

Neuwrith, Angelika, Andreas Pflitsch, and Barbara Winckler, eds. *Arabic Literature: Postmodern Perspectives.* London: Saqi, 2010.

Nussbaum, Martha Craven. *Hiding from Humanity: Disgust, Shame, and the Law.* Princeton, N.J.: Princeton University Press, 2004.

Orany, Ezzat. "'Nation,' 'patrie,' 'citoyen' chez Rifaʿa al-Tahtawi et Khayr-al-Din al-Tunisi." *Mélanges de l'institut Dominicain d'études orientales du Caire* 16 (1983): 169–90.

Parry, Benita. "Reflections on the Excess of Empire in Tayeb Salih's *Season of Migration to the North.*" *Paragraph: A Journal of Modern Critical Theory* 28.2 (2005): 72–90.

Pérès, H. "Voyageurs Musulmans en Europe aux XIXe et XXe siècles." *Mémoires de l'institut Francais d'archéologie orientale* 68 (1935): 185–95.

Pierpont, Claudia Roth. "Found in Translation: The Contemporary Arabic Novel." *New Yorker,* January 18, 2010, 74–80.

Protevi, John. *Political Affect: Connecting the Social and the Somatic*. Minneapolis: University of Minnesota Press, 2009.

Rastegar, Kamran. *Literary Modernity between the Middle East and Europe: Textual Transactions in Nineteenth-Century Arabic, English, and Persian Literatures*. New York: Routledge, 2007.

Reynolds, Dwight, ed. *Interpreting the Self: Autobiography in the Arabic Tradition*. Berkeley: University of California Press, 2001.

Roper, Geoffrey. "Ahmad Faris al-Shidyaq and the Libraries of Europe and the Ottoman Empire." *Libraries and Culture* 33.3 (1998): 233–48.

el-Rouayheb, Khaled. *Before Homosexuality in Arab-Islamic World, 1500–1800*. Chicago: Chicago University Press, 2005.

Rouhi, Leyla. *Mediation and Love: A Study of the Medieval Go-Between in Key Romance and Near-Eastern Texts*. Leiden: Brill, 1999.

Roy, Parama. *Alimentary Tracts: Appetites, Aversions, and the Postcolonial*. Durham, N.C.: Duke University Press, 2010.

al-Saffar, Muhammad ibn 'Abd-Allah. *Rihlat al-Saffar ila Faransa (1845–1846)*. Beirut: Al-Mu'assassa al-'Arabiyya li-l-Dirasat wa-l-Nashr, 2007.

Said, Edward. *Humanism and Democratic Criticism*. New York: Columbia University Press, 2004.

———. Introduction to Halim Barakat's *Days of Dust*. Washington, D.C.: Three Continents Press, 1983.

———. *Orientalism*. New York: Vintage, 1979.

———. *Reflections on Exile and Other Essays*. Cambridge, Mass.: Harvard University Press, 2000.

———. *Representations of the Intellectual*. New York: Vintage, 1996.

Salama-Carr, Myriam. "Negotiating Conflict: Rifa'a Rafi' al-Tahtawi and the Translation of the 'Other' in Nineteenth-Century Egypt." *Social Semiotics* 17.2 (2007): 213–27.

Salih, Tayeb. *Mawsim al-Hijra ila al-Shamal*. Beirut: Dar al-Jil, 1999.

———. *Season of Migration to the North*. Translated by Denys Johnson-Davies. Oxford: Heinemann, 1970.

al-Samman, Hanadi. "Out of the Closet: Representations of Homosexuals and Lesbians in Modern Arabic Literature." *Journal of Arabic Literature* 39.2 (2008): 270–310.

al-Samman, Muhammad Hayyan. *Khitab al-Junun fi al-Thaqafa al-'Arabiyya*. London: Riad el-Rayyes, 1993.

Sawaie, Mohammed. "Rifa'a Rafi' al-Tahtawi and His Contribution to the Lexical Development of Modern Literary Arabic." *International Journal of Middle Eastern Studies* 32 (2000): 395–410.

Schmidt, Leigh Eric. *Hearing Things: Religion, Illusion, and the American Enlightenment*. Cambridge, Mass.: Harvard University Press, 2002.

Sedgwick, Eve Kosofsky. *Touching Feeling: Affect, Pedagogy, Performativity*. Durham, N.C.: Duke University Press, 2003.

Selim, Samah. "Fiction and Colonial Identities: Arsène Lupin in Arabic." *Middle Eastern Literatures* 13.2 (2010): 191–210.

———. "The Narrative Craft: Realism and Fiction in the Arabic Canon." *Edebiyat* 14.1–2 (2003): 109–28.

———. "The People's Entertainments: Translation, Popular Fiction and the *Nahdah* in Egypt." In *Other Renaissances: A New Approach to World Literature*, edited by Brenda Dean Schilgen, Gang Zhou, and Sandra L. Gilman, 35–58. New York: Palgrave Macmillan, 2007.

Sells, Michael, ed. and trans. *Desert Tracings*. Middletown, Conn.: Wesleyan University Press, 1989.

Shakespeare. *Othello*. New York: Norton, 2004.

al-Shaykh, Hanan. *Hikayat Zahra*. Beirut: Dar al-Adab, 1998.

———. *Innaha London ya 'Azizi*. Beirut: Dar al-Adab, 2001.

———. *Only in London*. Translated by Catherine Cobham. New York: Pantheon, 2001.

———. *The Story of Zahra*. Translated by Peter Ford. New York: Anchor, 1996.

Sheehi, Stephen. *Foundations of Modern Arab Identity*. Gainesville: University Press of Florida, 2004.

al-Shidyaq, Ahmad Faris. *Ahmad Faris al-Shidyaq: Silsilat al-A'mal al-Majhula*. Edited by Aziz al-Azmeh and Fawwaz Trabulsi. London: Riad el-Rayyes, 1995.

———. *Al-Saq 'ala al-Saq fi ma huwa al-Faryaq, aw Ayyam wa-Shuhur wa-A'wam fi 'Ajam al-'Arab wa-l-A'jam*. Beirut: Dar Maktabat al-Hayat, 1966.

———. *Al-Wasita fi Ma'rifat Ahwal Malta wa-Kashf al-Mukhabba' 'an Funun Urubba*. Beirut: Al-Mu'assassa al-'Arabiyya li-l-Dirasat wa-l-Nashr, 2004.

Shimon, Samuel, ed. *Beirut 39: New Writing from the Arab World*. New York: Bloomsbury, 2010.

Shusterman, Richard. *Body Consciousness: A Philosophy of Mindfulness and Somaesthetics*. New York: Cambridge University Press, 2008.

Siddiq, Muhammad. "The Process of Individuation in Al-Tayyeb Salih's Novel *Season of Migration to the North*." *Journal of Arabic Literature* 9 (1978): 67–104.

Silverman, Kaja. *Flesh of My Flesh*. Stanford, Calif.: Stanford University Press, 2009.

al-Solh, 'Imad. *Ahmad Faris al-Shidyaq: Atharuhu wa-'Asruh*. Beirut: Sharikat al-Matbu'at li-l-Tawzi' wa-l-Nashr, 1987.

Spivak, Gayatri Chakravorty. *Death of a Discipline*. New York: Columbia University Press, 2003.

Swift, Jonathan. *The Works of Jonathan Swift*. 19 vols. Edinburgh: A. Constable, 1814.

Tageldin, Shaden M. *Disarming Words: Empire and the Seductions of Translation in Egypt*. Berkeley: University of California Press, 2011.

al-Tahtawi, Rifa'a Rafi'. *Al-A'mal al-Kamila li-Rifa'a Rafi' al-Tahtawi*. 4 vols. Edited by Muhammad 'Amara. Beirut: Al-Mu'assassa al-'Arabiyya li-l-Dirasat wa-l-Nashr, 1977.

———. *An Imam in Paris: Al-Tahtawi's Visit to France (1826–1831)*. Translated by Daniel Newman. London: Saqi, 2004.

———. *L'or de Paris*. Translated by Anouar Louca. Paris: Éditions Sindbad, 1988.

———. *Takhlis al-Ibriz fi Talkhis Bariz aw al-Diwan al-Nafis bi-Iwan Baris*. Beirut: Al-Mu'assassa al-'Arabiyya li-l-Dirasat wa-l-Nashr, 2002.

Tarabishi, Georges. *Al-Muthaqqafun al-'Arab wa-l-Turath*. London: Riad el-Rayyes, 1991.

Terada, Rei. *Feeling in Theory: Emotion after the "Death of the Subject."* Cambridge, Mass.: Harvard University Press, 2003.

al-Turk, Niqula ibn Yusuf. *Histoire de l'expédition des Français en Egypte*. Cairo: L'imprimerie de l'institut Français d'archéologie orientale, 1950.

Voltaire. *Lettres philosophiques*. Paris: Éditions Flammarion, 1986.

Wannous, Sadallah. *Al-A'mal al-Kamila*. 3 vols. Beirut: Dar al-Adab, 2004.

Zarkan, Muhammad. *Al-Jawanib al-Lughawiyya 'ind Ahmad Faris al-Shidyaq*. Damascus: Dar al-Fikr, 1988.

Ze'evi, Dror. *Producing Desire: Changing Sexual Discourse in the Ottoman Middle East, 1500–1900*. Berkeley: University of California Press, 2006.

INDEX